"For those readers who have grov lationships in their churches and genuine friendship, *Soulmates* is exactly the book for you! With refreshing spiritual insight, winsome humility, and delightful humor, Dr. Horn describes the nature of true Christian friendship and challenges each of us to settle for nothing less than the kinds of relationships that God designed us to enjoy."

—**Garth M. Rosell, Senior Research Professor of Church History, Gordon-Conwell Theological Seminary**

"David Horn's *Soulmates* is a welcome and unique contribution to our understanding and practice of interpersonal friendship and congregational community. There is an important overlap but it is in the contrast of (1) a freely chosen, mutually beneficial relationship (friendship) with (2) a divinely created, inclusive, obligatory fellowship of hospitality and sacrificial love (the church community) that Horn's insights most brightly and helpfully shine. Important reading for pastors and church leaders; exciting discussion possibilities for classes and study groups."

—**David W. Gill, author of *Becoming Good: Building Moral Character* and *Doing Right: Practicing Ethical Principles***

"This book is about practicing Christian faith within the complex fabric of the church. But it is entered through a discussion of the nature of, and differences between, friendship and Christian fellowship. All of these themes are treated here with rigor, uncommon insight, and a pastoral touch. The book's tone is warm, down to earth, and funny but there are profound truths in these pages."

—**David F. Wells, Distinguished Research Professor, Gordon-Conwell Theological Seminary**

SOULMATES

SOULMATES

Friendship, Fellowship &
the Making of Christian Community

DAVID HORN

Soulmates: Friendship, Fellowship & the Making of Christian Community

© 2017 Hendrickson Publishers Marketing, LLC
P. O. Box 3473
Peabody, Massachusetts 01961-3473
www.hendrickson.com

ISBN 978-1-61970-842-6

Printed in the United States of America

First Printing — March 2017

Library of Congress Cataloging-in-Publication Data

A catalog record for this title is available from the Library of Congress
Hendrickson Publishers Marketing, LLC ISBN 978-1-61970-842-6

CONTENTS

PREFACE

This book is about the nature of the church. As if we need another book about the church! Our Christian bookstores are stacked like cordwood with practical guides on ways to make our churches larger, our programs more inviting, our worship services more enticing, our leadership more productive, and our small groups more well-rounded.

Most recently, we have turned to other institutional models as a basis for refining what the church should become. Notably, the business world has become our template for doing church. There is now a virtual cottage industry of materials built around ways in which sound business practices can produce the right quantifiable products needed for what is perceived to be a growing and healthy church. Efficiency is the new value that needs to be added to that ancient list of Christian Virtues. After all, efficiency is absolutely necessary for churches where sanctuaries and parking lots extend as far as the eye can see.

Any church worth its salt is now being driven by well-conceived vision statements. Chances are you have probably gone through the process yourself. Your pastor and church leadership, having previously put their heads together, have dragged you and your congregation through a well-orchestrated period of corporate introspection to determine who you are as a congregation and what you should become. Indeed, this practice has seeped to the very edges of our church institutions. No longer is it enough that churches have vision statements; church nurseries now have vision statements, junior high youth programs have vision statements, outreach programs have vision statements, our church kitchens have vision statements.

As helpful as these strategies have been on one level, this trend that increasingly defines the church in functional terms, sometimes to the exclusion of it biblically and theologically, is a disturbing one. There are several scholars who have seen the church dangerously listing in this direction and are seeking to right the ship.[1] I leave them to their task. My task here is to suggest that the institutional functionalism that has taken over conversations about the church is not only wrong-minded, but it largely misses the point for most people in the church.

Listen closely to the average churchgoer. What do you hear in the corridors and foyers and fellowship halls of your church? (I am not talking about church leaders caucusing in the pastor's study.) What is being discussed in church members' living rooms? Listen. Can you hear what concerns them? Chances are they are not talking about vision statements or church bylaws or ways to make the committee structures work more efficiently. This book takes its cues from the informal conversations of those in our churches.

They are not well-articulated, these informal conversations around the watercoolers of our churches. They are not well reasoned. They cannot be easily reduced to PowerPoint slides. Notice especially that words trail off at the ends of sentences. What these conversations lack in logic, they make up in heartfelt conviction. In fact, these conversations are more about longing than anything else—longing for intimacy.

Ironically, it is perhaps the 20 percent or so in a typical congregation who flit from one church to another at any given locale who are the most articulate on this subject. Listen to these church nomads, these thirsty souls, as they seek to describe why they have left one church oasis in search of another: "I just didn't feel a sense of community." "The church wasn't very friendly." Or, "this church is so inviting." "I feel like a part of something here."

It is this impulse toward developing and participating in authentic Christian community that I want to discuss in these next pages. I begin by acknowledging two chief obstacles. The first has already been implied. For all of the rhetoric about Christian community, there is little clarity about what it actually is. What is this relationship we call "Christian community"?[2] More to the point, is the relationship unique to the church and, if so, how?

Second, most often what we understand to be Christian community tends to be overly sentimentalized. The concept too easily fits into a Hallmark greeting card. Perhaps this is understandable. Relationships are often discussed in such terms, especially highly personal ones. But given all that is at stake—given the depth of meaning within Scripture and other historical sources—I will attempt to look at this concept with greater clarity and depth of vision. I dare to do so from multiple perspectives.

First, as one who has shared in the fellowship of true community in a variety of church settings for my entire life, my commitment to this subject is deeply personal. I confess that I cannot look at this topic dispassionately. The practice of Christian community is nothing short of God's grace being manifest in our lives together. I have fallen victim to this act of grace in so many ways, and I long for others to do so as well.

Second, as one who has been in various forms of ministry all my adult life, I am well aware of the responsibility that pastors have in this area. As pastors look out over their sanctuaries every Sunday, is there a more challenging task set before them than to oversee the nurturing of authentic community within their congregations? Given the countervailing pressures of our culture, the increasing diversity of our people, the seemingly unending impulse toward conflict, and our tendencies toward sin, is true community even possible? How does one lead a church into true Christian community? Perhaps it is this nurturing of authentic community that is one of the lost spiritual disciplines that needs to be reclaimed, especially for pastors.

Third, as one who directed an institute for church renewal for over twenty years, I have committed myself professionally to observing and helping churches become vital and healthy communities of faith. It is one thing to experience vitality and harmony with a community of people at its institutional infancy; it is quite another thing to see a sense of community being sustained through the years as churches mature and grow into their dotage.

Finally, I am a sociologist and practical theologian by education and training. This last perspective reflects my methodological approach in the book. Although I will not attempt to deal with the biblical literature exhaustively, my approach is, first, to offer an understanding of Christian community from a biblical perspective. It is Scripture, after all, that provides the template by which we are to relate to one another as the body of Christ.

Second, my intention is to pick up this concept and turn it around in our minds, observing it from multiple angles from a sociological perspective. Like a canvas of a painting, how does the light catch it at this or that time of day? How do the shadows fall across it? More specifically, I would like to observe it as a unique relational type. In this, I pay homage to Max Weber's concept of "ideal types."[3]

One of the reasons relationships are difficult to understand is that they are so embedded in the warp and woof of human experience that we cannot see them clearly. Our understanding of how relationships work is mired in the specific conflicting emotions and prejudices that surround our lives. We are too close to life to make sense of it, as it were. To provide clarity, I propose we take a step back from this relationship as we see it being manifest in our day-to-day lives and observe the relationship more unambiguously as an abstract "type" of what we see in real life. In doing so, this ideal type is no less real than the practice of the relationship as it is experienced, but it is presented cleaned up of all the distracting contexts in which it is embedded.

Finally, to bring even greater clarity to this ideal relational type, I would like to look at Christian community as it contrasts with another important human relationship type. Isn't it true that sometimes the best way to see the beauty of a good novel or play is to read or observe a bad one? Sometimes the resiliency of a diamond on a jeweler's counter can best be appreciated when compared to the muted luster of zirconium. Although the relationship of "friendship" should not be viewed as less important or valuable than that of Christian "fellowship," I will use the similarities and differences of the one relational typology as a basis for identifying the unique characteristics of the other.

As I will explain later in detail, I purposely use the friendship relationship type as the ideal foil for understanding community because it is perhaps this relationship type more than any other that is mistaken for Christian community. In the confusion between the two rests the seeds of potential mistrust, unfulfilled expectation, and ultimately conflict.

It is the intersection between these two relationships that is being described in my choice of title for this book. "*Soul*mates" is a term that sits perched on the shoulders of both relationships. Does it refer to what sixteenth-century essayist Michel de Montaigne describes as the perfect, indivisible type of friendship that "possesses the soul and rules it with absolute sovereignty [that] cannot possibly be double?"[4] Or by "soulmate" are we referring to a whole new relationship instituted by the power of the Holy Spirit, whereby brothers and sisters in Christ are in the process of being transformed into a radical new community called the church of Jesus Christ? Or does it refer to both?

One final comment about the nature of this book: I have intentionally used personal anecdotes in the telling of the larger story of the book because of its deeply personal thematic nature. My intentions are that the *context* of the book mirrors its *content*. All the stories told are true. At points, however, some of the details have been altered and the characters camouflaged to "protect the innocent" as it were, and in some cases to better fit the point these stories seek to illustrate.

ACKNOWLEDGMENTS

I want to express my gratitude to two sources central to my early thinking on the contents of this book.

The first is my professor at Harvard University, Dr. Ralph Potter, who was instrumental in suggesting to me in a class during the early 1980s that I consider looking at informal, noninstitutionalized types of relationships in my study of sociology and religion. One of the texts in his class, Ethics of Relationships, was written by Gilbert Meilaneder and titled *Friendship: A Study in Theological Ethics*. It was this book that started my thinking, leading to my taxonomy contrasting friendship and fellowship.

I also want to thank innumerable brothers and sisters in Christ, many, many friends, and a few very close friends for acting as models for this book. You will remain nameless here, but you know who you are. Look closely and you will see yourselves written time and again on every page in black and white.

Particular thanks to Mike and Kathy and Bryan and Freddie. The irony is that it was the solitude you offered me—a raving extrovert—through the gracious offering of your places of retreat that was your greatest act of friendship to me. Your hospitality has been deeply imprinted in my heart. Special thanks to Patricia Anders, whose fine editorial skills are surpassed only by her patience and diplomacy in working with the likes of me. Thanks for embodying what this book is all about, friend and sister in Christ. Thanks, too, to Chad Ryan, my teaching assistant, who checked and rechecked my source materials in preparation for publication.

Finally, I want to thank especially my wife, Cec. She is a classic example of the mixed relational metaphor spoken of in chapter 1. She is a beloved and wise sister in Christ, a trusted and true friend, a faithful wife, a committed mother to our children, and much more, never ever has she been a stranger. You are written on every page, as are my children and daughter-in-law and son-in-law, Will and Bre and Molly and Johann, and my grandchildren, Sam and Annie. This book is dedicated to all of you.

CHAPTER ONE

THE MANY FACES OF RELATIONSHIPS

A Stranger in a Foreign Land

I was a stranger in a foreign land as I walked from the parking lot toward the church. There was no mistaking it was a church, not like one of those churches camouflaged as a school, a theater, or an industrial park building. This building looked like a real church, like a cathedral even.

It took some time to make it to the sanctuary as my hosts and I meandered around the church campus. There were two or three outlier education buildings to be seen, and the grounds were gorgeous! We finally ended up in the church portico just off of the sanctuary, which was laden with an assortment of pastries and coffee. I know it was against house rules, but I grabbed a pastry and ran for the sanctuary door. I figured that being a first-time visitor gave me special privileges.

My hosts and I were late, which probably explains why the elderly couple sitting at the welcome table hardly gave us a nod as we stood in the vacuous foyer. Being as discreet as possible, we opened the doors to the sanctuary—did I mention we were late?—and stood looking at the backs of 450 complete strangers and the face of one pastor who was well into the first point of his sermon.

What was it about this situation that sent such a shudder up my spine? Simple shyness? The result of our careless lateness? I have been a pastor and have visited new churches, many times in fact. But, as in any time when something is new, everything in the moment seemed more vivid and noticeable. Would my visit to this church meet my expectations?

As it was, the church service did meet my expectations in many ways. The sermon was excellent, both in content and execution—the pastor was a great communicator. The music was outstanding, traditional and liturgical just the way I like it. The sanctuary building was new and beautiful.

But what about my expectations relationally? How would this sanctuary of otherwise total strangers translate into becoming a sanctuary of brothers and sisters in Christ? After all, with the exception of what I presumed were a few seekers scattered about here and there, wasn't this what we were? Not brothers and sisters in the blood-coursing-through-our-veins sense, but real brothers and sisters in Christ, the kind who made such a difference in the first-century church when it all began! How would we all move from being strangers to something more?

From a look at the bulletin I was handed at the sanctuary door, this certainly seemed like a church making an effort to deal with the relational aspects of doing church. They appeared to be putting their best foot forward. I noticed that on Wednesday evening at 5:30 there was to be a fellowship dinner and lecture. Later in the month an annual Missions Festival was advertised that also had a dinner attached to it. For today after the second service, an Adult Lunch Fellowship would take place at an area restaurant for anyone who wished to attend. My goodness, this church liked to eat!

On the other side of the bulletin, I saw that there was actually a staff member specially assigned as a director of fellowship, and other staff assigned to lead small groups and prayer ministries. There was a meal ministry program that provided food for those in special need, and there was a special invitation to attend a variety of adult Sunday school classes.

Is there one word talked about more in churches than the word *fellowship*, especially in this day and age? If anything, the impulse toward fellowship as a central focus of church life has been growing in recent years. Whole new ways of doing church are being marshaled to extend a sense of warmth and friendship, particularly for the newcomer. Coffee bars now line the back of many sanctuaries, with parishioners encouraged to juggle mugs of hot java alongside their Bibles as they sit around tables during worship.

If the stiff formality of a Victorian parlor represented the ethos of the worship of yesteryear, then today's worship services are now clearly conducted with an eye toward sinking into the soft folds of a Barcalounger recliner. If worshippers were greeted with an invitation to call themselves to repentance and worship in the not-too-distant past, then today they are now first invited into the happy swell of visitor-friendly praise choruses.

Newcomers entering the front door of most churches for the first time will invariably be met by friendly greeters. In larger churches, there might be a Hospitality Center that offers friendly materials describing the life of a friendly church. Walk a few steps past the typical foyer and you will most likely discover the fellowship hall. This is a place to remember, because after the worship service that generally begins with a friendly welcome to strangers, everyone will end up in that same friendly place for Hospitality Hour.

If newcomers hang around for a few weeks, chances are they will get invited to a small group ministry, named by any number of titles, but all with the same goals in mind: Friendship Group, Community Group, Care Group, and so on. Although churches vary greatly in their capacity to pull it off, most don't suffer for lack of trying to be places of genuine fellowship and hospitality.

But what is this relationship we call "fellowship"? We speak so much about it that one would think we actually know what it means. When we talk about living in "Christian community," what are we really saying? For all the rhetoric, for all of our best intentions, for all of our programs, I am not sure we clearly understand how it is anything different from any other relationship we encounter on a daily basis. Or is it supposed to be any different?

Oh, enough daydreaming about fellowship! It was time for the benediction and the pastor had just invited us to "pass the peace." I turned around and looked into the eyes of two elderly couples as they extended their hands to me. We smiled at one another. Someone mentioned something about the weather. We shook hands all around. And then we all left . . . complete strangers.

Five Windows into the Soul of Christian Community

In thinking about what we mean by fellowship in our churches, I began to consider other places where we see it being displayed.

It's interesting that the smallest windows can sometimes offer access to the grandest horizons when faced from the correct side of the building. This is my motivation every time I climb the 148 steps (but who's counting?) up the north tower of the twin lighthouses on Thacher Island, north of Gloucester on Cape Ann in Massachusetts where I live. Cec and friends and I make a point of doing this climb every time we kayak to the little island. I am confident that what I will see at the top of our sweaty ordeal in the little foggy window is nothing short of the most splendid view of the rocky crags looking eastward out over the Atlantic Ocean.

Perhaps poets and novelists have this perspective in a way that most of us don't. If they have taught us anything through the years, it is that in the smallest, mundane details often overlooked in our lives are revealed the greatest truths. It is in the linnet's wings of Yeats, the common spiderweb of Frost, and the mundane daily voyage out to sea by Hemingway's fisherman that we find the largeness of life and death exposed.

Let me begin our look at the grand contours of Christian community by offering five small windows into the life of the church. They are thin stories in that they are not overly dramatic in themselves, but they are, nevertheless, ultimately thick with significance.

Window One: Thursday Night Live

Frankly, she just wasn't attractive. Her name was Mary Beth, and her long stringy hair fell flat against her forehead. You could tell she made an effort to dress up, but whatever she had done wasn't working that night. Nothing fit her very well. This was partly due to her being overweight and partly due to a limited clothes budget or a jaundiced eye toward fashion, or both.

It was fifteen minutes before the Bible study that night in the living room of my house on the North Shore of Boston. In real terms, this meant she sat down to fifteen minutes of awkward silence. Everyone in the Young Adults group I was facilitating—we called it Thursday Night Live—was pleasant enough. They certainly made the effort to nod their greetings, but she did not evoke anything close to natural warmth. There was nothing about her that offered a ready invitation to enter into conversation, even of the superficial kind. She didn't have it in her. Apparently, we didn't either.

After all, this was a well-established group with a social agenda to attend to. For five years now, this group had been evolving into a society unto itself, swelling to forty and fifty participants at a time. Weekly evenings around the fireplace and biannual retreats had cemented us together into a nice fellowship group. We had learned to mix light banter with the more official tasks of Bible study and prayer. We started off each night with a silly question that eventually led to more thoughtful conversation on the evening's text. Any initial thoughts of engaging in small talk with Mary Beth were quickly swallowed up by competing voices within the group.

The awkwardness of the moment could not go unnoticed as I stood there by the kitchen door that night. As pastor and facilitator of the group, I felt obligated to somehow draw her into the boat. But the water was up to the gunnels on this one. I confess that I wasn't particularly drawn to her myself and wasn't much help to our newest member.

As time went by, I wish I could say that the situation changed for Mary Beth and the group. She—we—made it through the first evening. I was somewhat surprised that she showed up a second and third and fourth time. In fact, Mary Beth eventually became a regular. That is, she became an attendee. But looking back, to the end she never really became a member in good standing. We became familiar enough with her and she with us. We gained a general sense of her background, yet none of us really engaged with her relationally. As the weeks wore on, our first impression of her was confirmed to be surprisingly accurate. Years of unpleasant experiences had shaped her into a needy person. One evening, Mary Beth didn't show up, and we never heard from her again. To this day, I am not sure what became of her.

Even now as I think back on Mary Beth, I can hardly remember her. She left such a light imprint on my mind and upon the life of the group. If it weren't for the fact that Mary Beth's little story is writ so large every day in churches around the country, it would hardly be worth mentioning here. But the sad reality is that the backdoors of our churches are littered with individuals like Mary Beth—people who come and go and hardly leave an impression.

Why aren't the Mary Beths of our churches able to enter into the life-giving community described so vividly in the New Testament? Left to themselves, they orbit the outer frontiers of our churches looking for ways to be included. Is it just a matter of limited social capacity? If so, then is the opposite the case—that the degree to which all of us enter into and partake in authentic community within our churches hangs on the thin threads of our capacity to be socially adept? Are the keys to the kingdom of God dangling around the thin fingers of only those who have the ability to be pleasant and gregarious?

More to the point, given its seeming maturity as a loving community, why couldn't our Young Adults group adequately make the invitation to Mary Beth? If the body of Christ is to be such a life-transforming community, then why do we duck inside doorways when we see the Mary Beths of our churches coming? We can make her an object of "ministry." But why do we have such a hard time truly making her one of our own?

Window Two: One Happy Family

They asked me to bring my vestments, and I was happy to oblige. However, I must say that not everything seemed to fit together that Sunday as I grabbed my robe to travel the forty-five minutes it took to get to the old Presbyterian Church in East Boston. As a fill-in for a pastor-colleague, I was happy to rework one of my sermons at the last minute, but why did they also ask me to serve as liturgist? And how was I going to be in a position to give announcements to a church I had never attended?

The story was soon to become much clearer. There was no one else to perform these functions. The exterior of the church was a large, impressive colonial brick building. But when I entered the sanctuary, I was greeted with approximately five hundred empty seats and seven full ones (when I say seven, I include the organist and the church sexton).

Perhaps the most curious moment was when I ascended the great steps of the elevated old pulpit, garbed in full liturgical attire, organ at full strength, to preach my formally constructed sermon to what in any other setting would have to be considered a poorly attended small group. The fact that my newly introduced parishioners sat scattered across the full expanse of the sanctuary made the scene all the more awkward.

What I was soon to find out was that what the church lacked in members it made up in endowment. Three elderly women literally kept the doors open with their thin, bone-weary arms as they hung desperately on to images of the church's Scottish-Irish heritage. Like debris on the side of the road, the church's northern European past had long since been run over by eighteen wheels of ethnic change. Years ago, the Scottish Presbyterians had fled to suburbia to soon be replaced by a vibrant African-American population. But this wasn't even the community that greeted me outside the church that day. By the time I visited the church, a new wave of Brazilian immigrants had taken over. The church had been mired in three changing layers of ethnicity, and they weren't about to change their ministry accordingly.

Nevertheless, the church continued to exist, opening its doors to the few who had long memories of a distant past. Is this an uncommon story for those of us who have chosen to live and minister in New England? Not really. With some irony, my colleagues and I work and live in what has to be considered the backwater of the American evangelical church. Any vestige of the strategic nature that the church claimed from its early past—particularly in the Great Awakening—has long since been swept westward and to the south. In its place is a landscape filled with small, once-vital, now-struggling churches.

As the director of the Harold J. Ockenga Institute for Church Renewal at Gordon-Conwell Theological Seminary, I came into weekly contact with students and pastors whose big dreams of great ministry had long since crashed on the rocky shoals of New England. Church growth manuals that seem to benefit churches in other parts of the country read like hieroglyphics here. It's not for lack of trying that we continue to seek God's favor.

But despite the seeming lack of growth and vitality of some of these small churches, the irony is that if one hangs around them long enough, one hears a great deal about community. Put your ear to the ground and listen in on these struggling churches, these faithful remnants who have banded together to keep the heat on and the pastor in part-time employment. You will be surprised. They do not lack for intimacy. In fact, the language is surprisingly accommodating in one sense. It is the language of "one happy family." This was the language I heard that Sunday in East Boston. These people cared for their sick. They administered their church fairs. They had church suppers. And they genuinely loved one another.

What do we make of this anomaly? Our heads tell us that these churches cannot be healthy. Their sanctuaries are three-quarters empty. They lack resources, both financially and in warm bodies to fill their roster of volunteer positions. Children no longer roam the aisles, to say nothing of teenagers. Programs sit idle. And yet, in their hearts, these small churches practice intimacy in ways that cannot be easily replicated in other contexts.

Window Three: The Magical Mystery Tour

We called it a Magical Mystery Tour. And so it was that we were all in a playful mood that day some fifteen years ago when we clambered aboard the plain yellow school bus in the church parking lot. There were forty-five of us, and we were all within one year of turning fifty. Playfully anointing our impending age with the soothing salve of laughter, we decided to celebrate our common birthdays together.

We spent the evening traveling up the seashore to a restaurant in Maine with the music of Creedence Clearwater Revival and the Grateful Dead in our ears and the taste of Cheez Whiz, Twinkies, and Ritz Crackers appetizers on our tongues. Some brave souls shoehorned themselves into their old bell-bottoms. We quizzed ourselves on sixties and seventies trivia along the way, and we even had a playful visit by John and Yoko of Beatles fame, played expertly by some of our younger fellow church members.

If the bus had slid off into the Atlantic that evening, heaven forbid, it would have been abundantly clear by looking at our church directory that it took with it the core leadership of the church. Such a disaster would have brought back memories, twenty years prior, to when that same group of then thirty- and forty-year-olds came in and helped transform our 275-year-old Congregational church, which had been on the brink of closing in the early 1970s. In God's providence, this group was at the center of bringing an antiquated New England church back to life.

The sum total of our little school bus tour describes very well the majority of churches in America. Churches are, by nature, generational. Like waves, through time they tend to grow, they crest, and, if not careful, they die in generational pockets. This is particularly true of the leadership within churches. Authority tends to pool in formative generations within the life cycle of churches.

What do we make of these generational pools? If a congregation is lucky, it might span two or three generations. In smaller churches, unfortunately, most often they span one, two at the most. In defining the dynamics of the practice of community in churches, so much rests on these generations. Which generation owns the sense of community in the church? Who has the power? How is authority shared and passed down from one generation to the next? All these questions sit quietly in the background and are most often left unanswered as churches live out their life cycles.

Window Four: Pastor as Friend

The things you realize at a funeral are quite amazing. There we all were—almost three hundred friends and family members, all of us there to honor my pastor-father who had passed away a couple of days earlier. They came from all over the Midwest. The older folks, representing his five full-time and several interim pastorates, sitting in the front rows to hear better, were the most conspicuous.

We laid my father to rest, and in doing so, we were really laying to rest sixty years of faithful ministry. It was my task to eulogize him for the family. As I looked out over the mourners that day, and particularly those tired souls in the front rows, I couldn't help but think of the kinds of relationships represented there before me.

How had they perceived my father? There my father was before us—first, seen through the eyes of a wife, certainly the most intimate of the relationships represented. And there were the four grown boys, less intimate but equally loving. Then there were four daughters-in-law. How did these daughters, tethered to this man all these years out of marital pledge rather than blood kinship, view him and his life? There were grandchildren and plenty of nephews and nieces too, who largely knew him past his prime.

There were only a few of his peers left who had observed him in his earlier days—no siblings, but a few brothers- and sisters-in-law. And finally, with the exception of the church custodian and the ladies who served lunch that day, all the rest sitting there saw this man through the lens of his ministry among them as their onetime pastor.

Of this latter group, I couldn't help thinking of one of Dad's most memorable sayings while I was growing up: "My best friends are ex-parishioners." Certainly he never made this little adage public, but there was something in Dad's past that always made him wary of getting too close to those he served. Perhaps it was a piece of pastoral wisdom that he had learned in his seminary days from the forties.

Whatever it was, in hindsight I think this self-imposed ministerial convention left my dad privately lonely. Publicly, no one would have guessed it. Dad was a big, gregarious man, and our home was a big, hospitable place. Our family life was cluttered with people from all walks of life. Dad's life was filled with relationships; but at the end of the day, few of those relationships could easily fall under the category of friendship, narrowly defined. Most of his friends sat outside the church door, at least of the church he was currently serving. Only when he left a church would he express friendship openly to certain special people.

The wisdom of this little saying of Dad's can easily be disputed. Is it wise for pastors to nurture friendships within their own congregations? If not, are pastors then doomed to a life of solitude? Aside from his or her family, where else is the source of community to come from for those who oversee community? Why was Dad so fearful? And what advice should we give young pastors as they enter into a profession that is enormously challenging, potentially filled with conflict, and often lonely?

Window Five: "Friendship Evangelism"

Andy lived on the "other side of the tracks" in every sense of the term. Everything about him told a deeper story. The insides of his shaking, yellow-stained fingers revealed a habit that he could not control and that matched his rasping cough. The continuous pursing of his lips revealed that he spent far too much time in the rural bars of Minnesota. The empty ring finger on his left hand did not tell the whole story—that he had been married and divorced three times—but it told us enough. If we could have seen the palm side of his arms under his long sleeves, I am sure we would have captured even more of his story.

He lived in a tiny house literally on the other side of the tracks that was three nails and a screw away from collapsing on him. And did I mention that he smelled terrible? Let's just say that his presence among us lingered for five or six minutes after he left the room. In every way, Andy was a lost soul.

This, in fact, is why some of the more committed members of the church befriended him. The phrase hadn't been coined yet, but if it had they would have said that they had committed themselves to "friendship evangelism" by taking Andy under their wings. Everything they did reflected friendship. Several of them had Andy over for dinner. They took him to church and sat with him. One of the members lent him money with the understanding that the chances the money would ever be seen again were slim to none. Many went out of their way to give him rides back to his little house. All of them were concerned for Andy and the state of his heart.

And, in time, Andy did have a heartfelt conversion experience. As the custom was in this little Baptist church, he even made a public profession of faith and went forward for all to observe. In the weeks ahead, he gave every indication of a changed life. He went to Wednesday night Bible study, joined the men's group, and faithfully attended church.

But sanctification is an interesting thing. The personal characteristics that were readily apparent before he became a Christian—but somehow overlooked—became all too apparent as time went on. Years of struggles with addiction did not end overnight. The very things that drove him to these habits lingered on. His neediness was exposed many times over as he drew attention to himself in inappropriate times and places. And his salvation apparently did not cure the smell that lingered around him.

In time, his "friendships" with those in the church became subtly strained. Certainly he was always welcomed to everything going on at the church. But fewer invitations to home-cooked meals were extended to him.

Apparently, fewer people were traveling his way, because fewer rides were offered. Andy often returned to his rundown little house alone and lonely. He was confused.

Andy's situation is not too different from many others who enter into the kingdom in our churches, but once there find themselves strangely alone. The empirical literature on religious conversion is filled with these kinds of stories. There is an entire genre of research that focuses on relationship theory and the way cults encourage converts by identifying persons in various forms of need as prime candidates for entering into their cult.[1] These psychologically and relationally deprived individuals are "ripe for the picking," and the literature confirms that they do indeed make excellent candidates.

Returning to the little Baptist church, I am certainly not suggesting too strong a parallel between Andy's situation and the well-orchestrated behavior of most cults. For one thing, those well-intended members were deeply committed to the biblical injunction to seek the lost and to make disciples. Their good deeds toward Andy were in no way manipulative and were offered honestly and with no strings attached. But why is it that their "friendships" with Andy could not be sustained when the purposes for which they pursued him were fulfilled? In what ways might "friendship evangelism" be unintentionally dishonest about the real motives for why a relationship is entered into and sustained?

Five Small Windows

Five small windows into the soul of the church: A young adult woman who seeks to fit into an otherwise vibrant faith community, a dying congregation that gives the appearance of community, a church responsible for passing the baton of community from one generation to the next, a pastor's unique relationship with the community he serves, and a new convert's first sojourn into the kingdom of God, who is wondering who he is going to sit next to in the pew.

Each of these situations poses a significant dilemma for the church. They highlight critical moments that if left unattended have devastating consequences on the relational lives of churches. If resolved, however, these would-be dilemmas frame places where Christian community flourishes and is at its best.

I want to look more closely into these windows later as the basis for better understanding the inner workings of the church, and to address practical implications of how community can be encouraged and sustained. For the time being, each story might well sit like light smudges in the backs of our minds. Let them leave an impression until we take care of some basic background matters. First, what do we mean by "Christian community"?

Relational Types in the Church

To speak of relationships within the church is to speak in surprisingly complex terms. Walk into any sanctuary on any given Sunday and you will find a vast diversity of relationships, each cross-pollinating across the aisles. Peel back the more institutional outer layers of relationships represented by such categories as pastor and laity, leader and follower, new attendee and member, believer and nonbeliever, and you will also find private, familial relations between husband and wife, parent and child, sibling relationships between brother and brother, sister and brother, and more extended kindred relationships between grandparents and offspring twice removed, and then there are the in-laws.

There is the special relationship between friends, the similar but more hierarchical relationship of mentor and protégée, and there is the instructional bond between teacher and student. Across the aisle, employers look over at their employees. Undoubtedly, there are commercial relationships; doctors sit next to patients, hair stylists sit next to (hopefully) satisfied customers. There are also civic and governmental relationships represented.

And there are some relationships we may not think much about. What about the relationship of "stranger-hood"? How do we relate to someone we do not know? What about that unfortunate relationship we call enemy, a relationship defined solely by conflict? And at one time, there was the relationship between master and slave.

These layers of relationships are not only represented horizontally across the sanctuary or fellowship hall, but also layered vertically within ourselves as individuals. At any given moment, a person can look across the sanctuary and see represented a brother in Christ, a boss or fellow employee, a teacher, the local politician, perhaps even a lending agent, all represented in one person.

Imagine the pastor who looks down in the middle of his sermon and sees a beloved sister in Christ in the front pew looking up at him. This sister in Christ also happens to be a voting member of the congregation and, therefore, one of his employers. Hopefully, she is also a friend. Upon closer inspection, this sister in Christ, who is a voting member of the church and his boss, and a friend, is also his wife. Imagine this all wrapped up into one lovely personification! How is that sermon going to satisfy all the relational roles laid out before her?

Much of what we find relationally in the church mimics precisely the social situation we face when we walk out into the streets of our community. Every morning when we wake up, we are required to navigate through layer upon layer of relationships. We grab our cups of coffee and venture into a wilderness of sometimes conflicting, often highly nuanced relationships that are stacked up at our doorstep waiting for us as we venture forth. It's a scary world out there!

The biblical text familiarizes us with many of these relationships. Scripture, from start to finish, is a tapestry of relational types. Putting aside for a moment the central covenantal relationship we have between Creator God and creature, we begin with the relationships of family. Marriage is a central relationship that finds its origins in the first two chapters of the book of Genesis. The relationship between Abraham and Isaac is one of the first of many descriptions of that most interesting relationship between a father and a son seen in Scripture. Not to be outmatched, the story of Rebecca and Jacob and Esau gives us a picture of the inner dynamics of mother to son, as well as that of brother to brother.

In the story of Moses and the relationship he had with the reluctant people of Israel, we find an example of the idea of family extended outward to tribes. We also see in him that complex relationship between leader and follower. In Saul, David, and David's son Solomon, we see the fundamental social contract between God's people being codified into nationhood. And in David especially, we see an example of friendship in his relationship with Jonathan. In the Psalms, David laments the reality of what it means to be an enemy.

Moving to the New Testament, the parables use the relationship of employee and employer several times as an illustration for larger truths. The parable of the Good Samaritan gives us a vivid description of what it means to be a stranger, a relationship that ranges somewhere on a continuum stretching between friendship and anonymity. Christ provides the supreme example of discipleship for his followers, later transforming this into a new relational type called apostleship. And today, what are we to make of the reality of that first-century relationship between slave and owner that Paul talks about? The list goes on.

Of course, we naturally don't think much about the relational complexities we face every moment of our day. The reality that every time we walk into a room we must negotiate ourselves around a complex matrix of relationships rarely rises to the level of our consciousness. When it does, it is because we have perhaps lapsed into a moment of self-conscious embarrassment that heightens these complexities; we face a socially awkward situation: "You are the wife of my older brother's boss, you say? I thought you were the maid, and I thought my brother was the boss!" Or perhaps we catch ourselves observing a socially maladjusted individual who has difficulty navigating his way from one type of relationship to the next: "No, Benjamin, you should not hug Daddy's boss in the same way you hug Mommy!"

Nevertheless, our ability to work around these relationships belies the fact that beneath the surface is an extremely complex web of rules that characterizes each of these relationship types. What is the source of sudden conflict that arises in our lives? Inevitably, we hit the trip wires of one of those hidden rules and don't even know it.

Relationship types are different in at least three ways. First, relationships are different in the specialized language that characterizes each of them. The language of an employer, for example, is the highly specialized language of the workplace and is used in special ways, particularly when talking to employees. Imagine using the vocabulary and tone of this marketplace language in addressing your infant son. "Son, get out of bed and take these spreadsheets and assess the viability of expanding our sales force into this area of the country!" Alternatively, imagine using the highly intimate language of a father to his infant child for purposes of talking to employees in the workplace: "All of you around the boardroom are so cute and cuddly!"

The language of therapists to their clients is even more specialized than that of commerce. Further, listen to the close parsing of words in the relationships between elected officials and citizens, or between lawyers and clients. On the other side of the spectrum, there is the language of siblings. The language of friendship is even more casual and imprecise. For close friends, a simple nod of the head or the slightest facial gesture can read like five paragraphs of single-spaced text.

Most interestingly, what is the language of a stranger when there is little shared context for saying or hearing what is being said? What is the language shared by two enemies? I could go on. Each is characterized by particular vocabulary, syntax, and, in some cases, tone and mode of expression. Imagine, then, using the language of a lover for a fellow employee. In our current sociopolitical context, there is a name for when intimate language intended for marriage is used in a workplace environment. It is called sexual harassment.

The second way relational types differ is in the conventions that define them as distinct patterns of behavior. Some of these set patterns of behavior reach to the level of ethical implications, as in the above example. Other conventions are less linked with presumed moral behavior. Some are implicit and hardly noted, and others are explicit and codified.

For example, Scripture is particularly clear on establishing moral parameters around the marriage relationship. But it is less clear how friends should relate to friends. There are clearly prescribed patterns of behavior for lawyers, especially as they stand before the bench. The conventions that define the behavior of a grandfather to his grandchildren might be less clear.

Most often these predictable patterns of language and behavior find their fullest expression in specific physical settings. The third way relationship types differ is in their unique contexts. Although a married couple might express themselves in a variety of private and public settings, the epicenter of the marriage relationship is in the bedroom. The context where the specialized language and behavior of an employee makes most sense is the workplace. The context of politicians to their constituents is the public square. The context of friendship ranges far and wide, as does that of brother to brother; but even here, these relationships tend to be defined by informal rather than formal settings.

There is much going on in relationships, both inside and outside of the church. With this in mind, what is this relationship we call "Christian community"? Walk into the sanctuary or fellowship hall, or even the living room of a member of your church's small group. What are your relational expectations? Are they being met? If they are not being met, then why not? If they are, then how might you encourage an even deeper sense of community?

Further, is this relationship we describe existing between brothers and sisters in Christ any different than, for example, what we might expect to be expressed at the monthly Lion's Club meeting? Is it special in any way? Should we expect more from it? Less? What language and conventions do we share as Christians that sets it apart from all other relationships?

Finally, if there is a unique relational type subsumed under the name of "Christian community," what are we to do with all the other relationships described above that are being expressed within our churches? How should being an employee, or a husband, or an elected official, or a salesperson of goods and services, or a teacher, or any of a number of other relationships be expressed in the gathered community of faith?

In the next several chapters, we will explore Christian community as a unique relational type that has the power to transform lives through the example set forth by Christ and empowered by the Holy Spirit. In order to do so, we will continue to explore a working definition of what we truly mean by "Christian community."

CHAPTER TWO

ON BEING A FRIEND

Perhaps "friendship" is the closest type of relationship that characterizes what we mean by Christian community. I'm thinking about my best friend. Aside from Cec and my immediate family, when I think of the most prized kind of relationship in my life, I think of my friendships. Is there a more profoundly personal, more deeply intimate, more wonderfully informal, more powerfully expressive, and more sought-after relationship than friendship? I don't think so.

Isn't this the relationship we see being displayed in clusters around the coffee urns and donuts in the fellowship halls of our churches? It would seem so, if the result of a simple click of the mouse is to be believed. The result of a Google search that cross-pollinates "church" and "friendship" registers 934,000 entries.

There is Friendship Church in Prior Lake, Minnesota; there is Friendship Baptist Church in Yorba Linda, California; there is Friendship Presbyterian Church in Athens, Georgia. Then there is Friendship Mennonite Church in Cleveland, Ohio, and Friendship Lutheran Church of Joy in Champaign, Illinois, and Friendship Missionary Baptist Church in Charlotte, North Carolina. And this represents just examples of churches from the first couple of pages of our search. Apparently, the linkage of friendship with church life spans the entire denominational and geographical landscape.

What is it in these churches that tethers characteristics of friendship so closely to our concept of community formation in churches? A click on the home page of the website of Friendship Church in Greenwood, Indiana, gives us a clue of the kind of traits that would seem to be at the core of community. The church beckons new people to "experience friendship: a kicked-back, relaxed, casual atmosphere." "Warm, inviting, friendly, cheerful, relaxed" are apparently the words that guests have used to describe the atmosphere of Friendship Church. The site further identifies the desire of the church to be the kind of church described in the Bible: "A church with relevant teaching, heartfelt worship, honest relationships, meaningful prayer, and compassionate care for the community around us."[1]

These, then, are apparently the words of Christian community: relaxed, casual, relevant, heartfelt, honest, meaningful, compassionate, warm, inviting, and cheerful. It is certainly not necessary to have "friendship" as part of the church masthead to realize that these same traits are almost universally valued in churches around the United States. Depending upon how far north or south one finds oneself from the Mason-Dixon Line, churches have more than likely institutionalized any number of conventions to display the practice of friendliness.

If friendship is so important for the church, then it is all the more important to be clear on what we mean by friendship. Rarely when we talk about friendship does it pass the Hallmark greeting card test mentioned previously. That is, this word *friendship* most often suffers from being over-sentimentalized in our present culture—over-sentimentalized and therefore trivialized.

The irony of this, of course, is that at a time when "being friendly" is growing ever more important to us, our understanding of what it means to be a friend is languishing. This is C. S. Lewis's lament when he observes that for modern man, friendship has become "something quite marginal; not a main course in life's banquet; a diversion; something that fills up the chinks of one's time."[2] Friendship has become ever so thin in our minds and hearts. It has been relegated from a position of serious obligation to, as Lewis sees it, a leisure-time activity.

One of the reasons for this is that friendship has come to mean almost anything. It is one of those big tent kind of words that expresses a whole range of relationships, from the person we just met five minutes ago to the person we have known and cared for all of our lives. Total strangers are called friends, work acquaintances are called friends, engaged couples are called "special" friends, and marriage partners are called friends. Our current usage of the term suffers from a serious case of grade inflation.

Accepting the reality that our capacity for friendship varies widely, both qualitatively and quantitatively, for the sake of clarity let's pull the strings tightly around this word and look at it narrowly, as if we are talking about our "best friend." We will look at the relationship as an idealized type of how it might appear at its best and most well defined. We will also confine our understanding of friendship to what we find embedded in Western cultural settings. We can predict that this relationship may possibly take on different shades of expression in other cultural contexts.

To set the record straight, you should know that this marginalization of our understanding of friendship is an anomaly of our time. In almost every other period of history, the concept of friendship was taken quite seriously. Looking back specifically in the Western tradition on the subject, it was a serious preoccupation for serious people, from philosophers and artists to religious leaders and social critics alike for many generations throughout history. As a result, a considerable body of literature grew up to describe it.

Walk with me through history to identify some of these contemplators of what it means to be a friend. Aristotle saw friendship (*philia*) as a major preoccupation in how a citizen is to live the virtuous life. He committed two full chapters of his *The Nicomachean Ethics* to his discussion of friendship, fully one-fifth of the treatise. For him, central to living a virtuous life is to exist in friendship: "For friendship is a virtue, or involves virtue; and also it is one of the most indispensable requirements of life. For no one would choose to live without friends, but possessing all other good things."[3]

Cicero follows suit with Aristotle and the almost unanimous chorus of other classical writers by anchoring the idea of friendship with the virtuous life: "Virtue (without which friendship is impossible) is first; but next to it, and to it alone, the greatest of all things is Friendship."[4] How important is friendship (*amicitia*)? For Cicero, one might just as well take the sun from the sky as friendship from life, "for the immortal gods have given us nothing better or more delightful."[5]

Augustine breaks into his *Confessions* with a sweet lament of a friendship lost too soon. With simple eloquence he speaks of his friendship as "one soul in two bodies," and puzzles how it is that he could still live while his "second self" be dead.[6]

This idea of friend as "soulmate" is expanded to systematic proportions in the sixteenth-century writings of Michel de Montaigne. Friendship is nothing short of two persons who have become one. Of his soulmate, he says, "but this friendship that possesses the soul and rules it with absolute sovereignty cannot possibly be double."[7]

In his essay "Of Friendship," Francis Bacon is less effusive but every bit as serious about the need for friendship: "For a crowd is not company; and faces are but a gallery of pictures: and talk but a tinkling cymbal, where there is no love."[8] He declares true friendship as nothing less than a human necessity, "without which the world is but a wilderness."

In Aelred of Rievaulx, we find the supreme achievement of medieval monastic reflection on friendship, but his spirituality is laced with the humanism of his central source on the topic of Cicero. Cicero's "virtue" as a backdrop to friendship is translated as Christian "charity" in Aelred's understanding of "spiritual friendship." From where does friendship come? Quoting his conversation partner, Ivo, Aelred states, "God is friendship."[9] Citing Amic, friendship for him is "mutual harmony in affairs human and divine coupled with benevolence and charity."[10]

Later in the late sixteenth and seventeenth centuries, Francis de Sales in *The Devout Life* speaks from the perspective of the cloister when he writes of a special friendship set apart from all others, which he calls "holy friendships."[11] The great divide between "true" and "false" friendships rests, for de Sales, at the wall of the cloister.

Not to be outdone by the Catholic monastics, the early Protestant dons also weighed in on friendship. In seventeenth-century England, the Right Rev. Jeremy Taylor (Lord Bishop of Down, Connor, and Dromore) speaks of friendship transformed by Christianity into a universal act of charity: "But then I must tell you that Christianity hath new christened it [friendship], and called this charity."[12] In his "The Measures and Offices of Friendship," he chronicles with minute detail the landscape of friendship as it is to be expressed both within religion and in nature in general.

George Berkley, an eighteenth-century Episcopal cleric, contemplated the principle of the mutual attraction of friendship by setting the relationship against the larger backdrop of the unity and design of creation. The inner unity of companionship is nothing less than a reflection of the order of the universe: "The system of thinking beings is actuated by laws derived from the same divine power undergirding the universe."[13]

In a quite different vein, Immanuel Kant spoke of friendship more as an ideal, an abstract idea to be spoken of at arm's length rather than realized, something to be discussed rather than cherished. He writes, "Friendship is an Idea, because it is not derived from experience. Empirical examples of friendship are extremely defective."[14]

This abstract concept of friendship that is held at arm's length can be matched only by the intellectual coldness of the French philosopher of the eighteenth century, Helvetius. For him, friendship is reduced to the shared wants that bind persons together.[15]

Emerson and his fellow traveler, Thoreau, return to friendship as something deeply spiritual in nature, but they believe that the source of this spirituality is found within. For Emerson, friendship is a natural divinity within the human spirit. In great Romantic fashion, he declares,

> My friends have come to me unsought. The great God gave them to me. My oldest right, by the divine affinity of virtue with itself, I find them, or rather, not I, but the Deity in me and in them derides and cancels the thick walls of individual character, relation, age, sex, circumstance, at which he usually connives, and now makes many one.[16]

Finally, in his *The Four Loves*, C. S. Lewis sifts through two other forms of love—affection and *eros*—to speak of friendship as the "least natural of loves; the least instinctive, organic, biological, gregarious and necessary."[17] He speaks fondly of the extravagant nature of two friends freely choosing to set themselves apart with no obligation other than to be friends.

And we could go on to include Plutarch, Epictetus, Seneca, and the church fathers, including Ambrose, as well as Ben Johnson and his friend Boswell, the writings of the Romantics—Keats and Wordsworth—William Godwin, and Sir Herbert Maxwell. All of these and many more represent a rich tapestry of thinking about the nature of friendship that is worth considering if we are to take this relationship seriously, particularly as it relates to the church.

What, then, are specific characteristics that make up friendship? What makes it such a compelling relationship set apart from the vast pantheon of other relationships we encounter every day? What makes it so special, especially (apparently) for those of us in the church who want to build our relationships around it?

There is certainly not full consensus in either principle or emphasis on every point in the literature on friendship. Each perspective has been mired in its own historical set of contexts and interests. But let's explore some of the characteristics that make up being a friend. For our purpose, think "best" friend.

1. Friendship Is Exclusive

One faithful friend is enough; it is even much to meet with one, yet we cannot for the sake of others have too many friends.—La Bruyere[18]

Has it really been thirty years already since I first trudged up that leeward side of the mountain to enter into what became, for me, one of the most compelling examples of Christian community I have ever experienced? It was in that little farming village—hanging so precariously on the side of the Rhone River Valley in Huemoz, Switzerland—that I lived and studied and worked and worshipped for five months with individuals from around the world at the L'Abri Christian Fellowship.

It was also there that I learned some important things about the nature of friendship. More to the point, it was there that a fellow student introduced me rather dramatically to a central insight into friendship. He told me how he had just finished a lengthy and gratifying conversation with his tutor on a subject near and dear to his heart. Apparently, captivated with the delight of new insights, combined with the warmth of a cozy fireplace and fortified by his own natural American openness, he innocently referred to his budding relationship with his mentor as being a "friendship." The response of his tutor was immediate and to the point: "You are not my friend. I have perhaps only three or four friends in my lifetime, and you are not one of them."

Perhaps only a German could get away with the raw honesty of this response. Dig back through the awkwardness of the moment for my fellow student, however, and there is the first truth that describes friendship as a unique relationship type. *Friendship is, by nature, an exclusive relationship.* Not everyone can be a friend. Of course, this may vary slightly from person to person, based upon personal disposition and other factors. Nevertheless, in comparison with other types of relationships, it is limited in scope.

Friendship, like any other relationship, has a natural horizon it looks out over. If we go beyond the natural horizon of any one relationship, we stretch the range of the natural identity, influence, and comfort level of that relationship. The horizon of a marriage, for example, is intimate, confined in influence and affections to the space between two persons. The horizon of a family is a bit farther out and is measured by bloodline, closer for immediate family, and farther out for extended family. Beyond this, the Old Testament offers plenty of examples of family relationships reaching out as far as the tribe. Joseph's horizon, for example, reached outward to the tribe of Benjamin.

Beyond the extended bloodlines of a family and tribe, the horizon that characterizes the relationship of fellow citizens reaches to the borders of one's sense of nationhood. Every time the pledge of allegiance is recited in the classroom, or the national anthem is sung at the ballpark, we share in the natural horizon of our citizenship. At these moments, we both include and exclude someone. We include ourselves with everyone in the classroom and the ballpark, or almost everyone. We exclude ourselves symbolically from noncitizens.

And we could go on to speak of the horizons of other relationships. The natural horizon of teachers with their students is extensive if one includes those who have previously shared the classroom with those who are currently under their tutelage. The horizon of salespeople in their commercial relationships with others, they hope, will be endless and reach to the farthest markets of the country and global economy. The horizon of being a stranger goes even farther, encompassing all those we have not yet had the opportunity to know.

The horizon of friendship, however, is very narrow. All of us are confined to the capacity of only a few friends. Cicero contrasts friendship to other relationships when he says, "You may best understand this friendship by considering that, whereas the merely natural ties uniting the human race are indefinite, this one is so concentrated, and confined to so narrow a sphere, that affection is ever shared by two persons only or at most by a few."[19]

What is it that makes this relationship so exclusive? There are several minimizing factors. The first may well be the most obvious. As awkward as this might sound, we just don't have enough *time* for more than a few friends. Imagine how this might sound to a room full of guests: "Excuse me, folks, I have something to say. I don't have enough time to make all of you my friends. Only a few of you are really my friends."

This sounds so strange, but it's true. Picture how you allocate your time differently to some people and less so to others. Ruminating on the natural limits of friendship, Aristotle says realistically, "For it is troublesome to have to repay the services of a large number of people, and life is not long enough for one man to do it."[20] Friendships—true friendships—take time and exist in time. Again, I am not speaking here of mere acquaintances. More will be discussed on this later, but it is enough here to say that the quality of friendship is defined by the quantity of its nurturing.

A second factor is equally basic. Friendship is limited by location. George Berkeley speaks of friendship as confined by the *geography* of one's close proximity:

> As in bodies, where the quantity is the same, the attraction is strongest between those which are placed nearest to each other. . . . A man who has no family is more strongly attracted towards his friends and neighbors; and if absent from these, he naturally falls into an acquaintance with those of his own city and county who chance to be in the same place.[21]

In this sense, I suppose it might be said that there are fifty or sixty individuals in New Zealand who could potentially be good friends of mine whom I will never have the chance to befriend because of geography. Alas, what a waste of good friendship!

But if it is the natural inclination of being drawn to persons of like cultural and social distinctions, the satisfaction of sharing a common place, or the regularity of association of one close by, then geography is an important factor in the confining limits of friendship. This, of course, is not to suggest that friendships cannot span geography. If "Friendship Tours" brochures are to be believed, the current shrinking of our world through opportunities for leisure and travel to virtually all parts of the world have somewhat altered the landscape of friendship in recent years. But the implications are nevertheless significant. The reality is that we are not friends with certain persons, because we are not where they are and they are not where we are. Make sense?

These factors might all be wrapped up more generally, if ambiguously, in terms of the limitations of *circumstance*. Friendship is limited by the common situations we find ourselves in. Sir Herbert Maxwell makes the point:

> Nevertheless friendship is largely the outcome of circumstance. The pursuit of a common object, the neighborhood of homes, community of language and environment—if these are not indispensable to friendship, they are at least the accidents by which it is engendered and kept in being: it is, indeed, difficult to imagine living friendships without one or another of these conditions.[22]

The accidents of time, place, and opportunity conspire to exclude certain individuals from friendship and include others. In this sense, the circumstances that surround the making of our friendships are downright fragile. C. S. Lewis imagines with us:

But in Friendship . . . we think we have chosen our peers. In reality, a few years' difference in the dates of our births, a few more miles between certain houses, the choice of one university instead of another, posting to different regiments, the accident of a topic being raised or not raised at a first meeting—any of these chances might have kept us apart.[23]

Picture Lewis's words in the context of your own best friends. Imagine if they were not at that precise restaurant or park bench when you met. Imagine if you were born two years later, or ten years, or three hundred years, for that matter. Our friendships hang on the narrow threads of circumstances that, in the end, are completely outside of our control.

Lewis is more precise in speaking of a fourth factor that makes friendship exclusive: *common interest.* Certainly he had in mind his long walks through wood and dale with his few good friends that ended inevitably with feet propped up over the hearth of an inn, a brew in hand, and great conversation between close friends. He speaks of companionship as being between people who are doing something together—"hunting, studying, painting or whatever you will." But Lewis sees friendship as more than just companionship, the sharing of activities. Friends, he says, "will still be doing something together, but something more inward, less widely shared and less easily defined."[24] Friendship for Lewis is using these external acts of companionship as opportunities to share intimately in each other's lives.

These criteria for friendship, of course, may have some exceptions. Some of you may be drawn to people with exact opposite tastes, but I think the criteria have some merit. When I look at my closest friends, not many of them spend a great deal of their time on Saturdays looking under the hood of their cars, nor will you find me there with them. I just don't look good with grease on my hands. There is a better chance that whatever friends I have will be sitting around a table with me talking about ways in which Harold Pinter affected the British theater scene in the late twentieth century.

A fifth factor that makes friendship exclusive is *personality.* If I am to be totally honest, I am drawn to some people, while others just get under my skin. Perhaps more than any other trait in this modern age, we emphasize personality as a measuring stick for what it takes to become friends.

Henry David Thoreau speaks of this in terms of "affinity": "Friendships take place between those who have an affinity for one another, and is a perfectly natural and inevitable result."[25] The quirky sense of humor or the studied introspection, the wry smile or the propensity for being impulsive, the naive openness or the rough frankness—there is something within certain persons that attracts friendship in highly complex and unique ways. Likewise, there are certain traits in others that become hindrances to friendship.

Finally, one wonders if *gender* is a limiting factor for friendship. Can best friends be members of the opposite sex, especially if you are married? I am not sure, at least not safely. Certainly this is a topic for debate based upon individual experiences. At the very least, here is an example of friendship being a potentially dangerous relationship under certain circumstances.

The debate on friendship and the opposite sex is complicated even further by opinions over whether males and females even perceive friendship in the same way. I watch Cec go out every month with her best friends to celebrate their birthdays with a special breakfast and gifts, and I wonder what they're doing. As a male, I hardly remember my wife's birthday, let alone any of my friends. We express friendship in different ways.

And speaking of Cec, what about friendship and marriage? Can husbands and wives be friends? I certainly hope so, but in doing so, they affect friendship with others. Victorian writer E. Lynn Linton says, "Marriage in itself is a formidable hindrance to friendship of any kind. It asks too much—seeks to occupy too large an area—seeks, indeed, to occupy the whole of the emotional area—it and the children resulting." And, again, she says, "No greater treachery to friendship can be done than by this false honour of mutuality in marriage."[26] Linton's observations here might very well be a product of her own Victorian age and may not reflect current sensibilities that link marriage and friendship closely together. Her point is, however, that marriage may well restrict other friendships from being expressed in that, by its exclusionary nature, it consumes time and commitment that would otherwise be expressed more broadly with other friends.

All of these limitations, then, conspire against friendship: *time, space, circumstances, personality and disposition, interest, gender, and even marriage*. In this it is an interesting relationship. On the one hand, nothing formally restricts us from being friends with almost anyone. None of the more objective criteria—such as bloodline that defines family, or a social contract that defines any number of social or commercial relationships—restrict friendship. Rather, it is these natural, highly subjective, and organic characteristics that make friendship, in the end, a highly exclusive relationship. Not everyone can be your friend!

2. Friendship Is Preferential

It is not man's way to embrace the whole world in his good-will; he prefers to restrict it to a small circle.—Immanuel Kant[27]

A second characteristic of friendship is that it is by nature *highly preferential*. Saying this is, admittedly, somewhat delicate. It is one thing to speak of friendship in exclusionary terms. It is quite another to speak of a relationship in less-than-democratic terms.

Imagine if we defined other types of relationships in this way. Picture two parents lining their three children up in the living room and selecting Melissa as their favorite child over Dana and little Jason. Or perhaps employees sense that they have been overlooked for a position because the boss happens to have a son. We call this nepotism. Or what about the prize student who purposely sits in front of the class and answers all of the teacher's questions? We call this favorite student the "teacher's pet," a not-altogether-positive term of endearment.

We find scattered about the world of commerce plenty of examples of individuals intentionally being made favorites. Airlines have what they call "preferred status" travelers. But even these relationships are carefully made and with certain public delineations in mind. When the flight attendant closes the curtain that separates the proverbial first-class sheep from the main-cabin goats, the only reason feelings aren't hurt—as some eat tenderloin on fine china and others eat their knees—is because specific assurances have been given that those with the linen napkins also have gold cards indicating that they are preferred because they paid more for their flight than those in the back.

But, without apology, every day we prefer certain people over others as friends. Why does this sound so jarring to us at first glance? Perhaps it is because we in the United States have built the opposite inclination into the very fabric of who we are as citizens. What has been created in the social DNA of our lives? "All men are created equal." Although it is the constitutional right of all persons to stand on equal footing with one another, our lives, and more so our emotions, contradict this fact every day and in so many ways! None of us view all people as equal. In fact, the very reason we need a formal social contract to assure us under the law that all persons are to be treated equally is precisely because, in our hearts, they aren't equal and, left to our own natural inclinations, we would not treat them as such.[28]

The language we use in discussing our friends is the best example of this. One would be hard-pressed to fight the impulse to put an asterisk or two next to certain individuals on a list we might make of our friends. We have friends, and then we have "better" friends, and then we might have "best" friends. We have "work" friends, and "church" friends, and "bowling" friends. The criteria for delineating these categories are most assuredly different for each individual, but the point is that friendship is highly preferential. If we look closely across the span of our familiar relationships, it would look like a pyramid.

Undeniably, the pyramid includes many layers of individuals we may consider friends, but friendship is narrow at the top. Regarding this, there is almost complete agreement from the past—"true" friendship is rare and is a highly selective process. Not everyone can be a friend, which Immanuel Kant insists:

> Is every man a possible friend for us? No. I can be a friend of mankind in general in the sense that I can bear good-will in my heart toward everyone, but to be the friend of everybody is impossible, for friendship is a particular relationship, and he who is a friend to everyone has no particular friend.[29]

Emerson speaks more poetically of true friends as "those rare pilgrims whereof only one or two wander in nature at once, and before whom the vulgar great show as spectres and shadows merely."[30]

The distinction that needs to be made here is one we rarely think about. It is the distinction of varying degrees of friendliness—of "being friendly"—with friendship itself. Jeremy Taylor says,

> It must therefore follow, that our friendships to mankind may admit variety as does our conversation; and as by nature we are made sociable to all, so we are friendly; but as all cannot actually be of our society, so neither can all be admitted to a special, actual friendship. Of some intercourses all men are capable, but not of all.[31]

Picture yourself in a social situation. There is a certain obligation built into most of us to be friendly with everyone present. By this I mean that we offer certain social graces to individuals of all sorts. To do so, however, is not necessarily to offer them our hearts. We may be under some obligation in social situations to "be friendly" but certainly not to become "friends."

So much confusion exists for most of us at this point as we seek to delineate levels of friendship for ourselves, and have them delineated for us by other would-be friends. Again, Taylor says, "There must be in friendship something to distinguish it from a companion, and a countryman, from a schoolfellow or a gossip, from a sweetheart or a fellow-traveler: friendship may look in at any one of these doors, but it stays not anywhere till it comes to be the best thing in the world [friendship]."[32]

There is actually much at stake in acknowledging the rare privilege of entering into a select society of one or maybe two friends. The integrity of true friendship itself rests on the unapologetic freedom we have in giving to a select few what we cannot nor should not give to the many. Can you see that offering friendship to every acquaintance we might make, as seemingly honorable as this might be on the surface, actually has the effect of cheapening the true friendships we have worked so hard on over the years?

So, what is it that true friends share that is so utterly selective? Some of the most transcendent descriptions of friendship surface in the writings on friendship at this point. Literature is filled with descriptions of the rare melding of souls, so much so that even individual identity between two friends is lost. Augustine speaks of friendship as the *second self* as he contemplates the death of his lost friend:

> I marveled more that I, his second self, could live when he was dead. Well has someone said of his friend that he is half of his soul in two bodies. Therefore, my life was a horror to me, because I would not live as but a half. Perhaps because of this I feared to die, lest he whom I had loved so much should wholly die.[33]

Montaigne speaks of the uncommon friendship set apart from all others he calls his *soulmate:*

> For this perfect friendship I speak of is indivisible; each one gives himself so entirely to his friend that he has nothing left to distribute to others . . . but this friendship that possesses the soul and rules it with absolute sovereignty cannot possibly be double.[34]

For Aelred, true friendship is nothing less than the complete *meshing of the wills.* In his dialogue with Gratian, he states, "I believed friendship was nothing else than so complete an identity of wills between two persons that the one would wish nothing which the other did not wish."[35] What interesting phrases these are: "second self," "soulmate," and "meshing of the wills." Here is highly preferential language suggesting that true friendship is so intimate, there is almost a sharing of identities!

Think about whom you consider your "best" friend. Is this not what you at least strive for, if not actually achieve? This is almost language we would reserve for marriage, of two people becoming one person, not physically, but in terms of our inner beings. Friendship at its best is when two people become one person. This kind of friendship is not to be given to just everyone. It is given only to a preferred few.

3. Friendship Is Reciprocal

One cannot be a friend without having one.—A. S. Hardy[36]

It is that awkward moment, especially for those in the public eye. It's that moment when you first sense another person hanging around too often and in unintended times and places. It's nothing inappropriate particularly, but you might sense the other person glancing at you. Or it's the nervous laughter, the misplaced phrase of the other person, the forced conversation, perhaps a stutter—the person obviously seeking approval from you. In time, it's the invitation to spend more time than you have to give. It is that awkward moment when you sense that another person is seeking friendship in ways that you know in your heart cannot be reciprocated.

Or swing the door to the other side. Have you ever found yourself the one with the nervous laugh, the stutter or the misplaced phrase, or the desire to spend more time with another person than what seems to be eagerly received? Have you ever sought friendship from another and not felt it recognized and appreciated? This leads us to our third characteristic of friendship. *Friendship must be reciprocal.*

You cannot be a friend with someone who is not a friend in return. It requires a mutual giving and receiving of oneself to truly be a friendship. Aristotle uses the most basic of illustrations to make this point:

> Friendship is not applied to love for inanimate objects, since here there is no return of affection, and also no wish for the good of the object—for instance, it would be ridiculous to wish well to a bottle of wine: at the most one wishes that it may keep well in order that one may have it oneself; whereas we are told that we ought to wish our friend well for his own sake. But persons who wish another good for his own sake, if the feeling is not reciprocated, are merely said to feel goodwill for him: only when mutual is such goodwill termed friendship.[37]

A bottle of wine does not a relationship make (of course, some would beg to differ!). Friendship cannot be a one-way street. It must include at least two people who are willing to give something of themselves to another person.

But can't we say this about any relationship in which something is always given and something is always received? Think of the feudal period in tenth-century Scotland. In the distant past, a good ruler gave his subjects protection and received in return their taxes and loyalty. Likewise, the subjects gave of their labor and adoration and received the protection of the ruler.

In our modern workplace, both employers and employees are always giving and receiving. An employer gives an opportunity for employment and receives the fruit of employee labor. In turn, employees give their labor and in return receive a paycheck from the employer. Both teachers and pupils give and receive: teachers their expertise, for which they receive a paycheck and hopefully willing minds. Students give themselves to hard work, and in return receive the knowledge passed down from their teachers.

In varying degrees, each of these relationships gives and receives, *but none in proportion to the other.* This is the difference. Put simply, if viewed from the perspective of a grocery aisle, one is not receiving a can of beans for a can of beans, or a box of cereal for a box of cereal. Nor is such given. Friendship is unique in that the mutual giving and receiving of oneself must be in relative proportion to itself in kind and extent. It receives what it gives and gives what it receives.

And what is it that is proportionately given and received? Certainly it must involve the sharing of common interests. Lewis makes this most basic of points when he says, "Friendship must be about something, even if it were only an enthusiasm for dominoes or white mice. Those who have nothing can share nothing; those who are going nowhere can have no fellow-travellers."[38]

I am not altogether sure what Lewis is doing with white mice here, but that aside, at its core friendship requires that individuals share an ever-growing reservoir of common experiences. In this sense, friendship is a transaction in which individuals trade their time and effort and shared interests with one another. Something must be given, and something of relative equal value must be returned.

Let me give you an example from my childhood. Although I was supposed to be upstairs sleeping, some of my fondest memories as a child are sitting on the top rung of the stairs, listening in on the conversations of my parents and their closest and longest friends as they sat around coffee telling stories to one another. I couldn't help but listen. Any thought of sleep was broken by their roars of laughter! Isn't this the glue that holds friendships together? We attend ball games together. We sit around the table laughing and telling stories together. We play cards together. We make travel plans together in order to share experiences.

And in sharing these experiences, friends over time begin to share more than the present moment of their common experiences. They begin to share a mutual understanding of one another's pasts and hopes for the future. Friends cannot help but tell their stories, and in retelling their stories, they begin to explore with one another the web of motives and incidents—both good and bad. They ask and answer for the other, "What happened? Why did it happen? And will you accept me despite what happened?"

Likewise, they explore and put the other person into their futures. Thoreau says, "The Friend asks no return but that his Friend will religiously accept and wear and not disgrace his apotheosis of him. They cherish each other's hopes. They are kind to each other's dreams."[39] Isn't this one of the great delights of friendship—not only to accept another person fully, despite who they might have shown themselves to be in the past, but also to be pulling for them into the future? It is to share experiences that have not even happened yet and that may only be in the other's mind as a hope and a dream!

All this is to say that although friendship includes mutual sharing of time and interests and experiences—of thoughts of the past and dreams of the future—it is even more than the sum total of all of these. It must include these things, but in the end friendship is the *mutual sharing of persons themselves*. In an elevated way that only Ralph Waldo Emerson can pull off, he says,

> So I will owe to my friends this evanescent intercourse. I will receive from them not what they have but what they are. They shall give me that which properly

they cannot give, but that which emanates from them. But they shall not hold me by any relations less subtle and pure. We will meet as though we met not, and part as though we parted not.[40]

In the end, friendship is not a commodity that is consciously shared with another person. It is not a product. True friends do not measure out what they have given and compare it with what they have received, like two children down on their hands and knees eyeing who received the larger piece of cake. Friendship is far less calculating than this. Rather, true friendship involves the natural giving of the self to another person, not with set expectations but with full confidence that it will be returned in kind.

4. Friendship Involves Equal Status

Defer to your friend as to an equal . . . for friendship knows no pride.—Ambrose[41]

There we were, three among seeming equals, as we rummaged around the dirt, moving daylilies from one side of the yard to another garden on the far side of the estate. Daily, weekly, monthly—we worked together for over three years, tending these gardens. And there they were, two elderly North Shore Boston Brahmins, working and sweating right next to me, their part-time gardener and part-time seminary student.

I would like to have considered Mr. and Mrs. Roberts as friends. We were always more than friendly to one another. If necessity required it of us, we certainly would have pronounced ourselves as friends, both publicly and to one another. They were always more than generous, at times treating my wife and me to periodic visits to the Marblehead Yacht Club with them. But at the end of every day when we got up off our mud-caked knees and they wrote out my check for the day's labor, beneath the cordiality the unspoken truth shared by all of us was that I was really their hired help. Every evening I left them to a life we rarely shared outside of their gardens.

Closely linked to the idea of the mutuality of friendship is that *friendship is a relationship of relative equality.* True friendship involves individuals who stand on equal footing, eye-to-eye, toe-to-toe, ego-to-ego. Unlike other relationships mentioned above—the ruler to the subject, the employer to the employee, the teacher to the student—friendship assumes a common status. Or as Aristotle says, "In all dissimilar friendships, it is proportion, as has been said, that establishes equality and preserves the friendship."[42]

I was struck a few years ago of this fact when Cec and I went with friends to the Museum of Fine Arts in Boston. At the museum, I noticed a sculpture that reminded me of this topic of friendship. Actually, to call it a sculpture without further explanation would be misleading. Made of heavy gauge wire, it showed two men standing face-to-face, ready to shake hands. You could see right through them. What struck me was how equally proportionate each of the statues was with the other, both physically and by expression. This is what friendship is. It is based on individuals with relatively equal proportionality.

More precisely, friends assume a relatively equal level of authority over each other. In fact, for Jeremy Taylor this is the difference between friendship and the parent-child relationship. He says:

> This friendship and social relation [parent-child] are not equal, and there is too much authority on one side, and too much fear on the other, to make equal friendships; and, therefore, although this is one of the kinds of friendship, that is of a social and relative love and conversation; yet in the more proper use of the word, friendship does do some things which father and son do not.[43]

The parent-child relationship, like many others, is by nature hierarchical, with levels of constraints and controls and assumed levels of submission built into one or other side of the relationship. The status of the one stands over and above the other. Friendship defies this kind of control, which poisons the spirit of what it means to befriend another. Especially in today's world, true friends see themselves sharing equally in the authority that exists between them, rather than having authority placed over one at the expense of the other.

But this hasn't always been the case. We find different perspectives at other times and places, when certain social roles were far more restrictive. One such time was nineteenth-century England when Lynn Linton in her essay "The Ethics of Friendship" speaks of friendship as narrowly confined to certain classes of people:

> The essence of friendship is equality. . . . Hence there can be no real friendship between people of very different social spheres, unless the superior is more democratic than is often found among Brahmins of any name or complexion. All the urbanity, even the familiarity of the high and mighty to those of low birth—no matter how thickly fortune has gilded the original clay pipkin [sic] is condescension, not friendship.[44]

Such a definition of friendship appears foreign to those of us in the modern egalitarian West, but Linton describes for us here a time when friendship was most vulnerable in the face of strong social controls. It is at those times when the hierarchical structures of authority and status are so strong that the more natural bridges between potential friends are least easily breached.

Especially in our day and age, friendship fades in the presence of this kind of condescension. But, as subtle as it may be, we find it fading even in informal situations where socially induced status doesn't seem to exist. Take, for example, the relationship between the mentor and the protégée. I spend a great deal of time with seminary students, mentoring them in their preparation for future ministry. Most often, this type of relationship is spoken of in the language of familiarity and friendship. Oftentimes, I will speak with my students in the language of friendship.

Certainly there is plenty of give-and-take in a typical mentoring experience and invariably I, like many of my colleagues, often declare I received far more than I gave. But even in the comfortable banter of advice making, strictly speaking, one side of the relationship controls the agenda and the other is a recipient. It functions hierarchically in the softest sense of the word and, at the very least, impacts how friendship is expressed.

There is another source of inequality that affects friendships that has little to do with external forms of status. Friendships are also affected by disparities in internal qualities. These may include differing levels of intellect, social graces, senses of humor, and so on. Friends tend to share comparable levels of personal characteristics. So it is that Cicero says:

> But here is another golden rule in friendship: put yourself on a level with your friend. . . . If any of us have any advantage in personal character, intellect, or fortune, we should be ready to make our friends sharers and partners in it with ourselves. For instance, if their parents are in humble circumstances, if their relations are powerful neither in intellect nor means, we should supply their deficiencies and promote their rank and dignity.[45]

Do opposites attract in terms of friendship? Perhaps in some cases, but generally friends tend to select themselves based upon qualities they share with one another, both in kind and in relative measure.

But does this mean that friendships cannot bridge the kinds of inequalities that exist in life, both externally and internally? Certainly there are plenty of examples to the contrary, the most dramatic being the biblical account of Jonathan, son of the king of Israel, and the then-lowly David, the shepherd/soldier. Innumerable other examples can be given of friendships spanning various boundaries of status in our lives. This is certainly, in part, because we tend to live in a less status-conscious social environment today that allows friendships to cross boundaries that in other times and places would be more difficult.

Friendships can span areas of inequality, but only if the areas of disparity in status are intentionally put aside for the sake of the friendship. Aelred states,

> Therefore in friendship, which is the perfect gift of nature and grace alike, let the lofty descend, the lowly ascend; the rich be in want, the poor become rich; and thus let each communicate his condition to the other, so that equality may

be the result. . . . Never, therefore, prefer yourself to your friend; but if you chance to find yourself the superior in those things which we have mentioned, then do not hesitate to abase yourself before your friend, to give him your confidence, to praise him if he is shy, and to confer honor upon him in inverse proportion to that warranted by his lowliness and poverty.[46]

If areas of status and disparities in inner qualities cannot be bridged in real life, then they must at least be reconciled and bridged by the friends themselves. True friends must truly see themselves as equal for friendship to exist. To do so means that they must consciously and continuously fight the pressures of disparity in status that surround them.

As an aside, it is worth stopping here briefly to reflect on more general comments made in chapter 1 concerning the subtle hazards of navigating around various relational types. What we observed there was that the source of conflict in relationships tends to be the result of tripping over the highly complex set of rules that exists under the surface of our lives. Those rules have to do with understanding the differences in the language, conventions, and contexts that exist in various relationship types.

This aspect of equality in friendship is an excellent example of how many trip and fall on their faces because they confuse the hidden rules of relationships. For example, some parents sometimes try too hard to be friends with their children when, in reality, they need to be parents. The hierarchical status of being parents over their children is a positive, even essential attribute for a healthy family structure. Parents may be compromising something of great importance in seeking to become strictly friends with their children.

Another example is in the ways in which employers and employees relate. Without suggesting that one must be a distant autocrat, it might be said that employers tend to lose some of their ability to lead effectively in direct proportion to the role friendship plays out with employees. Something is gained in seeking friendship, but not at the expense of important things being lost. All this to say that equality certainly is a virtue in friendship, but may not be in other relational contexts. With these words of admonition, we move on to further traits of friendship in the next chapter.

CHAPTER THREE

MORE ON FRIENDSHIP

W^e have now looked at four relational traits of friendships. Lest we get lost in the weeds on why we are talking about friendship, let me stop for a moment to remind us what we are doing here: We are seeking to understand the relationship that makes up the church. When we use the phrase "Christian community," what do we mean? What can we expect relationally of others in the church?

I am not speaking here of the institution of the church, what we might call the *square-ness* of the church with its programs, institutional ecclesiology, and roles—pastors, leaders, members, regular attenders, newcomers, and the like. Rather, I am speaking about better understanding the more organic *round-ness* of the church, its informal relationships. I am speaking here of church as "fellowship."

What individuals are relationally at the center of your church? Can you name them? Who is on the outside looking in, and why aren't they more engaged? Who holds everything together relationally in your church? With this reminder, let me continue. We are almost halfway there.

5, Friendship Is Self-Benefiting

Love implies want, and there is no friendship without it.—Helvetius[1]

Do you want an ideal picture of a traditional pastor's wife? Cut out her picture, put it on the refrigerator door, and point to it every time someone asks. She had all the qualities necessary to care for the churches she and her husband served for almost sixty years. As capable as she was in front of people, it was in what was seen by her husband and children in private that most marked her ministry: endless meals for sick parishioners or for the regular missionary who stayed overnight; late-night interruptions by persons in crisis; lesson plans put together at the last minute to cover for a sick Sunday school teacher; long hours of counseling, sometimes while experiencing one of her regular migraines; and, on top of all that, constant caring for her four less-than-appreciative, clueless sons.

Many of you know the kind of person that describes my mother. We put them up on the top of the relational scale along with those who are better known, such as Mother Teresa and St. Francis of Assisi. We call these people somewhat euphemistically "saints." There is a scent of altruism in the air when they walk by. That is, these women and men almost seem unapproachable in their virtue.

We call them saints because they possess one special quality. They share the ability or willingness—or both—to give of themselves selflessly to others without asking anything in return. They are like the plastic Virgin Mary statues placed on the car dashboards of the Catholic pious that placidly offer up the promise of roadway protection without any thought of receiving anything in return.

As unapproachably virtuous as these saints may be, they do not embody what is found in our next characteristic of friendship. Friends, by definition, are not saints. Let me clarify. Although individuals who happen to be saints may have friendships, and some of your friends might embody saint-like characteristics, the fundamental characteristic that describes these individuals is not descriptive of what it means to be a friend. Returning to our discussion on the reciprocal nature of friendship, true friends must give freely, but they must also receive freely in return. *Friendship is, by nature, self-benefiting.*

As strange as this might sound, the quality of any friendship can be measured by the quality of what is received by that friendship. Show me a friendship where one of the supposed friends isn't benefiting from the relationship, and I will show you a weak friendship, if it's a friendship at all. In the best sense of the word, friendship is a "selfish" relationship! Come again? Really?

Let me once again invite Aristotle to explain. He describes levels of friendship in terms of degrees to which friends are self-benefited. Admittedly, the lowest forms he describes are those motivated by pleasure or utility: "Friendship then being divided into these species, inferior people will make friends for pleasure or for use, if they are alike in that respect, while good men will be friends for each other's own sake, since they are alike in being good."[2] In these two lower levels, Aristotle acknowledges that both friends benefit from the relationship, but unevenly. In addition, longevity of friendships corresponds, he says, to their utility. Aristotle follows the logic: "Friendship based on utility dissolves as soon as its profit ceases; for the friends did not love each other, but what they got out of each other."[3]

Friendship at its best, however, is when friends benefit equally by their relationship. Aristotle continues, "In these cases also the friendship is most lasting when each friend derives the same benefit, for instance pleasure, from the other, and not only so, but derives it from the same thing, as in a friendship between two witty people, and not as in one between a lover and his beloved."[4] Returning to our previous discussion on the mutuality of friendships, friends are at their best when what is given and what is received are relatively proportionate to each other.

But friendship that involves genuine love and caring for another is not mutually exclusive of what is self-benefiting. Both need to exist for friendship to be healthy. Immanuel Kant says,

> If men, however, were so minded that each one looked to the happiness of others, then the welfare of each would be secured by the efforts of his fellows. If we felt that others would care for our happiness as we for theirs, there would be no reason to fear that we should be left behind. The happiness I gave to another would be returned to me. There would be an exchange of welfare and no one would suffer, for another would look after my happiness as well as I looked after his.[5]

The natural flow of a relationship where one person receives something is the impulse to give in return. It is this confidence that friends have in one another—that what is given is so valued that it is returned in kind; this is at the heart of friendship.

Let me return again to my best friend who will remain nameless. There is little I would consider as altruistic in our day-to-day relationship with each other. When we go out to see a movie together, or when we just sit around and have a mutually meaningful conversation on the current state of the Minnesota Vikings and their possible playoff chances, I am selfishly getting something out of our relationship. Even if what is being received is of no more physical worth than the return of companionship I see on his face, this is enough for me.

Just the common feeling of mutual respect, intimacy, and good will is enough for friendship to flourish. Cicero states it this way: "I do not deny that affection is strengthened by the actual receipt of benefits, as well as by the perception of a wish to render service, combined with a closer intercourse. When these are added to the original impulse of the heart, to which I have alluded, a quite surprising warmth of feeling springs up."[6] What great phrases we have here. Beneath every great conversation between friends is a "receipt of benefits" that leads to "services rendered." These are cashed in for a mutual sense of "warmth of feelings" between friends.

So it is that true friends long for the affection of another person. But to offer affection without anticipating anything in return robs the other person of a response required for intimacy to flourish. Would any of us not want to see our friends delighting in our company? So it is from the friend's perspective. The great gift of friendship is to so long for what the other is giving as to express that delight by returning that same affection.

6. Friendship Is Freely Chosen

You cannot extort friendship with a cocked pistol.—Sidney Smith[7]

This brings us to what I think is the central characteristic of friendship. To illustrate, what is it about a courtroom that is so confining? Even if you haven't actually been in one, you have certainly seen plenty of them on television. Think *Perry Mason* for those of you who can remember that show, or maybe you recall the words of Colonel Jessup, played by Jack Nicholson in the movie *A Few Good Men*: "You can't handle the truth!"

The dark wood paneling, the elevated judge's bench, the jury off to the side—all play a part of a well-scripted drama that, in the end, is somewhat predictable. We may not know the results of a specific case, but we certainly know the well-oiled theatrics. Lawyers scurry to and fro, freely giving their arguments and pleading their cases, but always within the limitations of the law. The judge rules, but he is obliged to do so under the heavy constraints given him by a code of jurisprudence. And no one is more constrained than the plaintiff, whose life is defined by the decisions made by the jury. Every role in the courtroom is defined by strict obligation to someone or something.

So too—but perhaps to a lesser degree—are all sorts of other relationships defined by preset obligations. Salespeople are obligated to offer products that meet the standards of customers buying the product. They are obligated to sell customers products that live up to their warranties. Doctors are obligated under the code of their medical profession to offer their patients the best care possible. In turn, patients are obligated to pay their doctors, no matter the results.

Even family members live under significant constraints. Siblings are certainly free to not be good brothers or sisters, but they have no choice in being brothers or sisters. Their bloodline gives them no choice. And marriage partners are obligated by the roles they play as husband and wife, both by the state and the church. All these are examples of relationships with limited choices attached—if not in terms of their behavior, then by basic definition.

It is this characteristic that sets friendship apart from all others. *Friendship is, by definition, freely chosen.* It is entered into without any set code of obligations. This is the rare relationship that is by nature unfettered and unstructured and consequently can many times be downright messy. No bloodlines, no social agencies, no rigid sense of outside obligation defines it.

And would we want it any other way? Consider how you would feel if after years of friendship you discovered buried in the deepest recesses of your best friend's desk a written contract indicating he or she was getting paid $50,000 to be your friend. Your best friend signed on the dotted line to be your friend! Or, maybe you discovered after years that your "best friend" saw you as "a ministry"! They felt sorry for you! They become your friend out of well-intended obligation. Would not these two discoveries affect your friendship with this person?

Is not the great delight in being a friend the complete confidence you have that your "friend" is just that, without any obligations to be such? No one is twisting his arm. There is no contract being signed that requires her to be a friend. There is no one with a gun to his head demanding friendship. No, true friendship rests on the confidence that the other person selected you over others freely and without obligation.

Montaigne makes this point when he contrasts friendship with family. Friendship is unlike families who are selected and sustained out of obligation to nature:

> And, moreover, the more these are friendships [between father and son] that the law and natural obligation impose upon us, so much less is there in them of our own choice and free will. And our free will has no creation more properly its own than affection and friendship.[8]

Not even nature binds friends to friends. They owe their relationship completely to what is freely offered and what is freely received. As a result, any expressions of affection can be received with assurance, knowing that they originate from within the friend.

What we are really saying here is that friendship is a relationship that is fundamentally unnecessary. It is utterly extravagant. Lewis says:

> Hence (if you will not misunderstand me) the exquisite arbitrariness and irresponsibility of this love. I have no duty to be one's Friend and no man in the world has a duty to be mine. No claims, no shadow of necessity, Friendship is unnecessary, like philosophy, like art, like the universe itself (for God did not need to create). It has no survival value; rather it is one of those things which give value to survival.[9]

Free from utility, as Lewis suggests, friendship has little functional value outside of its own expression. Friendship is an end in itself. It therefore focuses on the other friend for his or her sake and without any other agenda than the friendship it brings.

Certainly this freedom is expressed most clearly at the point of selection. Isn't this what is so delightful—especially for those of us who are extroverts—when we walk into a room and find there a veritable smorgasbord of individuals to select from to befriend? No one is telling us who to be friends with. The only thing in our way is whether our choices for potential friends respond in kind.

I recall the first year of college when I entered my undergraduate college campus for the first time at new student orientation. There it was spread out before me, a vast menu of potential friendships! For some of you introverts, this might have been scarier than for the likes of me. But, in time, you most likely did the same thing I did. I spent the next several months and years selecting my multilayered set of friendships, some of whom continue to be friends of mine to this day.

Further, once established, this freedom continues to be an important feature in sustaining these relationships. If there is anything that potentially compromises friendship, it is unwanted control on the part of one or both friends. Jeremy Taylor says it well: "Give thy friend counsel wisely and charitably, but leave him to his liberty whether he will follow thee or no: and be not angry if thy counsel be rejected: for advice is no empire, and he is not my friend that will be my judge whether I will or no."[10] In other words, in offering advice to friends it is important to allow the other to receive or reject it as he or she wills. Friendship is at its best when it is held lightly. Hold it too firmly and one risks squeezing the life out of it.

As an aside, isn't this what happens so often in failed dating relationships? The reason why relationships that otherwise might lead to marriage crash on the rocky shoals of heartbreak is because one or the other gets ahead of themselves. Unlike other cultures where marriages are arranged, the gold standard in the West for how relationships leading to marriage begin is as friendship. How a couple transitions from a relationship of freedom to one of obligation and constraint is delicate. Both members need to make the journey in complementary fashion. There is a veritable cottage industry of country music that chronicles the adventures where one person has wandered on ahead while the other has been left behind, still basking in the freedom of "just wanting to be friends."

7 | Friendship Is Dynamic

It takes us half our lives to learn who our friends are, and the other half to keep them. —Unknown[11]

I can't recall his name. I have spent hours massaging my brain, trying to remember—his first name, mind you. For a time I thought it was Robert, but now I am not so sure. Or was it Larry? How can this be? For two full summers during college, we were inseparable. We worked together at a summer camp, and the other staff members used to call us Zig and Zag, so linked we were at the hip. I thoroughly enjoyed Robert's (?) company, and he mine. For hours, we would sit around and laugh at each other's stories.

We laughed until we cried. We loved being in each other's company. We had all of the hallmarks of being "best friends."

How is it that now I cannot remember his name? Forty years later, should I still even call him a friend? Can friends forget their friend's name? Can friends be nameless? Perhaps you have such a friend. Or should we call them ex-friends? The very thought of Robert (?) leads us to our third characteristic: *Friendship is a dynamic relationship.*

Friendship is a relationship that is always changing. Certainly the relationship between a father and a son changes, as does the relationship between two siblings. What it means to be a father to a son when the son is three is significantly different than when he is forty. When siblings get older, they perhaps do not reflect the same childish pettiness with one another as in junior high. An employee may relate differently to her boss after fifteen years of employment. But in each of these cases—fathers, sons, siblings, employers, and employees—although they may change in some subjective sense, they do not change in terms of the fundamental roles each plays to the other. Fathers will always be fathers, no matter how old. Brothers will always be brothers or sisters to the other. Unless something changes rather dramatically at work, the roles of employer and employee remain the same.

But friendship is a relationship that is, by its very nature, always in flux. Linked closely to the previous characteristic—that friendships are freely chosen—to the extent that friends enter freely into their relationships with others, they are obligated to no one in the ways that their friendships progress. Friendship is dynamic and therefore free to go where it will. Always in motion, either friendship is rolling up a hill or it is rolling down. Friends are born and they potentially die. They never remain dormant.

In this sense, friendship is a deeply fragile relationship, fragile and therefore vulnerable. Thoreau speaks of it in terms of a "delicate plant" that needs to be continuously nurtured.[12] He says, "Friendship is never established as an understood relation. Do you demand that I be less your Friend that you may know it? Yet what right have I to think that another cherishes so rare a sentiment for me? It is a miracle that requires constant proofs."[13]

"Constant proofs," he says. Friendship can never be assumed (unlike, for example, the role of a mother-daughter relationship that can never die, even if expressed badly). Because it is always changing, it always needs to be tested, but tested not in the sense of two friends living in a state of paranoia with one another; rather, tested in the sense that friends need to be always aware of and nurturing the relationships they share.

This means that friendships grow, and they are potentially free to die. In terms of their growth, Aristotle insists that friendships take time:

Moreover they require time and intimacy: as the saying goes, you cannot get to know a man till you have consumed the proverbial amount of salt in his company; and so you cannot admit him to friendship or really be friends, before each has shown the other that he is worthy of friendship and has won his confidence. People who enter into friendly relations quickly have the wish to be friends, but cannot really be friends without being worthy of friendship, and also knowing each other to be so; the wish to be friends is a quick growth, but friendship is not.[14]

How much time friendship takes to grow certainly varies. When two people first realize they are friends and acknowledge such to each other, this may happen fairly quickly. But, as Aristotle suggests, the heart of friendship is the accumulation of shared company that in time confirms what may be hoped for and so stated at any time. What we call "long-lasting" relationships is the final proof of friendships worthy to be called such.

This concept of "worthiness" of friendship is a pervasive theme from the past and may seem foreign to the modern mind-set where everyone seems to be called friend. Several writers of friendship write about this. For true friendship to be valued, it must be tested and found to be worthy. Emerson speaks of buying entrance into the guild of friendship after a "long probation."[15] Aelred speaks of friendship as a process that goes through four stages that include a time of testing. He states, "You see, therefore, the four stages by which one climbs to the perfection of friendship: the first is selection, the second is probation, the third admission, and fourth perfect harmony in matters human and divine with charity and benevolence."[16] For Aelred, "selection" of friendship does not naturally nor necessarily follow quickly from "admission" as a friend.

True friendship, then, is measured by a set time when friends assess their true commitment to the other. How is this done? It may be done through testing that commitment when things go well and during times of difficulty. It may be done as friends observe how they measure up to others by comparison. It may be done through sharing stories from the past and dreams of the future, and observing how they are approved and shared. And it may be done by observing the sheer delight of affection when it is shared with the other.

But friendships are also open to dying. What kind of things would cause a relationship to die? The first, I suspect, is the source of my loss of friendship with Robert (?), the loss of proximity, measured in time and location. The reality of the matter is that the two of us have lived a continent apart for almost forty years. (Or have we? I am not sure where he lives.)

Like my past friend, Ben Johnson suggests that friendships die from being separated:

Friendship, like love, is destroyed by long absence, though it may be increased by short intermissions. What we have missed long enough we want it, we value more when it is regained; but that which has been lost till it is forgotten, will be found at last with little gladness, and with still less if a substitute has supplied the place.[17]

It is a sad thing, he says, when friendships are unknotted by the lack of time and effort put into them. But friendships require both, and when they are not expressed by the effort it takes to be present and available to the other person, friendships wither and die.

Kant also states that friendships die because of the natural changes that occur in individuals. He speaks of these changes in terms of "taste" versus "disposition":

So friendships may come to an end. In friendships of taste the relationship loses its basis when with the process of time taste changes and finds new objects, and so a new friend supplants the old. The friendship of disposition is rare because men seldom have principles. Friends drift apart because there was no friendship of disposition between them.[18]

Because friendship must not be controlling, friends must be allowed to grow and change in many different ways as individuals. They may change because of growth or decline in certain interests, outside commitments that once were mutually held, or in areas of intellectual inquiry. For friendship to grow, friends must be willing to change together—if not in every way, then in those ways that really matter to them.

Further, the source of the death of friendship for Cicero runs deeper. He speaks of the source of danger to friendship as a change in character:

Again, if a change in character and aim takes place, as often happens, or if party politics produces an alienation of feeling . . . we shall have to be on our guard against appearing to embark upon active enmity while we only mean to resign a friendship. . . . Our first object, then, should be to prevent a breach; our second, to secure that, if it does occur, our friendship should seem to have died a natural rather than a violent death.[19]

As Caesar was to find out in the last moments of his life as he looked into the eyes of his friend, Marcus Junius Brutus, friendship sometimes dies violently of intrigue: "*Et tu, Brute*?" (You too, Brutus?)

Jeremy Taylor is more specific when he speaks of character traits that may cause the death of a good friendship: "There are two things which a friend can never pardon, a treacherous blow and the revealing of a secret, because these are against the nature of friendship."[20] Of the former, trust is the cornerstone of friendship, and to breach a trust Taylor sees as near fatal to friendship. Of the second, Taylor understands secrets that are held between friends as "the chastity of friendship." The disclosure of what is held most privately with another is what he calls nothing short of "a prostitution and direct debauchery."[21] We will discuss this further in the last section.

And, finally, Aelred speaks of six things that break the bonds of friendship. He speaks of them as vices by which friendship are so injured as to dissolve what once was present. They are: "insult, attack, arrogance, betrayal of secrets, and the stab of the back . . . and one more: harm done to anyone for whom we have responsibility."[22] For him, friendship is eternal, and therefore to fall headlong into these vices suggests in the end that friendship probably never existed in the first place.

So friendships are always consigned to be moving targets. They are born, they grow, and if left unattended they decline and even die. There is nothing surrounding them to shore them up. Chances are if I were to reconnect with Robert (?) we might very well pick up our friendship where we left off. Maybe. Or maybe not.

8 / Friendship and Being Christian

Friendship can only exist between good men. —Cicero[23]

Would we have called them our "best" friends? Perhaps not, but if measured by the amount of time we spent with them, we could just as well have claimed them as such. We certainly enjoyed their company a great deal. We spent hours with them every week, all of us standing there with our thermoses or sitting there in our collapsible chairs on the sidelines as we watched utter chaos unfold before us. Our job was to yell words of encouragement to our little tykes as they sought to do something constructive with a ball, whether that be kicking it into the net or hitting it out of the infield.

But those days are now over for my wife and me. We are in that in-between stage before we have grandchildren old enough to take to their games. Returning to those earlier sidelines where we watched our children compete in Little League, those days were one of the main times in our married lives when we had sustainable contact with nonbelievers from our community. Now they are gone and so, too, is one of our major outlets for relating to those who may not be Christians.

Perhaps a confession is in order. This is the danger of being a pastor or working in a seminary. The focus in both these settings is so much on attending to the sacred spaces that we work and live in that it becomes surprisingly easy to isolate ourselves with like-minded believers and away from the secular world around us.

But what does this say about the nature of friendship? For believers, can we—should we—be linked to nonbelievers? Should the biblical injunction for marriage perhaps be extended to friendships; should we be unequally yoked? Should we have non-Christian friends? Further, is there a qualitative and/or quantitative difference between being a friend with a believer and being a friend with a nonbeliever? What are the barriers? What is missed if we don't establish friendships with nonbelievers?

In response to some of these questions, it is important to note that the explorers of friendship from the past have forever sought to plumb the depths to locate the outer frontiers of friendship. Where does friendship begin and end? Each began with a certain ideal of friendship, realizing that friendship is rarely expressed to the level of the ideal but, rather, is expressed imperfectly and on many different levels.

For example, for Aristotle friendship was defined as "the good." He said, "The perfect form of friendship is that between the good, and those who resemble each other in virtue."[24] But in saying such, he was quick to acknowledge that friendship is not limited to those who are virtuous. There are other lesser forms of friendship based on pleasure and on utility:

> Friendship based on pleasure has a similarity to friendship based on virtue, for good men are pleasant to one another; and the same is true of friendship based on utility, for good men are useful to each other.[25]

In these lesser forms of friendship, friends may exist on unequal footing, and consequently there might be limits in which friendship can be extended, but they nevertheless are part of a more universal notion of friendship. Friendships need not be confined to the ideal.

Jeremy Taylor transformed this classic notion of friendship as "virtue" into friendship as "charity." He says, "But when christianity [sic] came to renew our nature, and to restore our laws, and to increase her privileges, and to make her aptness to become religion, then it was declared that our friendships were to be as universal as our conversation."[26] Christian charity now defines friendship, he insisted, and it is charity that is the universal principle upon which all relationships are to be built.

But what of those who cannot share in Christian charity? As quickly as Taylor declared charity to be universal, he acknowledged that the sources of friendship extend beyond religion and include nature. He admitted of friendship that "all our graces here are but imperfect, that is, at the best they are but tendencies to glory, so our friendships are imperfect too, and but beginnings of a celestial friendship, by which we shall love every one as much as they can be loved."[27] Friendship does exist, then, beyond the reach of Christian charity, albeit imperfectly.

So, too, in an earlier time, Aelred reinterpreted the concept of Cicero's view of friendship as virtue into the notion of charity. And just as emphatically as Cicero, who insisted that "friendship can only exist between good men,"[28] so Aelred insisted that "true friendship" can exist only in Christ: "However, I confess that I am convinced that true friendship cannot exist among those who live without Christ."[29] He speaks passionately about "spiritual friendship" being "the mutual harmony in affairs human and divine coupled with benevolence and charity."[30]

But just as he claimed charity as universal friendship, so he extended the possibility that friendship could exist in other forms as well:

> Let us allow that, because of some similarity in feelings, those friendships which are not true, be nevertheless, called friendships, provided, however, that they are judiciously distinguished from that friendship which is spiritual and therefore true. Hence let one kind of friendship be called carnal, another worldly, and another spiritual. The carnal springs from mutual harmony in vice; the worldly is enkindled by the hope of gain; and the spiritual is cemented by similarity of life, morals, and pursuits among the just.[31]

These other lower forms of love came from multiple sources, including nature, duty, reason, or from affection alone.[32] All these, he insists, need to be distinguished from "true friendship" by law and precept, lest they ensnare friends by their slight resemblance to true "spiritual friendship."[33]

One final and dramatic example of how the notion of friendship as charity was linked to other forms of friendship can be seen in the words of St. Francis de Sales. Similar to Aelred's notion of "spiritual friendship," de Sales writes of the "holy friendships" that exist between brothers who are seeking to live a devout life in the world. These are friendships characterized by "glances [that] are sincere and modest; embraces pure and innocent; sighs only for heaven; familiarity is purely spiritual, its laments only concern failure in divine love; all of which betokens chastity."[34] They are necessary relationships that are critical for brother to be bound to brother living in the cloister. But is this the only kind of friendship?

No, says de Sales. To be avoided are what he calls "foolish friendships" that exist so pervasively outside the cloister. He describes these friendships as being based upon sensual and superficial qualities. By sensual, he is not merely speaking of sexual, but may include listening to a charming voice, the superficiality of accomplishments, and relationships characterized by young girls who focus on superficial talk, such as "he dances well, is very good at games, is well dressed, sings well; he is so nice to talk to, and so good looking."[35] Both are equally harmful qualities, says de Sales, the sensual and frivolous. Both are to be avoided if they are to achieve the ideals set forth for them in living a life of devotion.

In all of these examples, "ideal" friendship bleeds into what is viewed as lesser forms of friendship. We see here a reality that is confirmed in our lives every day. Friendship is a messy relationship that may not meet all of the standards set out for it. It nevertheless can be found flourishing in the most unpredictable ways and contrary to the values certain people put on it. From the ancients on down through the ages, evidence is provided that friendship can be shared across all times and cultures and types of people, good and bad. In today's world, it is displayed everywhere, from the athletic playing field to the war zone, from tribal commitments in Africa to childhood playgrounds in China.

But can it be displayed between believers and nonbelievers? It would seem so if we follow this train of thought from the tradition on friendship. Friendship is a universal relationship that certainly extends beyond the boundaries of what it means to be a Christian in the same way that it extends beyond multiple other cultural and social barriers.

In this sense, friendship is by definition not a Christian relationship at all, certainly not exclusively so. Non-Christians can have deep, meaningful friendships. Christians can have deep, meaningful relationships, and there is nothing to suggest fundamentally that Christians and non-Christians can't establish true, meaningful relationships with one another. This is not to say that friends can't be enriched in their relationship by what they share in Christian commitment and understanding, but these things by themselves are not necessary. Conversely, the things that make Christians distinctive— their faith commitment, their commitment to right living, their worldview— do not disqualify them in any way from relating meaningfully with those who do not share these same values. Go figure: Christians can be genuine friends with nonbelievers.

 Friendship Requires Knowing

When they are strangers or unknown, they cannot be
friends actually and practically.—Jeremy Taylor[36]

There they all were, sitting in front of me as I spoke: almost ninety Christians crammed together in the living room of a house church in the south of China. They were attentive, and their smiles could have lit up all of Shanghai. After my talk, I spent as much time as possible with several of these brave, committed souls. We had a wonderful time as we trekked around the city to see the sights. Somehow we bridged the language barrier just enough to laugh and kid with one another. We also made heartfelt plans and prayed together. I left with a lot of good feelings about many wonderful people during those days. But I left, nevertheless, without a friend.

This next-to-last characteristic may seem too obvious for serious consideration: *Friendship requires directly knowing the other person as a friend.* It requires actually having met another person and made a face-to-face assessment of his or her qualities over time.

Aristotle describes this quality in terms of direct communication of goodwill to another:

> And perhaps we should also add the qualification that the feeling of goodwill must be known to its object. For a man often feels goodwill towards persons whom he has never seen, but whom he believes to be good or useful, and one of these persons may also entertain the same feeling towards him. Here then we have a case of two people mutually well-disposed, whom nevertheless we cannot speak of as friends, because they are not aware of each other's regard.[37]

One cannot be a friend to another in the abstract. Just being aware of another's personal attributes—as worthy as they might be—does not a friend make. These attributes must be tested out and personified in another person's actual presence in order for friendship to occur.

In this sense, friendship is quite different from most other relationships. It is not a requirement—or a possibility—that most of us personally "know" our national leader, for example. He or she will lead and we will follow—if sometimes begrudgingly—whether or not we have intimate knowledge of each other and the lives we lead.

Nor do we need to really know the salespeople who serve us in the retail world. It might be an enriching experience. It might give us valuable information of their trustworthiness. It might make them better understand our needs and desires. But knowing each other will not change the fundamental status of our roles in these relationships.

Even more dramatically, it is not even necessary perhaps for children to know their parents and siblings. Adoption agencies are filled with family secrets that will never be revealed to children who have been given up for adoption. Again, for a father to know his son or a mother her daughter may be enlightening. But in the most basic sense, biological parents will always be parents, even if adopted children never actually get to know them. So, too, these children might have brothers and sisters despite the fact that they may always remain anonymous and therefore unknowable.

Why is this the case? Returning to our discussion about friendship as a relationship that is by nature completely free and without obligation, we see that friendship is not based upon an abstract role. Unlike these other relational types, friendship exists for itself and defines itself apart from a preset role. Consequently, to speak of being a friend can only mean to know someone in the most personal of ways.

What does this knowing look like? C. S. Lewis's portrayal of a long day with his friends describes wonderfully what it takes to know friends. He speaks of those times when his friends came together to bring out the best, wisest, and funniest in the others. These are the golden sessions, he says,

> when four or five of us after a hard day's walking have come to an inn; when our slippers are on; our feet spread out towards the blaze and our drinks at our elbows; when the whole world, and something beyond the world, opens itself to our minds as we talk; and no one has any claim on or any responsibility for another, but all are freemen and equals as if we had first met an hour ago, while at the same time an Affection mellowed by the years enfolds us. Life—natural life—has no better gift to give. Who could have deserved it?[38]

Whether at an inn, a ballpark, a reading group, or a playground, we hopefully can all identify with Lewis in this picture of common sharing of an experience with friends. It is in being face-to-face and side-by-side with a select group of others that we begin to know them and they get to know us.

Is it not our conversations that are the portals into which we know and understand each other? And is it not this highly personal knowing that is the actual fruit of friendship? The knowing of another person as friend requires a common commitment of time in order for it to grow. The more time the better. It also requires a commitment to a common place. Perhaps nowhere else is friendship stretched from its traditional moorings more than in this idea that friendship requires a common place.

All this, of course, brings up the current state of social media that has engulfed us in recent years. Technology has now pushed the idea of "being a friend" to its outer limits. So my two grown children can now spend hours on Facebook, social networking themselves into the lives of potentially hundreds, even thousands of "friends" around the globe.

I was especially reminded of this a few years ago while attending the Lausanne Conference in Cape Town, where I was one of the leaders of almost four hundred Stewards from around the globe responsible for the back-end logistics of the weeklong conference. Every morning I watched these college-age students line up at twelve computer stations to communicate with their "friends" from around the globe. Young men from remote tribes of Nigeria communicated with university students from Norway, and American students talked around the globe with their "friends" in China.

It begs the question: Are these technologically enhanced individuals actually "friends"? There are some wonderful studies that expand the conversation on technology started with the likes of Jacques Ellul, Marshall McLuhan, and Neil Postman. Much can be said on this topic that pertains to friendship that would send us off into directions we dare not go here. I leave us with only a few questions.

Given the nature of social media today, perhaps we need to re-clarify the path by which strangers take the journey from complete stranger-hood to varying degrees of acquaintanceship to true friendship. What is the journey and can technology adequately vet the process? Does it provide enough information for friendship to flourish? More to the point, to the extent that knowing a friend involves more than just having enough information "about" another, does technology offer enough context for "knowing" a person on a deeply personal level?

One gets the sense that we are only at the beginning of what technology will be doing in expanding our definition of relationships. Time will tell how it will impact our idea of friendship in the future.[39]

10 · Friendship and the Power of Secrets

When two friends part, they should lock up each other's
secrets and exchange the keys.—Unknown[40]

It was the smirk and the nod, though no one else in the room picked up on it. I could hardly see it myself. I hadn't seen that smirk and nod for almost five years because we now live halfway across the country from each other. But the little smirk that crossed one of my best friend's faces a couple of months ago during a visit read like a twelve-page essay with footnotes. And the nod added another couple of pages. Nothing else needed to be said. I understood exactly what was going through his head, and he knew I knew, so I returned the same smirk and nod. The result was uncontrollable laughter that had no context for the rest of the people in the room.

This smirk and nod is an example of the way friends communicate. True friends don't need long formal introductions or farewells. They don't even require fully structured sentences to communicate. The language of friendship, in fact, can be altogether inarticulate. It says all that needs to be said and nothing more.

This way of communicating is so contrary to standards in other relationships. Presiding judges in the courtroom require of lawyers that every single word be in order. Teachers require their students to communicate with clarity. The books they share reveal words, sentences, paragraphs, and chapters that speak of hours of editing before they are deemed acceptable. Parents are judged by the way their children speak in public. All these relationships are subjected to public scrutiny.

By contrast, the language of two friends is a deeply private language that often only they can understand and that may leave others bewildered. Its content frequently involves past shared experiences that need no real interpretation by the two friends. They read each other's pasts by heart. Thoreau speaks of this private language as being in direct opposition to what is social and institutional. He says, "We may call it an essentially heathenish intercourse, free and irresponsible in its nature, and practicing all of the virtues gratuitously."[41]

Oftentimes, friendship may even dissolve into silence. This, too, is language when two friends can sit in a room together for long stretches of time and not say a word. Georg Ebers says, "That friendship only is, indeed genuine, when two friends, without speaking a word to each other, can nevertheless find happiness in being together."[42]

As we discussed previously, because friendship is exclusive by nature, so too is the language that is shared among friends; it is exclusive. Above all else, friends have secrets. Living in their private world of inarticulate words and gestures, shared stories from their pasts, and even silence, they purposely exclude others by virtue of their lack of communication. They live in a world of secrets shared only by themselves.

Are these secrets wrong? On the contrary, say Taylor and Aelred; to expose what is most intimate between friends is a terrible breach in the relationship. It is these secrets that Taylor understands to be cause for the death of a friendship. To expose them to others is the proper cause of divorce that potentially "dissolves the union."[43] So, also, Aelred quotes Scripture: "He that discloses the secret of a friend loses his credit," and "to disclose the secrets of a friend leaves no hope to an unhappy soul."[44] Secrets held among friends are their highest possessions, and to expose them to others is to betray the trust central to being a friend.

CHAPTER FOUR

COMMUNITY IN THE MAKING

L et me summarize what I have described as the basic traits of friendship. First, friendship is unique in that it is limited in scope. It is exclusive. Not everyone can be a friend. Second, it is preferential. Not everyone is created equal. Friends prefer the few over the many. Third, friendship is reciprocal. One cannot be a true friend unless friendship is returned. Fourth, friendship involves relating to another with relatively equal status. Friends naturally see eye to eye and walk side by side.

Fifth, friendship is, by nature, self-benefiting. Found deep in the mortar of what it means to be a friend with another is the presumption of a return for one's relational investment. Friendship is defined as much by what is received as by what is given. Sixth, friendship is freely chosen in the sense that it is an end unto itself. The sheer delight we find in friendship ultimately rests in our confidence that our friends are motivated by no other obligation than just being friends. Consequently, and seventh, it is a relationship that is open-ended in the sense that friends are free to enter into and end their relationships at any time. Friendships grow and, sadly, even potentially die. They are dynamic by nature.

Eighth, friendship is potentially a messy relationship that does not follow the constraints characterized by other, more structured relational types. Certainly, it is not necessarily constrained by Christian identity and formation. Ninth, one cannot be a friend in the abstract. It actually requires directly knowing the other person(s). Finally, tenth, one of the delights of friendship lies in its secrecy. Listen in on a conversation between two friends, and it may very well be that what is heard and seen is difficult to comprehend.

The amalgam of these ten characteristics describes a relationship that is profoundly personal at its source. It is deeply intimate by nature. And it is wonderfully informal by disposition. Because it is not constrained by anything outside itself, friendship is expressive, even wildly expressive, by nature. And perhaps no other relationship outside of marriage is so governed by the affections of the heart.

Profoundly personal, deeply intimate, wonderfully informal, powerfully expressive, and filled with authentic affection: Are these not the very traits we strive for in the formation of community in our churches? Given the great deal of attention we have given to nurturing this relationship in our churches in the recent years, one would think so.

Is it friendship, then, that should be the goal of building authentic Christian fellowship? Put differently, should these be the relational expectations that brothers and sisters in Christ have as they enter our churches and, if so, how can these expectations possibly be met? To answer these questions, we would do well to turn now to the first-century church as described in the New Testament.

Three Scenes in the Making of Christian Community

Then all the disciples deserted him and fled.—(Matt. 26:56)

Imagine the confusion they must have felt, the confusion and hopelessness. Imagine the fear in their eyes. Jesus was now arrested in the garden of Gethsemane, declaring for all present to hear that he had not come to lead a rebellion but to fulfill prophecy. What did this mean, and what were they to do? They did what came naturally and ran for their lives, most likely scattering in ones, twos, and threes throughout the dark, inconspicuous corners of Jerusalem and beyond. Would we have done anything differently?

If we were betting persons watching those disciples heading for the hills that evening, we would not have expected anything more to come of these disciples of Jesus. Were three years of ministry to end here in the midst of events that became larger than their ability to comprehend, these few disciples caught in a perfect storm of Roman and Jewish authority combined with their lost expectations?

How is it that not more than a few days shy of two months after this event we find these same dispersed and terrified followers of Jesus back together again, participating in a remarkable display of life-giving community? These eleven Jews swelled to over three thousand true disciples who spoke in languages representing the entire known world. With confident humility, they worshipped and prayed together; they shared their earthly possessions; they experienced fellowship together. How did this happen? What kind of life-giving relationships had been forged among them that now serve as a template for what has been sustained for over two thousand years as the church of Jesus Christ?

Something both ancient and brand new was happening here: Christian community was being formed out of the vestiges of the faithful remnants of the past. Three scenes from the first two chapters in the book of Acts give us a glimpse of the church at its infancy. Each scene provides us with a picture of Christian community in the making.

Scene One: The Waiting Room (Acts 1)

"Do not leave Jerusalem, but wait for the gift my Father promised."—Jesus (Acts 1:4)

All they knew is that they were to wait and not leave Jerusalem. They were to wait for a gift. There were 120, which included the eleven of them, along with the women and the too few others who came to believe in Jesus during his ministry here on earth. All of them were Jews. And they were in an anonymous upper room. Perhaps they found themselves in the same room as their last meal with Jesus? They were asked to go there to wait, and wait they did.

But their waiting was not passive. Although we do not get it directly from the text itself, we can imagine how they spent their hours putting the puzzle pieces together of the past three years of their lives. Like individual observers just after an accident who each saw what happened but slightly differently and from varying angles, these disciples must have checked in with one another about what each had seen during those moments as they flashed by before their very eyes, those experiences leading up to and during the crucifixion. And how did they put their minds and hearts around the empty tomb and later the Savior leaving them one last time into the clouds?

Their own observations were certainly reinforced by those days when Jesus lived in their midst between the resurrection and his ascension. Jesus gave them convincing proofs that he was indeed alive and that the events they had experienced were nothing less than the fulfillment of events written long ago. Jesus taught them, the text says, for forty days. He must have brought new insights into the words and experiences they had heard and saw. We know they still had not fully flushed from their minds the expectation of a political kingdom here on earth.[1] There also must have been a lot of forehead slapping during those forty days: "Oh that's what you meant when you said . . . Oh, now I get it . . . Now I understand why you insisted . . . So, that's what the prophet Isaiah meant!"

But now that his great divine work of salvation was fulfilled, what was to come of his followers? We can only imagine Jesus speaking to them of how his teachings about the kingdom of God (*basileia*) were now to be revealed in the church (*ekklesia*). They were to be the new people of God. These followers of the Messiah, who had received the gifts of the kingdom of heaven through Christ's completed work on the cross, were to now carry that kingdom within themselves until some future day of completion, the *Parousia*. They were to be a people living betwixt and between, a community filled with a sense of satisfaction with what Christ had done for them already, yet still longing for something more.[2]

The text also says that they joined "together constantly in prayer." This word *together* is a deceptively complex word, seldom used by anyone else in Scripture, but a favorite word for Luke. Ten times Luke uses the word, and when he does use it, it has the power of more than simply describing being in the same place when they prayed. The sense here is that when these disciples of Jesus prayed in that upper room, they prayed with a deep sense of "being of one mind."[3] Now, as then, prayer has a powerful effect in not only uniting our hearts and minds with God but also uniting our hearts and minds with one another. The two go hand in hand, something of great importance to be remembered in the making of community.

Perhaps the selection of a replacement for Judas was the most telling sign that these upper-room occupants saw themselves eventually leaving their hideout to enter into a new sustaining mission. Why else would they have bothered to choose another disciple to add to their band of eyewitness apostles? After a roll of the dice, in God's providence, Matthias was invited into the leadership of the . . . what? In concrete terms, what was this kingdom of Christ being formed in their midst?

From Acts 1, we know they had been given the assurance of the Holy Spirit, who was to walk in their midst and from whom would come their authority. This was to be their gift. And with this promise of a gift, they had been given a commission of sorts, a commission that what they had seen and heard—what they had witnessed—was to fill the earth from Jerusalem, to Samaria, until the good news covered the entire globe. But, again, what was this new community to look like?

All through Acts we find subtle hints that something new was afoot. For example, it is a small thing, but in the listing of the disciples in this passage, why was the order of the inner circle changed? The standard pairing of the two sets of biological brothers—Simon and Andrew, James and John—now bore a new logic of priority—Peter, John, James, and Andrew. Surely this reflected a new order of what was to become the leadership in the new church, but was there not a hint that brotherhood was being transformed before their very eyes? A new brotherhood in Christ was being formed that moved beyond bloodlines. And with this brotherhood, the women—the Marys, Joanna, and Susanna—were added in full communion.

Scene Two: The House of Many Nations (Acts 2)

When the day of Pentecost came, they were all together in one place.—Luke (Acts 2:1)

The gift finally came, and when it came, did it ever come! All of what took place in that day in the house at Pentecost certainly could have a natural explanation behind it. There was the natural sound of a violent wind, the natural sight of flaming fire, and the natural sound of people talking. But when the gift came upon them, all these sights and sounds left no doubt in anyone's mind that what engulfed them was nothing short of supernatural. Imagine being caught up and transformed by such an event as Pentecost!

Beyond the immediate effects of the moment, it was the mighty wind and the divided tongues of fire that gave lasting audible and visual evidence that whatever was to come was to be defined by the presence of the Spirit in their midst. The wind revealed the vast power of the Spirit; the fire symbolized the great purity and holiness that is to be a part of our life together. Here was an inauguration of a new era of the Spirit that was to be the evidence and means by which we are now to live our lives.

The fact that these tongues of fire landed upon all who were present, and that the words spoken beneath these fiery tongues embodied the languages of many nations, reflects the scope of this new community. This Spirit was to be distributed beyond the confines of the then established religious order and was being displayed across the globe as they would have seen it. Here was the story of the Tower of Babel in reverse. The new community of the Spirit was to be for all nations and all peoples.

Peter's subsequent sermon at the end of Acts 2 put words to what was being experienced at Pentecost. First, in reaching back to the prophet Joel, he located this time of the Spirit's coming to a specific place and time:

> "In the last days, God says, I will pour out my Spirit on all people. Your sons and daughters will prophesy, your young men will see visions, your old men will dream dreams. Even on my servants, both men and women, I will pour out my Spirit in those days." (Acts 2:17–18)

These new Spirit-filled believers at Pentecost, says Peter, were now living in a time that had long been anticipated and had finally come. They were living in the last days, a time when all God's people were made prophets by virtue of the Spirit manifest in their midst, a day that lingers on in the church today.

Peter's sermon further identifies this new community of the Spirit in the life and work of Jesus. Again, reaching back to the Old Testament but this time to the Psalms, Peter speaks as an eyewitness account of Jesus' story, chronicled in six parts: A man divinely attested by miracles; put to death according to God's purposes; raised to life as the prophets had foretold; exalted at the right hand of the Father and manifest by the Spirit; forgiving all who repent, believe, and are baptized; and now willing to add all of these into a new community under his name.

It is under Jesus' name that this new community is to be known. In the future, Jesus is not to be understood as a distant memory, a figure stuck in time, but as Peter described him: a vital, living reality who transforms our lives and who is the object of our belief in the present. It is through the Spirit that the reality of Christ is extended through time and space within the context of the church as his body. So it was that three thousand new converts, speaking multiple languages but receiving repentance and saving faith, were baptized under this name Jesus.

Scene Three: The First Church of Jerusalem (Acts 2:42–47)

All the believers were together and had everything in common.—Luke (Acts 2:44)

It was these three thousand Jews, temporarily living in Jerusalem but soon to disperse back to whence they came, who made up the first local church of Christianity. What was this church to look like? Fresh from their first-century revival, how were these new converts to conduct themselves? How was the Spirit to work in their midst, not only in them as individuals but corporately as brothers and sisters connected in Jesus' name? How were they now being asked to live their lives?

One would think, with the effects of the grand display of the Holy Spirit at Pentecost still ringing in their ears and blinding their eyes, that mystical experiences would be the first thing that characterized this church. Certainly signs and wonders performed by the apostles continued to instill awe and amazement in these new believers. Yet it was the apostles' teaching ministry that was mentioned first. As in Jesus' day, miraculous signs were an important means of authenticating the truth of God's word. But the first thing the Holy Spirit did was to open a school, and these new students had the opportunity to sit at the feet of those who actually had been in Jesus' midst. As Jesus taught them, so these eyewitness apostles taught the early church.

A second characteristic of this new church tends to get the most attention by most of us free market capitalists, because it makes us nervous. All the believers held "everything in common." That is, they sold their possessions and goods and gave to those in need. It should be duly noted that first-century Palestine was a place of stark need for so many, and we presume for many in this first church. Does this mean that private property was eliminated? No, because later in this passage there is indication that invitations went out to break bread together in homes presumably still owned by those in the church. But the larger point is that here is a church that spontaneously expressed radical generosity to one another by holding gifts that God had given them in common with others in need.

What would provoke such generosity, especially to many who, we assume, were strangers only a few days prior? The word being used here says something about the source of their motives. The word is *koinonia*, and it means to have "fellowship," "communion," "participation." Although this word is never used in the Gospels, the apostle Paul uses it thirteen times. He never uses it in a secular sense; rather it is always used religiously. Even more precisely, he only uses the word to communicate fellowship in something beyond itself. Paul has no sense of a community grounded in human relationships; rather, it is fellowship grounded in Jesus.[4] In 1 Corinthians 1:9, for example, he speaks of "fellowship with his Son"; in 2 Corinthians 13:14, he speaks of "fellowship of the Holy Spirit"; and in Philippians 1:5, he speaks of "partnership in the gospel." The fellowship these Christians shared was a mediated relationship in that it always referred back to Jesus, the source of their generosity.

As an extension of having everything in common, they were also a worshipping church that devoted itself to the breaking of bread and to prayer. The definite article suggests of the former that they were already committing themselves to an act of remembering Jesus' work on the cross in the Lord's Supper, probably as part of a larger meal. It also suggests that prayers were corporate prayers. Where did they worship? Apparently they worshipped both formally in the temple courts as well as informally in their homes. They worshipped everywhere. And how did they worship? They worshipped with spontaneous joy and sincerity.

Finally, this wonderful little description of the first church captures an often-overlooked last feature. Here is a community that did not get so caught up in all the wonderful things it was doing—learning, fellowshipping, and worshipping—that it ignored the grand commission given it by Jesus not too many days prior at his ascension. Not more than a stone's throw from their own conversions, these young converts also beckoned others to conversion. The same Spirit who poured himself out on these people from all nations at Pentecost poured himself out continuously to all those who would hear and believe. And the result was that "the Lord added to their number daily those who were being saved" (Acts 2:47).

Under the Shade of the Church Tree

These three scenes in the early chapters of the book of Acts are a descriptive preamble to the community of faith. They reveal in small part a church that is both as old as the hills and as new as today's manifestation of it. Its roots go deep down into the stories of God's covenantal work with the likes of Abraham and Moses and David. It sits on the trunk of the life and works of Jesus Christ. And its canopy spreads out for all to see through the work of the Holy Spirit inaugurated at Pentecost.

Under this great tree we find a community of believers learning to relate to one another in altogether new ways. Certainly these early—mostly Jewish—believers came out of a great tradition where the people of God had been worshipping God together for generations. But something new was happening here under the guidance of the Holy Spirit. They were being called to relate to one another in radically new ways.[5] What characterized this new community of faith? As in our assessment of friendship, at least ten aspects characterize Christian fellowship.

Fellowship Is Nonexclusive   / .

> *Neither Jew nor Gentile, neither slave nor free, nor is*
> *there male and female.—Paul (Gal. 3:28)*

Imagine the 120 Jews from the upper room after their wait, observing the Spirit of God on that day of Pentecost manifesting himself upon three thousand God-fearing Jews from all parts of the known world. What must they have thought? Here they were observing people who had been swept away into all areas of the Diaspora. They included visitors from as far south as North Africa, westward across the Mediterranean to Rome and beyond, and eastward through Mesopotamia. They included such diverse groups as Arabs and Cretans, perhaps even Armenians. Many were born Jews, but others wore their Judaism like secondhand suits. They were converts. All of them were known that day by alphabets, words, and syntax cast about like ships on a rolling sea.

It happened so quickly, like the rushing of wind and the flashing of fire. What were they to think of this new community in the making that defied the laws of religious gravity as they knew it? What seems so obvious to us now was earthshaking to these first-century Jews who were so deeply embedded in a tradition that stretched their hearts, minds, and sympathies all the way back to the promises of Abraham and the law of Moses. We know as we journey on through the New Testament that language and race were only the first distinctions broken down in this new more inclusive community. They were soon to be confronted with the breaking down of barriers heretofore deemed impenetrable to them.

What were they to make of Paul's radical declaration in his letter to the Galatians that true sons of God now included peoples who only yesterday were considered religiously unacceptable to the Jewish community? From Paul's admonishment of his fellow apostle only a chapter earlier, apparently even Peter had difficulty acclimating himself to the horizons of this radical new community.[6] Who are to be included as sons of God? Paul declares, "There is neither Jew nor Gentile, neither slave nor free, nor is there male and female, for you are all one in Christ Jesus. If you belong to Christ, then you are Abraham's seed, and heirs according to the promise" (Gal. 3:28–29).

How can this be? In a single stroke of his pen, Paul seemingly sweeps away the residue of prejudices built on religious nationality, social status, and gender that had been accumulating for centuries. Even Gentiles were to be made full and equal members of this new community of Christ!

The very courts of the magnificent temple built by Herod the Great on which these same apostles certainly stood tell much of the story. There were three courts surrounding the temple proper, all anchored on the same elevated platform: The Court of the Priests stood predominantly at the center; to the east stood the Court of Israel for the layperson; and further east still was the Court of Women. Any Gentile's viewpoint of these three temple courts would, at best, have been eye level to the temple floor, as they would have had to look up nineteen steps from the Court of the Gentiles.

Further, gazing up those nineteen steps, the sight line of these Gentiles would have been at least partially blocked by a stone wall one-and-a-half meters high. The ominous warning on this impenetrable barrier would have prevented them from ascending the last five steps up to the level of the other three courts and temple itself. Inscribed on the wall in both Greek and Roman was a warning that no foreigner could go beyond the wall *under pain of death*. The great divide between Gentile and Jew was rock solid, written large in their laws and psyche.[7]

Is it this dividing wall that Paul speaks of in his Epistle to the Ephesians as being torn down? To these uncircumcised Gentiles peering up over the barricade that surrounded the temple, he declares:

> But now in Christ Jesus you who once were far away have been brought near by the blood of Christ. For he himself is our peace, who has made the two groups one and has *destroyed the barrier*, the dividing wall of hostility, by setting aside in his flesh the law with its commands and regulations. His purpose was to create in himself one new humanity out of the two, thus making peace, and in one body to reconcile both of them to God through the cross, by which he put to death their hostility. (Eph. 2:13–16; italics added)

Paul declares that they are no longer strangers and sojourners; these Gentiles are now to be viewed as "fellow citizens with God's people and members of his household" (Eph. 2:19).

Both Jews and Gentiles have access to the Father through the Spirit. Using language from the Old Testament community, both together are to become a temple that becomes a dwelling place for God. Less than two chapters later, this once-divided community is admonished by Paul to be vigilant to maintain inclusiveness and unity because "there is one body and one Spirit, just as you were called to one hope when you were called; one Lord, one faith, one baptism; one God and Father of all, who is over all and through all and in all" (Eph. 4:4–6).

If only these early first-century eyewitnesses of Jesus had eyes to see, then Paul's words would not have surprised them. After all, Jesus' entire life and ministry had already been about the business of constructing a whole new kingdom of God in their midst that was far more expansive than many were comfortable with. They would have seen it in the eyes of the Samaritan woman Jesus talked with at the well in John 4. They would have seen it in the eyes of the sinners and publicans with whom Jesus sat at table, much to the consternation of the religious authorities. They would have seen it in the desperate eyes of an unclean, misplaced woman who touched him in the midst of the crowd, and equally in the eyes of the daughter of the well-respected synagogue ruler who was brought back to life in Mark 5 with Jesus' simple touch.

It is with some irony that the disciples seemed to be the last to see this new society in the making. The religious authorities immediately saw what Jesus was doing, and their reaction to him throughout the Gospels was nothing short of their efforts to divert the train wreck that was about to crash into their long-held, highly exclusive establishment.

Here, then, is a picture of a new kind of relationship that is utterly *breathtaking in its inclusivity*. The words of Jesus and the apostle Paul echo through a world that transcends the then unthinkable chasm between first-century Jews and Gentiles, extending to barriers at one time thought unbreakable. Who are our brothers and sisters in Christ? The community that Christians are now to share is not only unbound by ethnic and racial distinctions, but also includes—in Paul's words in Galatians—certain social distinctions that during his day were difficult to bridge, particularly between master and slave and male and female. And with these, we can also include distinctions bound by time or space, by circumstances, by preferences, personality, or interests.

We have only to consider the iconic role of the nightclub bouncer as a basis for appreciating the expansive nature of what binds us together as a community of Christ. Picture the bouncer giving up his night job at a trendy Manhattan club to take up new responsibilities on Sunday morning at the front door of one of our churches. Let's even make it one of our more trendy churches, for the sake of realism. He stands there, larger than life, bull neck, shirt unbuttoned down to his belt, gold chains, perhaps a few well-placed tattoos, his clipboard in hand, measuring people as they enter. Given the witness of Scripture and evidence of what we find in churches around the world, what criteria would he use to admit individuals into the church? Who will he allow entrance into our churches, and who will he reject? Perhaps geography could be a tangible criterion. There are currently 2,272,800,000 Christians in the world today.[8] About 256,500,000 make up the American church. Certainly not all of these are what we would consider "born-again" believers, but a good percentage of these numbers would be permitted to enter.

Before he closes off the door with his velvet rope, what about the millions from the non-Western, majority world church where most of the current growth of the church is occurring, individuals we don't know or may never hope to know in person? What of those living high up in the mountain churches of Peru, or in the swampy lowlands of the country once known as Burma? How about our Anglican brothers in Uganda, or the Japanese businesspeople in Tokyo? Estimates vary widely concerning the size of the church in China. Left quietly stewing in Communist seclusion for sixty years—once opened, what do we now find? Some are estimating upward of ninety million or a more conservative seventy million.[9]

If we were to peer over the shoulder of our bouncer into this global church, we would certainly find believers from all parts of the globe reflecting every circumstance imaginable. Well-scrubbed Western Christians will be present, sitting there in straight-back pews, all nicely in a row. But next to them would be tens of thousands of Christians from the seventh most impoverished country in the world, Chad, sitting shoeless on the dirt ground. Some of them may be worshipping Jesus for the first time, even as they wipe the last confusing vestiges of tribal religion or Islamic teachings from their minds and hearts.

On the other side of our church, perhaps we might see our Ukrainian charismatic brothers and sisters. But these sisters and brothers wouldn't actually be in their pews; they would be on their feet, praising God in the aisles. And next to them would be our brothers and sisters from Papua New Guinea sharing a hymnal with us. But, here again, we would have to make adjustments in our worship; only one of us would be reading, not just because of the language barrier between us, but because only one of us has the ability to read.

Imagine this congregation unfolding before our very eyes: well-scrubbed and rich sitting next to dirt poor; PhD candidates next to candidates ready to read for the first time; the culturally rich by Western standards and values next to the culturally rich by Ugandan standards and values. All of these individuals—caught in multiple and varied circumstances—are brothers and sisters in Christ. Values, lifestyle, and life circumstances don't seem to matter as criteria for this relationship.

But if geography and circumstances are not sufficient criteria for determining who are bona fide members of our common fellowship in Christ, then perhaps our bouncer might search for more subjective criteria. Maybe certain personality traits might be more reliable for defining who we are relationally. What if he were to subject all churchgoers to some kind of psychological instrumentation as a basis for who we should associate with as brothers and sisters in Christ? Maybe he could use the Myers-Briggs personality inventory.

For those not familiar with this personality test, it measures four different tendencies in people on four different continuums. First, it measures a person's capacity to interact with people. Some people are extroverts who are actually energized by a crowd; others are introverts who flee from any thought of a crowd, because people sap them of their energy. The very thing that brings vitality to one person diminishes the other. The test also measures a person's capacity to think about things. Some individuals process the world around them in linear, empirical fashion: "Just give me the facts!" For others—those intuitive souls—life comes to them in one big whole. They are typically deemed "big picture" persons. Third, the test measures how individuals tend to make choices based upon the information they receive. Thinking people tend to use their cognitive processes to measure their environment; while for "feeling" people, their world is measured more through their affect. Finally, some people measure time and space in highly controlled fashion; they not only have a calendar but actually use it. They like closure. Understandably, they are called "judging" people. Their counterparts are individuals with perceiving tendencies. Their entire approach to life is open-ended: "Appointment . . . what appointment?"

Putting aside the limitations of these types of measurements, the larger point is that people are born differently with temperaments that naturally send them down life's road in unique ways. We all have certain lenses through which we see our lives and life in general. Add the complex layering of circumstances that serves as a backdrop to our lives—good and bad— and we are all shaped and defined into unique personalities. Some of these personalities we are drawn to; some we are not. Some personalities we are willing to invest in because we more readily share the same life lens; others we are less inclined to invest in. Frankly, some people we like and others we do not by sheer force (or dullness) of their personalities.

What about personality as the criterion for determining the quality of our fellowship? Should the velvet rope of the bouncer be held open or closed based upon a person's inner qualities? A quick look inside our churches reinforces what we find in Scripture. Our congregations are filled with all sorts of personalities. Some, if we are to be honest, are a bit odd. (Apparently our sanctification in Christ doesn't necessarily eliminate the eccentricities some of us share.) Scripture itself reflects all types, from Peter's impulsiveness, to Jeremiah's gloom, to the apostle Paul's tenaciousness. There is no evidence in the Bible that our lives in Christ are determined in any way by temperament.

Well then, maybe, just maybe, our nightclub bouncer can make his assessment of who is in and who is out based upon shared commitments. Maybe our common interests are sufficient means by which we are called to relate to one another. What is your interest? Sports (Red Sox or Yankees, Celtics or Lakers?), cooking, camping, reading poetry, reading romance novels, NASCAR, painting miniature toy soldiers, computer games, shopping? Human associations have forever been defined by individuals huddling around the warmth of common interests that fire their time and imaginations. We relate to people who like the same things we do.

Are common interests the criteria that might be used to define our common life together as brothers and sisters in Christ? As a conscious matter of strategy, perhaps it is here that the Western church has used certain criteria for defining church life in a way that is potentially harmful. Specifically, the trend in recent years to build our churches in homogenous clumps as an actual strategy for growth needs to be reconsidered. We call these groups "affinity groups." Of course, there are certain pragmatic efficiencies in inviting the same people to the same party, as it were. It is easier for people to interact more freely when they have common affinities in terms of social status, age, and interests. Certainly the river of growth and prosperity in a church is stronger without all the annoying tributaries that siphon off the major force of what we might want to accomplish in our master plans for our churches. Homogeneity makes pragmatic sense for multiple reasons.

But take away the diversity of the people of God; take away the means by which we have the opportunity to see God working in each individual believer in a multiplicity of ways; take away the relational challenges in a church, the solutions of which can be attributed only to the Spirit of God working supernaturally in the midst of the church; take away evidence of the future of the kingdom of God working in our churches now in light of how it will be displayed in eternity in all its diversity as described in Revelation 7; take all of this away, and we really don't have Christian fellowship at all. Rather than being a challenge to community, the diversity we find in our churches, in all its layers and richness, is the very evidence that the kingdom of God is actually being manifest in our midst!

If the truth were to be told, we may silently share our bouncer's disappointment as he looks down at his clipboard. At least our actions often suggest such. Peer over his brawny shoulders at what actually goes on in the life of our churches: We like our communities exclusive and uncluttered. Imagine what our churches might look like if we let just anyone in. And once in, imagine including everyone equally in the life of the church.

Alas, our Manhattan bouncer is left with very few criteria for determining who is to be allowed into the church. If it is not common ethnicity, geography, and circumstances; if it is not through common attraction resulting from personality or shared interests; if it is not through a narrow band of complementary values, then how can we determine the ways in which we can relate to one another?

Jesus lays out for us only one criterion for defining our life together, which is surprisingly light to the touch. The only criterion that holds us together as a common relational entity is the mercy we share together that leads to a shared faith in Jesus Christ. Only one check mark goes on that ubiquitous clipboard—and it is shaped like the cross.

Fellowship Is Nonpreferential

> My brothers and sisters, believers in our glorious Lord Jesus
> Christ must not show favoritism.—(James 2:1)

How quickly the tide shifted in that early church. If only the little snapshot described in scene three at the end of Acts 2 could be sustained. Like so many utopian visions that have littered the landscape of history, this picture of new converts devoting themselves to a seemingly perfect balance of teaching, fellowship, giving, worship, and evangelism seems almost too good to be true. The end result of their communion together was that the church numbers increased tremendously—so much so, it says in Acts 6, that even a large number of priests from the temple court became obedient to the faith and entered into their fellowship in the Jerusalem church. If only this experience could be bottled up and used as a template for our own church experience.

But we can bask only briefly in the altruism of this moment in the life of the early church. In Acts 7, we find Stephen, one of the newly coined deacons, standing before the Sanhedrin preaching a glorious sermon of how the work of God in the Old Testament story points directly to Jesus, the Messiah. In short order, his sermon leads to his stoning, and his stoning leads to a great persecution of the church at Jerusalem. In succinct fashion, Luke describes for us at the beginning of chapter 8 that the early church was scattered beyond the safe confines of Jerusalem into Judea and Samaria, and eventually beyond. Come hell or high water, in God's providence, Jesus' commission in Acts 1:8 to be witnesses not only in Jerusalem but to Judea and Samaria and the world was to be fulfilled by this young, timid church.

We can only assume that among those sent packing were some of the three thousand Jewish converts at Pentecost who returned home. Perhaps it was some of these Pentecost Christians who were part of "the twelve tribes scattered among the nations," whom James would soon write to in his letter (James 1:1–2). Perhaps some of these Christians encouraged James to "consider it pure joy" when they experienced trials of many kinds, because the fruit of their struggles produced perseverance, maturity, and ultimately faith.

In these scattered churches we find evidence of the second characteristic that uniquely describes the relationship of the gathered community we call the church. Christians are to be colorblind. Like those who lack the capacity to see clear distinctions between red and green, Christians are to lack the capacity to see the social and personal distinctions that exist naturally outside the walls of the gathered church. Christians are to be *blind to favoritism* of any kind. James is straight and to the point: "My brothers and sisters, believers in our glorious Lord Jesus Christ must not show favoritism" (2:1). In the context of these words, James is particularly speaking of a form of favoritism he had found in their midst based upon economic status.

The scene he paints could not be more vivid: the setting is the gathered place of worship, perhaps a messianic synagogue (James 2:2–4). As we read the story in the second chapter, perhaps we notice the glint of gold on a finger as the sun hits it, and then we see the elegant purple robes. Clearly, this person who just entered the synagogue is someone of distinction. We cannot help but notice him, and if noticing him is our only fault, then perhaps we would be all right. But it takes only this first glance at the visitor for the social gravity of the place to take over. Like a rock, the rich visitor rolls to the front of the place of worship. There he finds perched at his feet a poor man without a ring and void of a colorful robe. Let the worship service begin.

According to Roman social standards of the day, this scene played itself out perfectly. Roman law explicitly favored the rich. Persons of lower class could not bring accusations against those higher up in the social food chain, and even if they could, they would not have had the means to follow through with their lawsuits. In addition, persons of lower class were given harsher penalties if convicted of any crimes.[10]

But James would have none of it in this passage. The relationship that characterizes the church is to be radically different. He does not mince his words: In making the distinctions based upon outward appearance, he says, "Have you not discriminated among yourselves and become judges with evil thoughts?" (James 2:4). For true fellowship to be expressed, no distinction should be made between the rich visitor and the poor person at his feet.

The irony of this scene, of course, is in the fact that James reminds them later that the very rich friends of this rich synagogue visitor are the persons who oppress the church by exploiting and slandering them and dragging them into court (James 2:6–7). Later in his letter to them, James has even stronger things to say about these rich persons, telling them to "weep and wail" for what is coming their way, because of their false dependency upon their money and because of the injustices they have brought on the poor (James 5:1–6).

But resentment toward the rich is not the reason why James demands that the church be a no-preference zone. Unlike the motivation behind the social movements in the nineteenth century that were the antecedents to twentieth-century Communism and socialism, James's intentions here are not to level the social playing field by setting up one group against another for the sake of social equality. Nor do we find here a recipe for more current trends in political correctness that assume that everyone has natural rights to be socially equal. Rather, James's argument for a community void of false distinctions can be understood and claimed only within the unique context of the shared community of God's people.

First, argues James, such preferential treatment of the rich is wrong because it stands contrary to God's own attitude and thus his character. When those in the church make such distinctions, he says, they dishonor the poor, and in dishonoring the poor they behave contrary to the entire narrative of the Old Testament where we see God time and again acting on the side of the poor and oppressed. The specific passage James is probably referring to here is Leviticus 19:15, "Do not pervert justice; do not show partiality to the poor or favoritism to the great, but judge your neighbor fairly."

This same narrative extends to Jesus' own words as he inaugurates the kingdom of God in the Gospels: "Blessed are you who are poor, for yours is the kingdom of God" (Luke 6:20). What need not be construed from these words is that the poor, in themselves, are to be more highly favored than the rich. Rather, what is being declared here—to the extent that the poor display spiritual richness in the face of their physical poverty and to the extent that they have faith—is that they embody a lasting testimony of God's work in their lives. So James can declare, "Has not God chosen those who are poor in the eyes of the world to be rich in faith and to inherit the kingdom he promised those who love him?" (James 2:5).

James's words here closely parallel Paul's own attitude in 1 Corinthians 1: It is in the weak and least influential by the world's standards that God's power is most clearly displayed. Paul declares:

> Brothers and sisters, think of what you were when you were called. Not many of you were wise by human standards; not many were influential; not many were of noble birth. But God chose the foolish things of the world to shame the wise; God chose the weak things of the world to shame the strong. God chose the lowly things of this world and the despised things—and the things that are not—to nullify the things that are, so that no one may boast before him. (1 Cor. 1:26–29)

For these early Christians, many of them from lower social strata, we can well imagine the power these words had on them as they sought to live their lives in a status-starved world.

James continues. The second reason the relationships expressed within the church should be void of preferential treatment is because such distinctions are against the "royal law." James makes it plain that much is at stake here. The consequence of acting with partiality toward others in the church is that they will bring judgment upon themselves by doing so. Acting with favoritism is against the law. What is that law? It is the law of love first expressed in the Decalogue of old and summed up by Jesus as the commandment that is to govern the hearts and minds of all in the new kingdom as he has inaugurated it for the church: "Love your neighbor as yourself" (Matt. 22:39). The law of love can find its fullest expression only when those who live under its precepts are treated with complete impartiality.

This precept of the law of love is most powerfully expressed in the words of Jesus in response to the request of the mother of disciples James and John for a privileged position of power in the new kingdom. Jesus could just as well be speaking directly to the situation James is facing with the churches addressed above:

"You know that the rulers of the Gentiles lord it over them, and their high officials exercise authority over them. Not so with you. Instead, whoever wants to
become great among you must be your servant, and whoever wants to be first
must be your slave—just as the Son of Man did not come to be served, but to
serve, and to give his life as a ransom for many." (Matt. 20:25–28)

Partiality cannot exist under such strictures. If we are called to be servants,
then no one under this new law is in a position to stand over another.

These words from James, as well as Jesus and Paul, beg the question:
How are we to fellowship with one another in our own church contexts?
If we expand the picture beyond the one offered us by James, then we find
that the preferences we are to avoid extend well beyond economic status
distinctions. As with the exclusiveness already discussed above—the ethnic
distinctions between Greek and Jew found in the early church—we are challenged with ethnic diversity in different ways by those who arrive weekly at
our churches' doorsteps, especially as the world gets smaller.

What about cultural differences, such as in the ways we construct our
lifestyles and personal worldviews, behavior defined by basic values in ways
we look and eat, or the way we wear our hair? Even more so, as has already
been discussed in the last section, what about personality distinctions that
determine who we are most drawn to, or not drawn to, for that matter ("I
just can't stand being around that person")? And what about those people in
our churches who, for one reason or another—perhaps it is the social limitations carved early in their lives and psyche because of a terrible childhood—
we just have a difficult time being around?

Who have we avoided lately in our church? Take notice of the way we
position ourselves within our own sanctuaries. Are we not often pulled by
the same natural gravitational pull as our brothers and sisters in the book of
James? Do we not find partiality displayed in so many times and places in
our own churches? Duck our heads into our fellowship halls after the morning service. What do we find? Or walk through our youth group events. Or
even show up at our small groups in the various homes of our community.
Who do we find ourselves continuously talking to? More to the point: Who
do we never think of talking to? The society we find ourselves in within our
churches is often a tapestry of layers of personal preferences.

I am not, of course, speaking here of preferences that might be displayed
as a result of the day-to-day functioning of the church. Prudent leadership
leading to an orderly life together sometimes requires that some be elevated
above others by virtue of the expression of their gifts, both natural and
spiritual. Leadership and giftedness might very well point to more public
and regular forms of affirmation by the body as a whole. But even here—
especially here—our preferences must bear the marks of the discipline of

true humility on both sides. Against all natural impulses to do otherwise over time, leaders must continuously learn the discipline to not see themselves above those they serve. Equally, the community as a whole must be vigilant to not offer those who lead a level of status that would eventually be destructive to both themselves and those to whom they give authority.

The most dramatic example of preferentiality is in the celebrity status we give to some within our churches at large. Don't we offer certain individuals in our Christian circles celebrity status that mimics the larger culture around us? *People* and *US* magazines have nothing on us in this regard. If we were to compare the lists of celebrities who are hot commodities in the Christian world at any time, our lists would be remarkably similar. We should resist this celebrity culture for the sake of these individuals as well as for our own.

Finally, the greatest dangers in our churches in this regard may be the most subtle. Discussions involving the status of churches themselves inevitably will elicit a clear profile of what would conventionally be considered "healthy" or vital churches versus those considered not so. Any pastor committed to the current canon of literature involving numerous church growth models in circulation will know that the "sweet spot" in any congregation involves attracting young couples in their twenties through their forties who have lots of children and youth to fill church programs. These are the productive years in the lives of families; the hope is, of course, that some of this productivity will translate into productivity within our churches as well. Conversely, when discussing less productive churches, the most natural description is that they are small churches "filled with old people."

There is undoubtedly logic to this profile that has a great deal of merit to it, and it has, by and large, passed the test of time for pragmatic reasons. But stepping back far enough to see this perspective against the larger backdrop of the kingdom of God, does this profile of church life not illustrate precisely what James rails against in his example of what is not to go on in the churches he is writing to in first-century Asia Minor? Like those who saw the gold ring and purple robe of the wealthy visitor, we give preferential treatment to the most productive in our midst. It is for these that we reengineer our worship services, sometimes to the objections of a prior generation. It is for these that we develop our best programs. And it is these we seek to attract and accommodate. We do these things while those we may deem less productive—the aging, sometimes singles, or the economically challenged—tend not to get as much of our attention. Even our descriptions of them suggest that we view them somewhat as liabilities to our church life.[11] Of this, I will only repeat James's admonition: "My brothers and sisters, believers in our glorious Lord Jesus Christ must not show favoritism" (2:1).

Fellowship Is Nonreciprocal 3.

"Lend to them without expecting to get anything back."—Jesus (Luke 6:35)

Picture the upper room again where 120 disciples sat waiting patiently for something to happen. Caught between Christ's death, resurrection, and ascension on the one hand and Pentecost on the other, they waited for something that could only vaguely be imagined: the coming with power of the Spirit in their midst. Certainly forty days of being in the presence of Jesus as he taught them about the kingdom of God just prior to this time would have brought some clarity to their minds and hearts. In terms of their understanding, what a difference Jesus' teachings—often veiled in parables—now would have made when looking in hindsight at the events of his life and death and new life again.

Perhaps for the first time in that upper room, these disciples began to unravel some of the hard sayings of Jesus that perplexed them during the past three years as they sat listening to him on those Galilean hillsides. And hard sayings they were. Who said being a follower of Jesus was easy? At times, the threshold Jesus set for them seemed impossible to reach.

Nowhere did Jesus demand more of them in his teachings than in how they were to relate to one another. Perhaps, for example, the disciples' minds wandered back to Jesus' parable of the Good Samaritan. This teaching certainly would have first brought to their minds the slight smirk on the face of that teacher of the law who set the stage for Jesus telling the parable in the first place. The lawyer asked "What must I do to inherit eternal life?" (Luke 10:25) as if he really wanted to know. Jesus made him cough up the answer to his own question: "Love the Lord your God with all your heart and with all your soul and with all your strength and with all your mind," and "Love your neighbor as yourself" (Luke 10:27). Eternal life requires faith being manifest in active love for God and, subsequently, for one's neighbor.

It was the lawyer's follow-up question that actually provoked Jesus to provide the parable: "And who is my neighbor?" To this, Jesus offered up a person who could not have been reviled more in this lawyer's life. A Samaritan! In the midst of the throes of the Assyrian exile, these opportunistic, half-breed Jews inhabited land that was not rightfully theirs, so said the religious establishment of which this lawyer was a member. These Samaritans were traitors and not to be trusted: people whose true colors came out in where they chose to worship—in their temple on Mount Gerizim rather than in Jerusalem. Indeed, they very well might be viewed in the same way as the demon possessed.[12] Perhaps even the disciples had a hard time getting their minds around Jesus' use of this figure as the one who displayed true neighborliness in the parable.

But the power of this parable is not limited to Jesus' choice of central character. Its power lies in what the Samaritan did, in contrast to what the two members of the religious establishment did not do in leaving the stranger lying helpless on that dusty patch of road somewhere between Jerusalem and Jericho. Moved with extraordinary compassion, not only did the alien Samaritan stop and care for the sufferer, but everything he offered the stranger on the road was given without any thought of anything in return. This is the mark of true compassion; the love that the Good Samaritan showed was wholly one-sided, even as he gave the innkeeper two coins and a promise for more with no thought of repayment as he left.

Planted deep in this little parable is the third characteristic of what lies behind the kind of love that we, as Christians, are to manifest toward one another. The relationship that Jesus describes here is a relationship of compassion characterized by a complete absence of expectation for repayment. This is the gold standard upon which we are to live our lives together. To practice love as Jesus describes it is to express it *without any sense of reciprocation.* It is to be a relationship completely one-sided in terms of any expectations we might have on the front end and any benefits we might seek on the back end.

If this is the kind of love that is to be shared between complete strangers, as illustrated in the parable of the Good Samaritan, imagine what that love would look like to our enemies. Jesus gives us an even more dramatic example of the kind of lopsided relationship that should characterize our fellowship with one another when he calls us to love our enemies in Luke 6. Jesus' teaching here is so simple and forthright that it almost loses its impact on us. He commands, "Love your enemies, do good to those who hate you." Come again? "Bless those who curse you, pray for those who mistreat you." Once again? "If someone slaps you on one cheek, turn to them the other also." And, finally, "If anyone takes your coat, do not withhold your shirt from them. Give to everyone who asks you, and if anyone takes what belongs to you, do not demand it back. Do to others as you would have them do to you" (Luke 6:27–31).

How lopsided is this relationship? This teaching of Jesus makes no sense under the standards by which we normally live. In fact, it runs crosscurrent to everything we hold dear. Not only is it illogical, but at its core it seems unjust. Someone steals your cloak and not only do you not try to get it back, but you give the person who steals it your other garment? You fervently pray for the unjust person who maligns and mistreats you? Let the person who hits you for no just reason hit you again? This teaching of Jesus seems to lack a sense of justice; one could say it even sets a dangerous precedent. Once this kind of behavior got around, imagine what it might do to our much-coveted sense of basic human rights. Our system of jurisprudence would crumble under the weight of such a teaching.

Yet as impractical, counterintuitive, illogical, and unjust as it may seem to us, this is the standard that Jesus calls us to in loving one another. At its core, again, is this concept of *love being nonreciprocal.* The logic he gives us is, in fact, set against the logic and behavior of this world:

> "If you love those who love you, what credit is that to you? Even sinners love those who love them. And if you do good to those who are good to you, what credit is that to you? Even sinners do that. And if you lend to those from whom you expect repayment, what credit is that to you? Even sinners lend to sinners, expecting to be repaid in full. But love your enemies, do good to them, and lend to them without expecting to get anything back." (Luke 6:32–35)

It is precisely because we can expect nothing in return from our enemies— in fact, quite the opposite since we can expect bad things—that our relationship with them is the standard that Jesus uses for us in our love for others. No wonder the world out there—the "sinners"—must look in on the church, on its good days, with utter amazement.

These, then, are two examples that Jesus gave us as a pattern for our relationships: a stranger—a much maligned alien at that—and an enemy. If the motive behind loving a complete stranger is hard to grasp, then being motivated to love one's enemy is even more difficult to comprehend, let alone act upon. What is it in the Christian that would motivate us to express love for one another under these sets of circumstances?

The answer lies in Jesus' final words in his command to love our enemies: "Then your reward will be great, and you will be children of the Most High, because he is kind to the ungrateful and wicked. Be merciful, just as your Father is merciful" (Luke 6:35–36). God the Father is to be our example here. He sent his Son to an ungrateful and wicked people, and received nothing but neglect and evil in return. Likewise, our relationships should bear the same evidence of mercy for others that we have received ourselves through the work of Christ on the cross.

These relationships of the despised stranger and the enemy might well be disquieting examples for us in the church because, at the most subterranean level, we know that mixed motives are baked into almost everything we do and every relationship we foster. Even our best intentions are often tainted by quiet self-interest.

Who of us, for example, hides motives for intimacy and positive self-regard behind the gifts we give to one another? Buried deep behind every gift is a desire for acknowledgement of our love for another person. There is certainly nothing wrong with this, but if we emptied our pockets every Christmas to total strangers rather than to family and friends who expect our gifts, then we might learn something about ourselves and our motives for giving.

Or what of the altruism behind the gifts we find, say, displayed on almost every university campus we walk through in the country? Chances are many of the buildings we pass are tagged with a wealthy donor who has sought some level of immortality on the walls of his or her alma mater. Although there's nothing wrong with gifts from generous donors, contrast this with the anonymous gift of the donor whose only restriction is that no one knows his or her name. What of the nameless buildings on these campuses that reflect the silent legacy of a truly nonreciprocal gift?

I wonder what our churches would look like with more relationships characterized by this total lack of regard for reciprocity. I wonder, for example, how we would even select the very churches we attend. Do we not come to this decision based upon the menu of what local churches offer us and our families that is of most value to us: the best worship, the cleanest nursery, the most organized small group ministry, or the most teenager-attractive youth program? Certainly there is nothing wrong with any of these congregational assets, but what if we selected our churches strictly based upon how we can serve? What a radical notion! What if our churches were filled with people whose first and most natural impulse was based upon the unbridled service they would bring to that congregation, without any thought of anything in return?

Fellowship Is Not Concerned for Status 4.

But that its parts should have equal concern for each other.—Paul (1 Cor. 12:25)

Imagine the time it took for the calm to return after the din of the overwhelming roar of wind at Pentecost, much like a tornado. Picture dilated eyes finally finding their normal pupil size as these disciples left the room after observing the bright light of what looked to be thousands of tongues of fire. Consider what it took for the minds and emotions of these three thousand to finally settle after they heard and understand languages they were never taught. And think about the time it took for the prophecy-filled words of Peter's sermon at the end of Acts 2 to settle into their hearts and lives.

The early church that evolved from the upper room of Pentecost experienced a mighty supernatural display of the Spirit of God unlike anything seen before or since. But the Spirit was not left at the doorsteps of the room that day. The three thousand or more believers were not left with merely a supernatural experience. Indeed, the Spirit was to be the evidence that they were a community bound together in Christ.

The overwhelming sense of the presence of the Spirit in that room was really the promised return of God's presence to dwell among his people in a personal way. It is the same Spirit who filled the tabernacle and the temple where God dwelled among his people, as seen in Exodus 33. It is the same Spirit of the Lord talked about in Isaiah 63:9–14, in Psalm 106:33, and in Jeremiah 31:31–33, where God proclaimed, "I will make a new covenant . . . and write it on their hearts." This presence is linked later in Ezekiel 36:26 to the Spirit who will "give you a new heart and put a new spirit in you." Here is the promise of a renewed presence, as we see in Ezekiel 37:27: "My dwelling place will be with them; I will be their God, and they will be my people." And it is the same Spirit of the new covenant promised by the prophets Jeremiah (33:31) and Ezekiel (36:27), who would indwell God's people and cause them to live as a community that would follow his ways. At Pentecost, he came in dramatic fashion.

We tend to think first of this presence of the Spirit in highly individualistic and personal ways. The Spirit does, indeed, take up residence in the lives of people individually, as Paul discusses in 1 Corinthians 6:19–20. But Paul speaks more often of the evidence of the Spirit in corporate terms, as the Spirit manifesting himself in the midst of people of God. For example, Paul writes to the Ephesians of a new community being raised up together to become a holy temple of God, "a dwelling in which God lives by His Spirit." In Jesus Christ, he says, "you too are being built together to become a dwelling in which God lives by his Spirit" (Eph. 2:21–22).

Not only is the Spirit present in the midst of his people; he is the very structuring principle upon which this new community of believers is built. For this, the apostle Paul uses a wonderful, far-reaching metaphor that describes both *who* we are as a community of believers and also *how* we are to function together as a community. We are a "body," he declares in 1 Corinthians 12. Reflecting back in part to the baptism received initially at Pentecost, he declares, "For we were baptized by one Spirit so as to form one body—whether Jews or Gentiles, slave or free—and we were all given the one Spirit to drink" (1 Cor. 12:13).

In the context of these words, Paul gives an extended anatomy lesson of how the individual members are to work together to serve the body as a whole. For the "common good," he says, each member of the community is given one or more gifts by the Spirit to be used for the edification of the others, including (but not exclusively) the gifts of wisdom, knowledge, faith, healing, miraculous powers, prophecy, discernment of spirits, speaking in tongues, and the interpretation of tongues. In 1 Corinthians 12:7–11, Paul makes it clear that these gifts cannot be attributed to anyone other than the Spirit; they are his gifts and his alone. As such, it is for him to disperse them according to his own desire.

In verses 14–20 of the same chapter, Paul continues his lesson on the anatomy of the body. In these verses, his primary concern is in how the manifestations of each of the gifts of the Spirit dispensed to individual members serve to instill unity within the body as a whole. He then asks a series of rhetorical questions that provoke the reader to consider how it might be if one member of our body chose to function separately from all the others. What a predicament we would be in if hands, feet, eyes, ears, and nose did not work together. We would be uncoordinated at best, nonfunctional at worst.

In the specific context in which Paul is writing—where certain gifts in the Corinthian church, such as tongues and prophecy, seemed to have been given a disproportionate emphasis, causing disunity within the church—he further considers what might be the source of the body's lack of coordination and disunity. Is it not caused by a false sense of value placed on some gifts in comparison to others, based upon how they are being manifested publicly? Some gifts are viewed more highly than others. So Paul says of those parts of the body who insist that they don't need the others,

> On the contrary, those parts of the body that seem to be weaker are indispensable, and the parts that we think are less honorable we treat with special honor. And the parts that are unpresentable are treated with special modesty, while our presentable parts need no special treatment. But God has put the body together, giving greater honor to the parts that lacked it, so that there should be no division in the body, but that its parts should have equal concern for each other. (12:22–26)

A quick scanning of our own physical bodies confirms what Paul is saying in spiritual terms. We might very well be more drawn to our classic nose or our large right bicep than that awful-looking piece of tissue, our liver. Or who of us would deny that the bones of our inner ear might be at least as important to our daily functioning as that playful little dimple on our right cheek we are so proud of? Members of the body who might seem to have less important functions in the body of Christ are as indispensable as those who might appear to have greater importance. In this sense, all parts of the body are to be equally valued.

Paul's use of the body in 1 Corinthians, and also in Romans and Ephesians, is a powerful metaphor for describing how the church is to function. Might not this picture of the functional nature of the church also serve as a model for how Christians are to express themselves in their fellowship together? As the Spirit works in the church through the manifestation of his gifts, these gifts in turn shape the ways in which the members of the body relate to one another interpersonally. In this sense, just as those gifts that appear to be weaker prove to be indispensable to the health of the body, so too are not the weaker brothers and sisters among us to be viewed as equally indispensable? Should they not be viewed as honorable? And just as those gifts that are less noticeable are treated with special treatment, should not the weaker of our brothers and sisters be treated accordingly?

Unlike other types of relationships that assume a form of common equality as a basis for their meaningful expression, Christian fellowship is a relationship *without concern for status*. It is not necessary for Christians to be on equal footing with one another to relate meaningfully. In fact, quite the opposite; the hallmark of Christian fellowship is that it bridges all manner of disparities, both formal and informal. There is to be no pyramid of relationships in the kingdom, where we find some perched higher on the narrow point at the top and others down further near the broader base.

A brief look at the first-century church provides multiple examples of ways in which the fellowship those in the church shared was marked by the breaking down of social and cultural barriers of many kinds. We need not look any further than the scene at the end of Acts 2. The first church of Jerusalem clearly included individuals who cut across social and economic strata, as wealthy members of the church sold their possessions and, as a supreme act of *koinonia*, gave to their poor brothers and sisters in need.

Or what of the small church at Philippi? Although the story is not told in detail, it can be conjectured from Acts 16 that Lydia, the wealthy dealer of purple cloth whom Paul first met on a riverbank, eventually sat shoulder to shoulder with her more humble sister, the ex-demoniac slave girl, and her new brother in Christ, the rough, pagan centurion jailer. The book of Philemon also bridges a social ravine that would not have been crossed in the first-century Roman world. Imagine, slave and master as brothers in Christ! Paul's admonition to these two was to act like the equal siblings in Christ they now were. We are brought back again to Paul's wild claim that the fellowship we are to share with one another extends in all directions: "There is neither Jew nor Gentile, neither slave nor free, nor is there male and female, for you are all one in Christ Jesus" (Gal. 3:28). All persons are to be viewed as equal.

Nowhere is this commitment to equality better illustrated for Paul than in his own admonitions to his Corinthian brothers and sisters in 1 Corinthians 11. Here we find Paul painting a picture for us of a first-century house church typically divided into two rooms: an inner, more elaborate room containing a low table with stacked pillows surrounding it; and an outer room where most of daily life went on, including cooking. If we had an opportunity to see what Paul was responding to that day, we would have seen some privileged few in the church sitting around the table in the inner room, breaking bread and taking the Lord's Supper, while many others in the church were forced to sit on the dirt floor in the outer room. Of this scene, Paul declares,

In the first place, I hear that when you come together as a church, there are divisions among you, and to some extent I believe it. No doubt there have to be differences among you to show which of you have God's approval. So then, when you come together, it is not the Lord's Supper you eat, for when you are eating, some of you go ahead with your own private suppers. As a result, one person remains hungry and another gets drunk. (1 Cor. 11:18–21)

To those sitting on pillows around the table in the inner room, Paul has some strong words. He declares to them a warning, which we repeat somewhat innocuously as part of most of our Communion services:

So then, whoever eats the bread or drinks the cup of the Lord in an unworthy manner will be guilty of sinning against the body and blood of the Lord. Everyone ought to examine themselves before they eat of the bread and drink from the cup. For those who eat and drink without discerning the body of Christ eat and drink judgment on themselves. That is why many among you are weak and sick, and a number of you have fallen asleep. (1 Cor. 11:27–30)

What these few who elevated themselves above the others were doing was deemed by Paul as "unworthy" behavior. There is no room for these distinctions in status. To allow such to happen is not only the source of division in the church, but it actually opens those in the church up to judgment. Paul would not stand for such in the body.

We need to be careful here, however. Our tendency might be to see the basis for this equality as brothers and sisters in Christ written between the lines of the political documents that govern our lives in the West, our various constitutions. But we do not rely on man-made documents. Why are Jews and Greeks, slaves and freepersons, males and females equal? Why must there not be dividing walls where some eat in a more privileged inner room and others sit in a less privileged one? We are made equal only as a result of Christ Jesus. We are made so because we "are all children of God through faith, for all of you who were baptized into Christ have clothed yourselves with Christ" (Gal. 3:26–27). The source of our equality is not something we find in ourselves, nor is it something we can claim as an "inalienable right." As brothers and sisters in Christ, we are equal only because Christ has made us so. He is the great leveler of our relationships because we are made equal at the foot of his cross.

I wonder what a church fellowship would look like if this kind of equality were on full display. Imagine, for example, the makeup of the typical ruling board of our churches. Why are church leadership boards in many churches filled with the successful and prominent? Why are they populated by those who have risen to the top of the vocational and economic food chain? Where are the blue-collar union workers, the agricultural workers, and those working to clean our hotel rooms and care for our gardens? What if our leadership more broadly reflected the socioeconomic spectrum of our churches?

And what of our children and youth? If they truly claim the name of Jesus, young as they are, how much more would we value them in the church if we saw them as brothers and sisters in Christ? Imagine looking into the eyes of a six-year-old sister in Christ, or a fifteen-year-old boy, and seeing in them equal partners for the sake of the gospel. How might this perspective change the way we do children's and youth ministries?

Further, what roles might our less talented members play? Why is it that we push our most gifted and attractive individuals to the front where they are most visible? Finally, how can we honor those in our sanctuary who, in any other place, would be marginalized?

Of course the picture is more complicated than this. A person's contribution to our shared fellowship is based upon more than just issues of status. Paul himself makes distinctions in the gifts and how they are to be manifested, at one point suggesting that we seek the "greater gifts" (1 Cor. 12:31). But the manifestation of these "greater gifts" for Paul was not based upon being more authoritative in the sense of having greater power; rather, these gifts were made higher in light of the effect they had in the needs of the body.[13] Further, understandably some in our fellowship make greater contributions to the fellowship of our communities than others. Some are more talented and more resourceful. Some are in a better position in life— the established adult over the child, the gifted musician over the tone-deaf man—to make a contribution. But never should these contributions be the source of elevating one brother and sister over the other.

Imagine the example our churches would be to outsiders who looked inside our doors and saw a community strangely unaffected by the status structure that otherwise permeates our world. Imagine the unemployed, disheveled person in joyous relationship with well-heeled businesspeople. See the mother of five talented, well-adjusted children sitting next to the single mom who feeds her three children on food stamps. Imagine the "least of these" as persons of prominence in our midst. What an amazing sight it would be for the outsider to see people loving one another freely and without the slavish constraints of status that so afflict their own lives.

CHAPTER FIVE

MORE ON THE MAKING
OF COMMUNITY

For the discerning reader, it should be readily apparent by now that the relationship that defines the early church is quite different from what we see today as friendship. What do we see in Christian fellowship that compares to friendship? If friendship is by nature exclusive, then what we know as Christian fellowship is nonexclusive. If friendship is preferential, then Christian fellowship is nonpreferential. If friendship is mutual, then Christian fellowship is non-mutual. If friendship involves equal status, then Christian fellowship is not built upon status at all.

Not only are the two relationships different, but they are, in fact, conceptually exact opposites. In significant ways, the nature of friendship runs contrary to what is espoused in the building up of Christian community as described in the New Testament. What might this mean? Could it be that being a member of the community of Christ is more than just extending friendship to others? Perhaps having fellowship with Christian brothers and sisters is not fundamentally an exercise in friendliness at all. Or, put differently, expressing friendship with another may ultimately have little correspondence to extending true Christian fellowship.[1]

Certainly this might come as a surprise to most of us. In the seventeenth century, Jeremy Taylor made an observation that is striking in its directness for us today:

> The word "friendship," in the sense we commonly mean by it, is not so much as named in the New Testament and our religion takes no notice of it. You think it strange; but read on before you spend so much as the beginning of a passion or a wonder upon it. There is mention of "friendship with the world," and it is said to be "enmity with God:" but the word is nowhere else named, or to any other purpose, in all the New Testament. It speaks of friends often; but by friends are meant our acquaintance, or our kindred, the relatives of our family, or our fortune, or our sect; something of society, or something of kindness, there is in it; a tenderness of appellation and civility, a relation made by gift, or by duty, by services and subjection.[2]

Although the relationship we understand as friendship is surely scattered sparingly about in the New Testament, Taylor is right when he observes that it is not centrally located in the New Testament. More to the point, it is not the primary relationship that describes the first-century church.

To reinforce Taylor's observations, one way to delineate the one relationship type from the other is through the general distinction made in the biblical use of two meanings of the word for "love" in the New Testament: *phileo* or *philia* and *agapao* or *agape*. We must be careful here. The distinction is not a perfect or complete one, and there are some noted exceptions; but the two uses of the word generally stand out as describing two different types of relationships when used in the New Testament.[3]

Philia indicates general fondness toward a person or thing: in general, to have affection for another. Its more particular usage is to describe love, friendship, hospitality, or devotion toward a friend or relative.[4] *Phileo* means a friend or relative. As we have already seen, particularly in the writings of Aristotle and Cicero, it is the dominant word in classical usage that goes all the way back in antiquity from Homer onward. It does not have a clear religious emphasis on its own. For this reason, perhaps, in the New Testament, the word *phileo* is used infrequently: five times in Matthew, thirteen times in John, and seven times elsewhere. The noun *philia* is used only once in the New Testament, in James 4:4.

Further confirming Taylor's observation, Matthew 10:37 is a typical use of *phileo*, where natural love is derived from family connection: "Anyone who loves their father or mother more than me is not worthy of me; anyone who loves their son or daughter more than me is not worthy of me." The apostle John generally characterizes love according to whether the world is viewed as God's creation or in enmity with God. When the world is viewed as God's creation, natural love has a legitimate place, as in John 11:3, 36 where Jesus' bond of friendship with Lazarus is declared. When the world of darkness is described as being against God, love of the world is expressed in direct opposition with God, as in 1 John 2:15: "Do not love the world or anything in the world."

Further, *philos* is used several times to denote a friend to whom one is under a basic obligation. Luke is particularly fond of this usage (for example, Luke 7:6; 11:5; 15:6, 9, 29; Acts 10:24; 27:3): It is the friends and neighbors in Luke 15:9, whom the woman calls to rejoice with her when she finds her lost coin. In most of these cases, friends are often mentioned alongside relatives. In John 19:12, Pilot is concerned about losing his honorary title as "Friend of Caesar."

Finally, at points *philos* is used to describe God's love for the godless, as in Matthew 11:19 where Jesus is called the "friend of tax-collectors and sinners." It is this usage that most dramatically describes Jesus' description of his disciples as "friends" in John 15:14ff.[5] Jesus loves them in spite of the fact that they are enemies, just as God loves the world that hates him. They come to him as sinners and became his friends through his sacrificial love. So, now, instead of the love and friendship they enjoyed while belonging to the world, they are in new fellowship with the family of God.

By contrast, *agapao* and the noun *agape* are the least specific terms for love in classical usage, meaning "to honor or welcome." Interestingly, in its classic usage, *agape* carries with it hardly any of the warmth of *phileo*. This will have implications for our discussion later in the next chapter. Its etymological origin is unknown and its meaning is generally colorless and indefinite. The verb often means no more than to be content with something, or to welcome somebody with a courteous greeting.

Agape, however, does have a deeper meaning when it indicates striving after something, or liking somebody or something; at times in general usage it can denote sympathy or mutual respect and friendship of equals. Specifically characteristic are instances where it takes on the idea of preference, and means to put one value or aim above another, to esteem one person more highly than another.

As colorless as the word is in classical usage, when taken up in the New Testament, *agape* is used in very particular ways to speak of the love of God or the way of life that is based upon that love. The word is used to describe God's activity as love, to speak of God's relationship with humankind, and the relationship that God's people have to share with one another. This word dominates the New Testament. Sixty-three times *agapao* is used in the Gospels for "to love." The noun, *agape*, is used nine times. Although not his only word for love throughout his Epistles, *agape* ("love") and *agapao* ("to show love") are the words Paul uses predominately, 109 times together.[6]

In the Gospels, *agape* is the word that most clearly describes divine love. It is the love God has within the Godhead (John 3:35). Further, it reflects the divine love God has for his Son. In John 10:17, for example, Jesus says, "The reason my Father loves me is that I lay down my life." The word also speaks of the divine love God has for the world and all he created, as we find in John 3:16—it is the reason why God gave his Son.

Notably for us here, it is this divine love described in the Gospels that sets the standard for how we are to love others, as in John 13:34 where the disciples are to love one another "as I have loved you," using Jesus as the standard. This same injunction is repeated in John 15:12—"My command is this: Love each other as I have loved you." Further, in John 13:34, Jesus declares, "A new command I give you: Love one another. As I have loved you, so you must love one another." It is the very mark of this love that sets his disciples apart from all others: "By this everyone will know that you are my disciples, if you love one another" (13:35).

Paul's use of *agape* is equally extensive. At the heart of Paul's message is the love of God (*agape*) in Christ. We find it most clearly in Paul's description of Christ's atoning work on the cross; for example in Romans 5:8, "But God demonstrates his own love for us in this: While we were still sinners, Christ died for us." Or we find this same usage in Ephesians 2:4–5, "But because of his great love for us, God, who is rich in mercy, made us alive with Christ even when we were dead in transgressions."

Interestingly, the word is used to describe love that is limited in scope to some and apparently not to others. It is love that is for the predestined and elect, and those who are children of God, as in Romans 9:13—"Just as it is written: 'Jacob I loved, but Esau I hated.'" Saving love, says Paul, comes through a relationship only with Jesus Christ, as in 1 Timothy 1:14: "The grace of our Lord was poured out on me abundantly, along with the faith and love that are in Christ Jesus." It is not love that can be self-attained or conjured up from within. Rather, this love comes through the work only of the Holy Spirit as God pours his love into the human heart. In Romans 5:5, Paul declares, "And hope does not put us to shame, because God's love has been poured out into our hearts through the Holy Spirit, who has been given to us."

Consequently, this is love to be manifest as a joyful response to the grace of God that comes through the work of Jesus Christ on the cross. It should naturally overflow to others. To the Colossians Paul says, "My goal is that they may be encouraged in heart and united in love, so that they may have the full riches of complete understanding, in order that they may know the mystery of God, namely, Christ" (Col. 2:2). Time and again, Paul admonishes the community to seek love: "Be devoted to one another in love. Honor one another above yourselves" (Rom. 12:10), and

> therefore, as God's chosen people, holy and dearly loved, clothe yourselves with compassion, kindness, humility, gentleness and patience. Bear with each other and forgive one another if any of you has a grievance against someone. Forgive as the Lord forgave you. And over all these virtues put on love, which binds them all together in perfect unity. (Col. 3:12–14)

In considering all of these uses, then, it can certainly be said that the use of *agapao* for describing love uniquely dominates the New Testament. Again, acknowledging some noted exceptions in the way the two words are sometimes used interchangeably, the general shift of the use of *phileo* and *agapao* for love suggests that a new relationship transplants friendship as the central source of deep-seated intimacy and relational connectedness in the first-century community of Christ. Narrow in its focus, divine in origin, and motivated by God's grace manifest through the work of his Son, these Christians were to be characterized by a love unlike any other.

What a dramatic difference this new relationship is from the Greek and Roman worlds of Aristotle, Cicero, and the other classical writers who understood the underpinnings of society and its institutions built upon a concept of friendship! Even as the first-century Christians lived in these cultures, they were being called to relate to one another in altogether new ways that extended beyond and even contradicted this predominant idea of friendship. Spilling out of the teachings of Jesus and seeping into the writings of the New Testament was a concept of a radical new society characterized by the reutilizing of a much-neglected word in classical usage, *agape*. And within this new society, we find expressed an entirely new way of relating love to one another as brothers and sisters in Christ.

The implication of this reality for us today is nothing short of stunning. Is it not the case that in our effort to develop fellowship with one another as brothers and sisters in Christ, we frequently falsely use friendship as our modus operandi in the church? This is often the logic that drives our understanding of Christian fellowship: If the neighborhood bar "where everybody knows your name" is a friendly place, or if the neighborly Lion's Club is a friendly place, then the church just needs to be a bit friendlier to set itself apart. If the friendship we find exhibited in a group of colleagues is deep and heartfelt, then we just need to be more heartfelt by comparison!

But as important as friendship might be in the church, being "friendlier" than other kinds of relationships might very well miss the point. God calls us to an entirely new way of relating to one another that is radically different from any other relationship around us, including friendship. Nowhere else do we find this relationship expressed in a way that defines us as brothers and sisters in Christ than in the church.

To further illustrate this new relationship, we continue now with our description of Christian fellowship. It should come as no surprise that, as in the last chapter, the community to which we are called as Christians continues to run cross-grained to that of friendship.

5. Fellowship as Self-Giving

See that you also excel in this grace of giving.—Paul (2 Cor. 8:7)

It is almost as if Luke didn't think his readers had a clear enough picture of the early church in the one he painted at the end of Acts 2. He needed to back up and once again paint a portrait of this new church in Jerusalem at the end of Acts 4. He begins by describing the church at Jerusalem: "All the believers were one in heart and mind" (Acts 4:32). Defying the ban the Sanhedrin placed on their preaching, they continued to testify to Christ's resurrection "with great power."

And then he makes this amazing claim: "There were no needy persons among them" (Acts 4:34). Not one needy person throughout the entire church of Jerusalem? Surely this must be hyperbole. How could this be? But there it is: "No one claimed that any of their possessions was their own, but they shared everything they had." Seeing the needs of others, men and women in that early church sold property and houses and laid the proceeds at the apostles' feet for their distribution to the poor.

With some irony, this next trait of what it means to be in Christian fellowship is perhaps the most difficult for those of us in the affluent Western church. Built into the very fabric of what it means to be in community with one another is the *impulse for radical self-giving.* One would think that given the advantages of time and space—given the relatively excessive wealth and leisure afforded us at this time in history—this trait would be the most natural for us to express. To be fair, with one small step into the next chapter of Acts, we find evidence that giving of themselves was not, perhaps, much easier for those early Christians. The story of Ananias and Sapphira is an early reminder of the claim our possessions have on our lives.

Buried deep in one of Paul's Epistles is a wonderful example of what is asked of us if we are to be in true fellowship with one another on this count. The group of churches we find Paul describing in 2 Corinthians 8 was the modern-day equivalent of the runts of the litter. They would have been at the end of the line in terms of our expectations. After all, the churches of Philippi, Thessalonica, and Berea—the Macedonian churches—were experiencing severe poverty themselves, probably as a result of undergoing persecution. And yet, these were the churches that Paul used as an example to spur on their more affluent fellow believers from the Corinthian church to express generosity to the equally destitute church in Jerusalem. Paul says it was these weak little sister churches that were first in line to give far beyond their means for the sake of their fellow believers at Jerusalem and as an expression of the grace that God had given them.

The kind of giving we find that characterized these Macedonian Christians was threefold. First, they gave spontaneously. Paul says, "Entirely on their own, they urgently pleaded with us for the privilege of sharing in this service to the Lord's people" (8:3–4). The word used here is *koinonia,* which again has the common meaning of "sharing, participation, and fellowship." For these believers, to enter into fellowship with their brothers and sisters was naturally to share of themselves. Here is an example of a relationship in which no pleading was needed for them to participate in other people's suffering. The begging itself implies a lack of prior manipulation on Paul's part. There was no counting of shekels, no drawn out calculating of figures, no worried pondering on the part of these believers. The privilege of sharing with others was entirely reflexive on their part. In their rush to participate, they gave from the basic impulses of their hearts, not from the prior calculation of their heads.

Second, they gave sacrificially. Paul says of these Christians, "In the midst of a very severe trial, their overflowing joy and their extreme poverty welled up in rich generosity. For I testify that they gave as much as they were able, and even beyond their ability" (8:2–3). These Christian brothers and sisters gave out of their poverty and not out of prosperity.

This kind of giving involves a mind-set foreign to our own economic sensibilities. It echoes Jesus' own observations as he sat in the shadowy corner of the temple court, as recorded in Mark 12, and observed how various people gave. The economics just don't seem to work in the conventional way. Jesus claimed that the value of the thin little coins of the widow's offering hitting the bottom of the collection container was far greater than the hefty clank of the coins given by the wealthy.

Here is an economic system that was not built on the actual value of the dollar, or the shekel as the case may be. The currency of the kingdom from Jesus' perspective was based on the value of the giver. More to the point, it was based on the value the giver had placed on the Giver of all things, great or small. This is why the Macedonian Christians could give so freely from out of their own poverty. They knew the Source from which all things were given.

This leads us to the third characteristic of giving by the Macedonian churches. These believers gave selflessly. That is, they gave with no sense of return on their investment from the others. The overarching theme in this passage of Paul's request for the collection of a gift to the Jerusalem church is that of offering a gift of grace. What an amazing phrase! Offering a gift of grace. Whatever was being done here was all about grace. Paul's stated use of the Macedonian church as an example for the Corinthian church was not focused on their gift per se; rather, it was as a result of the gift they had already received from God (8:1).

Again, what was to be their motivation for giving? In contrast to our most basic impulses, the giving we find displayed here by these Macedonian Christians has nothing to do with a hoped-for gift in return. Nor, as Paul reminds the Corinthian church, is it something to be done out of obligation (8:8). Nor, for that matter, is it a way to illustrate how much they could do for God. The sole motivation behind their giving was their overflowing response to what God had already given them.

The gift of the Macedonian church—and the hoped-for gift from the Corinthian church—was to be nothing less than the joyful recognition that they were the beneficiaries of far more than anything they could ever give. So Paul reminds them: "For you know the grace of our Lord Jesus Christ, that though he was rich, yet for your sake he became poor, so that you through his poverty might become rich" (8:9). The only true Giver is God, and this was to be the entire focus of their giving.

If this is the case, then what is the ultimate effect of this kind of giving? Surely the church at Jerusalem benefited from the gifts they received in tangible ways. Certainly the act of giving must have been satisfying to the givers. Of course, the example of giving set by the Macedonian churches had the intended contagious effect on others, including the Corinthian church. But Paul makes it abundantly clear that the ultimate purpose for giving has little to do with those who give and those who receive. Later, in the following chapter of 2 Corinthians, he says:

> This service that you perform is not only supplying the needs of the Lord's people but is also overflowing in many expressions of thanks to God. Because of the service by which you have proved yourselves, *others will praise God* for the obedience that accompanies your confession of the gospel of Christ, and for your generosity in sharing with them and with everyone else. (2 Cor. 9:12–13; italics added)

If the act of giving is ultimately an act of acknowledging God's grace in our lives, then the net effect is God's own glory. Their generosity brought thanksgiving to God.

Now drag this example of the Macedonian churches from the past up to the present in the context of our own giving. Has there ever been a time and place more capable of giving generously than presently in the West? In recent years, it is estimated that 80 percent of the world's evangelical wealth rests in North America.[7]Although researchers do not agree completely on exact amounts, there is general consensus that between $1.54 trillion and $6.72 trillion in assets are at the disposal of American evangelicals, excluding the value of their primary homes.[8] Of these Christians, only one-third to one-half financially support their churches.[9]

To put all this into perspective, in 2007, Americans spent over $40 billion on their pets.[10] In 2010, it was projected that they would spend over $60 billion on weight-loss programs.[11] If Paul were to look around for another example of gracious giving to be offered to the Corinthian church, it would seem logical that he would point our direction. He would be sorely disappointed, if not downright embarrassed.

The Macedonian churches in 2 Corinthians have much to teach us about the way we should give as an act of fellowship to our fellow believers, at home and around the globe. Measured by their spontaneous impulsiveness to give, we may find ourselves wanting. Unlike the example of these churches, our giving is often calibrated as if we were holding a test tube in one hand and a pipette in the other. Every drop of energy we expend, every ounce of our time, every cent in our wallets is measured out in precise detail and registered with precision. But for our fellowship to flourish like these early churches, we need to be far less calculating, perhaps even careless and sloppy. What would it look like if one of the most anticipated moments of our worship service was the time of offering, and our giving every week flowed over the lips of our offering plates? What a wonderful mess it would be!

The challenge here, however, is not to admonish us to give more out of obligation, to grit our teeth and force another dollar out of our wallets and into the till. Rather, the example of the Macedonian churches is really an invitation to enter into a new mind-set that frees us to serve one another under the strictures of a whole new economic system. We are all receivers of far more than we can ever give. The grace we bestow on others, by way of the grace God has bestowed on us, should flow from us as nothing less than excess spillage.

I saw a small taste of this new kingdom economics a few years ago at an event in Europe in which wealthy donors spent a week with ministry leaders from around the Middle East. For seven long days, we had the opportunity to hear, sometimes in heartbreaking detail, of the hard work of the gospel in these predominately Islamic countries. Time and again, we heard about how the poverty of resources confronting these faithful churches was easily matched by rich expressions of God's work being manifest through hundreds and thousands of conversions. By the end of our time together, the value of the dollar in the hearts and minds of these donors became increasingly small in comparison to the task at hand. This is what kingdom giving will do for us. It will turn poverty into riches and riches into poverty. In both ways, our fellowship with our brothers and sisters will be made all the richer.

6. Fellowship as a Divine Command

"My command is this: Love each other as I have loved you."—Jesus (John 15:12)

Following is a completely fictitious rendering of a biblical narrative. It is completely fictitious, but I hope with just enough perspective to make a point. Picture, if you will, the situation of the 120 disciples in the waiting room after the events of Jesus' death, resurrection, and ascension. Imagine the room being not quite large enough to comfortably fit everyone. Maybe it is stifling with the heat of bodies and Middle East humidity. We can well imagine the sun beating down on that anonymous room during those long days of uncertainty. We know they prayed and carried on some business. Their primary task there was to wait, but wait for how long? Maybe there was still some residual fear and trepidation in the air that put some of them on edge as they waited.

Imagine the vast display of personalities stewing in this tiny melting pot, each person in that room relating to the others on various and multiple levels. Some, we know, were family members; some were fellow apostles who walked with Jesus for three long years and knew one another well; some were probably close friends; and some perhaps only knew the others in the room as passing acquaintances. Stripping back the enormity of their task—which those of us see who have the privilege of hindsight as we read the biblical text—at least one of the immediate tasks confronting each of them was the messy business of relating meaningfully to one another day by day, hour by hour, moment by moment.

With this picture in mind, we could just as well play this story backward and imagine the day-to-day relational pressures and delights of the twelve disciples as they lived in the close quarters of their journeys through the Palestinian countryside. Three long years they went about the business of relationship building. We could also play the story forward and observe the relational landscape of the first church of Jerusalem as recorded at the end of Acts 2, or any number of other churches as they were being formed in those early years—the Corinthian church, the church at Philippi, or those who came together as a community at Antioch.

Returning to the upper room, imagine now if Bartholomew, or per-haps Simon the Zealot, perhaps Stephen from the south side of Jerusalem, or—pick a name, it doesn't matter—one of these men decided that they'd just about had it up to here with Peter's authoritarian attitude, or Philip's skepticism, or—it doesn't matter—perhaps it was James's holier-than-thou attitude. Someone needed to leave the group or conflict was going to erupt. Everyone entered the room freely, after all, so they should be able to leave freely as well. Maybe the only way that relationships could be salvaged would be to take a vote and decide who would leave this "island" of new Christ-followers as they were being shaped into a new community.

As implausible as this scenario may seem, it raises the question as to the mechanism by which those in Christian community with one another enter and leave their relationships. To what extent is Christian fellowship a freely chosen relationship? Our best instincts deceive us at this point. Most of us measure our most intimate relationships by the degree to which we can freely enter and leave them. How does the Hallmark saying from the '70s go? "I am I and you are you, and if by chance we meet that would be groovy!" Isn't our freedom with one another as Christians the very thing that makes our fellowship so deep and endearing as brothers and sisters in Christ?

The answer to this question might surprise us. If we were to run our hands across Jesus' teachings on love, we might find our fingers getting snagged on some hard realities that are surprisingly ragged to the touch. Putting aside our sentimentality over the intimacy we expect from fellow-ship with our fellow believers, when Jesus speaks of loving one another he does not speak of it in warm, volitional terms. He speaks of the love that is to characterize his followers as a command to be followed. To be in true fellowship with one another is nothing less than *a nonnegotiable obligation*.

What is it Jesus says of love? In response to the prodding of the Pharisees concerning the greatest commandments, Jesus declares:

> "'Love the Lord your God with all your heart and with all your soul and with all your mind.' This is the first and greatest commandment. And the second is like it: 'Love your neighbor as yourself.' All the Law and the Prophets hang on these two commandments." (Matt. 22:37–40)

Love is a commandment. In Jesus' response to the Pharisees, he is clearly speaking of a new demand placed upon us. Standing squarely in the ethical tradition of Hillel, the command to love trumps all others, Jesus says. All other commandments fall in line behind the obligation to love.[12]

Therefore, to love God is to love him as a slave (Luke 17:7ff.), by faithfully obeying his orders and submitting to his lordship over all of life (Matt. 6:33). If love is a choice for Jesus, then it is a dramatic one: "No one can serve two masters. Either you will hate the one and love the other, or you will be devoted to the one and despise the other" (Matt. 6:24). For Jesus, love is a matter of the will and of doing, not feeling or choosing.

Further, obedience to Jesus' nonnegotiable command is the only visible hallmark by which the outside world knows that we are one of his. He explains:

> "A new command I give you: Love one another. As I have loved you, so you must love one another. By this everyone will know that you are my disciples, if you love one another." (John 13:34–35)

These words of Jesus seemingly defy all reason. Contrary to what we would expect, disciples of Jesus will not be known by those on the outside by their freedom to choose to love their fellow disciples. One would think that the quality of love for one another should best be measured by our open willingness to express love for one another.

Not so. Jesus says we will be known by our willingness to obey the command to love others, just as we receive his love in us. Therefore, loving others is not ultimately about us and our ability to choose love at all; it is about Jesus' love for his disciples and their willingness, in turn, to mimic his love to others.

The apostle Paul picks up this language of love as a command in Galatians 5 when he speaks of the freedom we share as fellow believers:

> You, my brothers and sisters, were called to be free. But do not use your freedom to indulge the flesh; rather, serve one another humbly in love. For the entire law is fulfilled in keeping this one command: "Love your neighbor as

yourself." If you bite and devour each other, watch out or you will be destroyed by each other. (Gal. 5:13–15)

Certainly Christ makes us free, says Paul, but this freedom does not come unfettered in the context of Christian community. The choices we make in Christ are bound by obligations we have to the perfect law in Christ.

It is for this reason that Paul could choose so freely to bind himself to others for the sake of the gospel in his first letter to the Corinthians: "Though I am free and belong to no one, I have made myself a slave to everyone, to win as many as possible. . . . I have become all things to all people so that by all possible means I might save some" (1 Cor. 9:19–22). To the Jew he becomes a Jew, to those under the law he comes under the law, and to the weak he becomes weak.

The ofttimes freely swinging barn door of relationships we find in our churches today suggests that we might not fully take seriously the implications of the fact that Jesus' call to love one another is, first and foremost, *a divine command*. In a society consumed by choices of every kind—just walk down the cereal aisle of your local grocery store—it is not difficult to identify the source of our addiction to choice as it plays itself out in every aspect of our lives. I daresay that the predilection toward greater choice has buried itself so deep in our Western culture, we have lost our ability to consciously realize its impact on us. Choice is now a state of mind, a basic assumption of life, an inalienable human right.

So, how has this assumption of choice impacted our lives together as brothers and sisters in Christ? It has impacted it in every way and at all levels. Once again, observe the vast migration of transient churchgoers, for example, as they follow their consumerist instincts to cash in their coupons for the next great deal in the next great church in the area. How many individuals in the United States leave their current church only to transfer to yet another in any given year?

Of course, there are good reasons for some of us to switch churches at times; but regardless of motive, what are we leaving as we move to our next church home? If we are to take seriously the biblical view of Christian fellowship, then we are leaving relationships of serious obligation. We are leaving individuals God has commanded us to love, and we need to be careful how we leave these obligations. In this highly mobile age, perhaps we cheapen Jesus' command on our lives if we act as if these relationships are easily expendable as we move on to our next set of relationships.

On a more local level, this idea of fellowship as something we choose freely rather than out of divine obligation is reflected in the way we have fellowship within individual congregations. Our tendency is to enter into fellowship with our brothers and sisters freely at will based on such criteria as personality, socioeconomic status, and sociability. As a result, our fellowship together is parsed out in pockets throughout our congregations. Just observe who is sitting next to whom in your fellowship hall. Why is it we feel such liberty to move from one of these pockets of sociability to the next based upon the social criteria we use?

Setting aside the formal institutional structures of the church—where the pastors and leaders are at the epicenter and everyone else in the church is layered institutionally, spiraling to the outermost frontiers of the church based on their responsibilities—every congregation also has an informal relational structure. This structure is oftentimes less obvious; but if we look closely, every congregation has its own relational typography, with a small minority at the center who represent the relational epicenter of the church. They are the 20 percent or so who make church life an important part of their social life. You can recognize them by the fact that they tend to linger after every service and often have a coffee cup in hand. But radiating out from this soft intimate center are layers of less relationally invested souls from regular participants, to partially interested attendees who show up periodically, to fringe spectators who may identify themselves as card-carrying members of the church but almost never participate in the informal life of the church.

Of course, there are many reasons why individuals choose not to enter into the relational life of the church—some good and some bad—but look again, and you will invariably find at the very outposts of every congregation an additional few who continuously circle around the outer rim of the life of the church, wanting to join the warmth of the community at the center but never quite able to fit in. Perhaps they are socially ill equipped to navigate in a complicated social situation. Maybe they have lived morally compromised lives. In some settings, racism may raise its ugly head. Maybe they are just broken people. Whatever it is, they are not drawn into the center.

Who are these individuals in your church? Upon what basis do they have any hope of entering into the life-giving fellowship of the church? How do they have any possibility of participating in our fellowship with one another, other than being viewed as an object of someone's ministry? If choice were the criterion upon which they were included, then there would be no chance for these individuals. We know this because, left to our own inclinations, we would never find them sitting around our tables in our homes or in our small groups.

It is for these individuals, if no others, that Jesus' call to fellowship is one of command and not of free-flowing inclinations. It is interesting that time and again in the Gospels we find it is these kinds of people with whom Jesus chooses to surround himself—the Samaritan woman, the little man Zacchaeus, the unclean woman who touched his robe in a crowd, the drunkards and prostitutes—people we would not include in our circle of friends if it were not for the fact that Jesus commands us to love these as we would love our dearest friends.

We are a people bound by divine obligation to love whomever claims the name of Christ. The same criteria we might use to enter into relationships outside of the gathered community cannot be used by us within the church. They cannot. We are commanded—*commanded*—to love. Thanks be to God for our own sakes, for the sake of the least of these, and for the sake of his church.

7 Fellowship Is Eternal

There before me was a great multitude that no one could count, from every nation, tribe, people and language, standing before the throne and before the Lamb.—John (Rev. 7:9)

We can only assume that three years of sharing a common experience with Jesus had established the disciples into a close-knit group. We can even assume that many of their relationships evolved into close friendships, perhaps not fully as a group, but in twos and threes or more. We can well imagine that through the years two one-time strangers such as Philip and Bartholomew, for example, began to share more of themselves with one another than just their common tasks and commission as fellow apostles. We can see these two drawn together through common interest or similarity of personality, sitting next to each other at almost every meal. Or maybe if we lingered behind the group on their journeys through the Galilean countryside, we would catch them predictably off to one side exchanging a laugh or two. Maybe they sometimes included Thaddeus in their friendly escapades—the "three musketeers," the others would have called them. Perhaps.

Through their special times together with Jesus, maybe Peter and Andrew gradually began to see in each other more than what they shared in a common father and mother, or as common business partners, for that matter. Possibly, for the first time in the presence of Jesus, they were able to put aside their sibling rivalries—"who's the better fisherman?"—and they became truly good friends.

But one wonders what would have happened to these disciples as a group if the events of the last week had ended differently. From a relational perspective, what if they had not experienced together the events of the cross, resurrection, ascension, or the forty days with Jesus afterward? So much of eternal consequence depended upon the events of Holy Week.

But what of their relationships one with the other? Would they have found themselves together again, waiting in that upper room prior to Pentecost?

Maybe Philip and Bartholomew would have met periodically; Thaddeus joining them every other year. Certainly, we could see enough points of connection for Peter and John to remain together. Indeed, we find them back together fishing again in the Sea of Tiberius soon after the resurrection in John 21. Perhaps the others would have found themselves together less often, meeting sporadically to share increasingly distant memories of days gone by when Jesus was alive and in their midst.

But the glorious truth is that the events of the close of the gospel story did not end at the cross. The claims of Jesus could not be relegated to the rearview mirrors of their memories. It was this sense of the living reality of Jesus—that he died, rose again, and ascended miraculously to the heavens—that brought these disciples together again in the upper room that day where they waited for the next thing to happen. It was this reality in their lives and not any personal relational inclinations they might have had toward one another—their friendships—that brought them together again to form a new fellowship of believers that reverberates to today as the church.

The eternal nature of the cross under which we stand as Christians raises the question of the temporal nature of the relationship that binds us together as a church. Perhaps above all other characteristics we have discussed thus far, the one thing that most sets Christian fellowship apart from any other forms of human interaction is that *it is an eternal relationship.* All other human relationships will die, but not this one.

The implications of this are significant and should shape the way we relate to those who sit next to us in our pews every Sunday. We better get used to our brothers and sisters sitting across the aisle from us in our churches—those who are true believers in the resurrected Christ—because these relationships will characterize our relationships in eternity. The fellowship we share today in the old kingdom will continue into its perfected state in the new. Apparently not even marriage survives this transition.[13]

The apostle Paul captures the eternal scope of this unique relationship we share in Christ best in his wonderful Epistle to the Ephesians. In this, his Epistle of the church, he sets our new relationship with one another against the larger backdrop of eternity. For Paul, the church is not to be viewed merely in terms of its present physicality. Rather, he casts our understanding of it against the larger backdrop of eternity and allows us to see ourselves now in light of who we are becoming.

The blessing at the very beginning of his letter gives evidence of this larger backdrop. God, the Father of our Lord Jesus Christ, blesses us "in the heavenly realms" (Eph. 1:3). Nowhere else in his Epistles does Paul use this phrase, but he uses it here and four more times throughout Ephesians. In doing so, he reminds us of the eternal landscape upon which the church is built. This landscape certainly looks off into a future horizon, but it also describes the church in its present state. He describes the "heavenly realms" as where Christ is seated after being raised up to rule with power and authority, "not only in the present age but also the one to come" (Eph. 1:21). In 2:7, it is the seat upon which we are raised by God with Christ in order that "in the coming ages he might show the incomparable riches of his grace, expressed in his kindness to us in Christ Jesus." And it is that sphere upon which "rulers and authorities" continue to operate even now in the church (Eph. 3:10; 6:12).[14]

As if to mark the temporal parameters of these spiritual blessings in the "heavenly realms," he immediately carries us back to the very beginning of creation, before creation in fact. When did our adopted sonship begin? Paul says,

> For he chose us in him before the creation of the world to be holy and blameless in his sight. In love he predestined us for adoption to sonship through Jesus Christ, in accordance with his pleasure and will—to the praise of his glorious grace. (Eph. 1:4–6)

He predestined us to be his sons and daughters—to be in communion with him—well before we were even created.

And when do the blessings we share in Christ end in the "heavenly realms"? If our adoption as sons and daughters of God began before the very creation of the moon and stars, then it reaches its fulfillment in Christ when time meets eternity. Paul declares of God,

> He made known to us the mystery of his will according to his good pleasure, which he purposed in Christ, to be put into effect when the times reach their fulfillment—to bring unity to all things in heaven and on earth under Christ. (Eph. 1:9–10)

In Christ all things will be united in eternity. The verb here, *anakephalaioo* ("to unite" or "to sum up"), has the sense of bringing all things together. In Christ, time will be united with eternity; Christ's headship over his people will finally be fully expressed; those who are living and those who are dead—the church on earth and the church in heaven—will finally express themselves as one church, and the creation that we currently hear groaning (Rom. 8:18ff.) will sing a whole new tune with the heavenly chorus (see the book of Revelation).[15]

In between these expanses in time and eternity, Paul describes in detail the new society we are to share as adopted sons and daughters of the "heavenly realms." We have already spoken previously of the "mystery" (Eph. 3:2–6) surrounding the reality that Greeks and Jews are no longer to be divided as "foreigners and strangers," but are to be "fellow citizens with God's people and also members of his household" (2:19). He continues to describe this new united people in summary fashion throughout Ephesians as those who are to exercise gifts freely given to them by the Spirit (4:11–13); as ones who are to be imitators of God (5:1); as those who are to live as children of light (5:8); and as those who are to put on the full armor of God (6:10–18), because the world is not what it seems: "For our struggle is not against flesh and blood, but against the rulers, against the authorities, against the powers of this dark world and against the spiritual forces of evil in the heavenly realms" (6:12).

If this is who we are to be as adopted sons of light, then all of our relationships must bear perspective on the sonship we have in Christ. Paul goes on to speak specifically of the relationship of wives and husbands, who are called to love and serve each other with love and servanthood (Eph. 5:22–27). He reminds children and parents that they must maintain relationships laced with obedience and respect for one another (6:1–4). And he insists that even the relationship between slaves and masters must reflect the kind of respect and obedience that can make sense only in light of their mutual relationship with Christ (6:5–9).

It is the marriage relationship, in particular, that Paul points to as the model upon which the church is built. Or is it the other way around? Paul says in 5:25–27,

> Husbands, love your wives, just as Christ loved the church and gave himself up for her to make her holy, cleansing her by the washing with water through the word, and to present her to himself as a radiant church, without stain or wrinkle or any other blemish, but holy and blameless.

The template upon which marriage is to be built is Christ's church. Marriage should bear the traits of holiness, selflessness, and purity because these are the traits the church should reflect.

If then we are present and future bearers of the "heavenly realm," if we are adopted sons and daughters of Christ from creation all the way to our fulfillment in the future, if we are truly the bride of Christ, then how might this perspective shape the way fellowship is displayed in our churches on any given Sunday?

It will shape us in three ways. First, it will shape us in the way we behave toward one another. C. S. Lewis observes in *The Weight of Glory*:

> It is a serious thing to live in a society of possible gods and goddesses, to remember that the dullest and most uninteresting person you talk to may one

day be a creature which, if you saw it now, you would be strongly tempted to worship, or else a horror and a corruption such as you now meet, if at all, only in a nightmare. All day long we are, in some degree, helping each other to one or other of these destinations. . . . There are no ordinary people. You have never talked to a mere mortal.[16]

In seeing our own lives in light of eternity, we need to see one another in the same light. There truly are no *ordinary* people in our midst as followers of Christ.

Our fellowship with one another should reflect this reality in the way in which we love and serve one another. Lewis goes on to further describe what is to be our attitude and behavior toward our brothers and sisters:

> Our charity must be a real and costly love, with deep feelings for the sins in spite of which we love the sinner—no mere tolerance or indulgence which parodies love as flippancy parodies merriment. Next to the Blessed Sacrament itself, your neighbour is the holiest object presented to your senses. If he is your Christian neighbour he is holy in almost the same way, for in him also Christ *vere latitat*—the glorifier and the glorified, Glory Himself, is truly hidden.[17]

Our behavior toward one another should reflect the seriousness to which we approach our brothers and sisters. If we are important to God, then this should say something about how serious it is that we value one another.

Second, having an eternal perspective might well expand our understanding of those with whom we are in fellowship. The writer of Hebrews 11 does us a wonderful service on this account when he describes our fellow sojourners in the faith. Imagine this parade marching through the pages of Scripture in front of us. There is ancient Enoch the God pleaser, and Noah who built an ark out of "holy fear." There is Father Abraham, who was given an inheritance only to have it tested in the severest manner, and Sarah his barren wife. There is the scoundrel Jacob who worshipped God while leaning on his staff as an old man blessing his sons, and there is Moses who led God's often-disobedient people rather than enjoy the pleasures of Pharaoh's palace. There is Rahab the prostitute who welcomed the spies, and Gideon, and David, and Jephthah, and so many more. The writer finishes by reminding us that many of these fellow believers lived destitute lives, some were mistreated, and, some were even persecuted, but all were "commended for their faith," even though they were not privileged to receive what had been promised (Heb. 11:39–40).

We can go on and speak of those who run off the edge of the biblical account and onto the pages of church history. There is Augustine the Confessor and Tertullian the Apologist. There is Luther standing in front of the door at Wittenberg, and Tyndale in front of the printing press. There is Wesley and his coworker Whitefield. There is the good parson Baxter and the great preacher Spurgeon. And there are individuals we might not recognize without the lens of eternity. There is the small band of friends who huddled under that haystack in 1806 and changed the course of modern missions, and there are generations of simple immigrant churchgoers who have faithfully put away their tools of the trade on Sunday to worship together. All of these, great and small, stand before us every Sunday—only we don't see them.[18]

Perhaps we need not be from a high church tradition to reclaim the expansiveness of our fellowship at this point. Caught oftentimes in the smallness of our own local congregations, could not our worship be made all the richer if we were to open wide our eyes for a moment and see these multitudes that look over our shoulders each Sunday, the multitudes not only measured vertically—of our fellow Christians sitting in places remote to us, such as South Africa, Peru, or Fargo, North Dakota—but also the multitudes measured horizontally in time leading to eternity?

All of these vertically and horizontally placed individuals are our brothers and sisters in Christ. They are individuals with whom we will spend eternity, and whether physically alive or dead, they are part of the living community of the faith that is now and will be ours forever more. Imagine if our worship services were conducted in such a way that reminded us that we are not the sole objects of God's delight but also part of a larger community that extends beyond the thin walls of our own sanctuary. Imagine.

Third, the implication of the eternal nature of our fellowship confronts us with an anomaly. Christian fellowship is, at its core, *a static relationship*. As counterintuitive as it may seem, the fellowship we share with one another within the gathered community does not grow, in the same sense that it does not die. It is not fundamentally a dynamic relationship in one sense.

But this reality seems to contradict everything we know about vital relationships. Do we not want to see ourselves and our fellow believers grow in understanding and appreciation of each other, and should not our fellowship be measured by the extent to which this kind of growth occurs, not only in terms of the mundane facts of our lives but also emotionally and spiritually? Is this not the great delight that comes with entering into relationships with another; to relate more and more meaningfully together as time goes by?

Certainly all this is true at one level, but at a more fundamental level our fellowship with one another remains rigidly unchanging in its character. Perhaps a small illustration will help clarify this important and necessary truth. I take you back many years to when my daughter turned seven. For a Christian parent, can there be a moment more meaningful than when a child enters into the kingdom of God? This is when my daughter became a fellow believer in Christ with me. Both of us stood there that day—a seven-year-old little girl just beginning life, and a grown man well into his career and established in his education—now equally brother and sister in Christ. Flash forward to the present. I am heading toward my dotage; Molly is now well into her career and anticipating (gasp) marriage. Are this father and this daughter any more or less brother and sister in Christ now than they were eighteen years ago? No. In this sense, our fellowship with one another—although possibly more mature now in terms of how we relate together—is precisely the same.

This is the nature of the communion we share with one another. It certainly changes and matures in one sense, as all relationships do. But hidden beneath the relationships we share in Christ is the even more profound bedrock confidence that the grace bestowed on us as brothers and sisters at any given moment is no more and no less than what it will ever be. It will never die because it cannot die. It is eternal and unchanging in every way.

8. Fellowship Is a Mediated and Thus an Exclusive Relationship

There is one God and one mediator between God and mankind.—Paul (1 Tim. 2:5)

Certainly it was not by force of citizenship that they were there together that day. The supernatural invitation to the Pentecost moment was to people "from every nation under heaven" (Acts 2:5). Neither was it by force of family sentiments. Only in the broadest sense as Jews could they trace their common bloodline. Nor was it as a result of a political or commercial contract. They couldn't even speak to one another with the same language. And it was not out of friendship and affection.

Acts 2 indicates that these three thousand were part of a multitude who came together for the same reason that they had been coming together for centuries at this time of the year. Scattered far and wide across many nations, they were drawn to Jerusalem once again to celebrate *Shavu'ot*, the Day of Pentecost. But in the midst of the hustle and bustle of a city bursting at the seams with festival-goers, how was it that these three thousand found themselves in the same room?

We can only conjecture how they broke away from the others that fateful day. There is no evidence that they came as a result of an organized campaign. We cannot imagine a couple of disciples out there, breaking away from the other 120 waiting in the upper room, putting up posters in the city inviting people from around Jerusalem to a Pentecost event. Even if they could have planned it, who was it who would have had the forethought and the right database to bring together this precise ragtag group of God-fearing Jews from every nation? The text doesn't tell us, but the implications are that the Spirit nudged those in attendance in ones and twos and threes and more toward the same room at that same precise time in order that the Spirit would descend upon them.

Of course, once the Spirit gave evidence of his presence with the sound of the mighty wind and the amazing display of fire and the hearing and understanding of many languages, and once Peter started preaching, there surely was plenty reason to be together, if for no other reason than that they would have shared a common experience. But before the wind and the fire and the voices and the preaching, what was it? Can we imagine any scenario that would have motivated these particular men and women to come together and enter into the relationships that we find displayed at Pentecost? The Spirit in their midst was the only reason why these men and women came together. Take away the Spirit in their midst, and any thought that this new society would have been formed is gone.

Perhaps this seems too self-evident but it points to the next characteristic of the relationship of the fellowship shared by brothers and sisters that is unique above any other type of relationship. Christian fellowship is a *mediated relationship*. That is, the relationship that binds the gathered community together is not direct. As Dietrich Bonhoeffer puts it in his *Life Together*,

> Christianity means community through Jesus Christ and in Jesus Christ. No Christian community is more or less than this. Whether it be a brief, single encounter or the daily fellowship of years, Christian community is only this. We belong to one another only through and in Jesus Christ.[19]

It is only through an intermediary that true fellowship can exist, that we can relate to one another face-to-face as brothers and sisters in Christ. Take away Christ in the center and the relationship crumbles before our very eyes.

Paul explicitly identifies this intermediary in 1 Timothy 2 in the midst of his instructions to his young charge, Timothy:

> For there is one God and one mediator between God and mankind, the man Jesus Christ, who gave himself as a ransom for all people. This has now been witnessed to at the proper time. (1 Tim. 2:5–6)

The background for this word *intermediary* involves the idea of "negotiator" and has the sense of one who establishes a relationship that would not otherwise exist. Further, in the above passage the word *antilytron*, which means "to redeem," has the sense of payment. Paul is saying here that humans are desperately in need of mediation and that God provided Jesus as a go-between in order to reconcile fallen humanity to himself.[20]

It is this Jesus, our Mediator-Redeemer, whom the Holy Spirit came to bear witness to in our lives and in the life of the church. The Spirit is forever before his people within the church, reminding them who this Jesus is. So Paul boldly says, "Therefore I want you to know that no one who is speaking by the Spirit of God says, 'Jesus be cursed,' and no one can say, 'Jesus is Lord,' except by the Holy Spirit" (1 Cor. 12:3).

In revealing Jesus to us, the Holy Spirit performs many functions. He is our teacher (2 Pet. 1:21) and our great counselor in need (John 14:16–17). He prays for us (Rom. 8:26) and is our guide in the midst of life's perplexities (Rom. 8:14). He warns us (1 Tim. 4:1) and sometimes rebukes us (Gal. 3:2). He is a guide for our conscience (Rom. 9:1). He is the source of our joy and peace (1 Thess. 1:6), he equips us for the tasks before us (Heb. 13:21), and he loves for us (Rom. 5:5). Finally, and most importantly, he is the deposit that guarantees our inheritance moving into the future (Eph.1:13–14). Of our sonship through the work of Jesus, he is forever reminding us that "the Spirit himself testifies with our spirit that we are God's children" (Rom. 8:16). In all these things, it is the Spirit of God who is in the midst of his people acting in all of these ways for our own edification. We are the people of the Spirit, and as such it is the Spirit that defines our relationships with one another.

This reality, however, is often overlooked in the midst of our relating to one another as brothers and sisters in Christ. Left to ourselves, our default mode is to act as if we relate through force of our own personal and inter-personal capacities. But contrary to our own instincts, it is not the powers of personal attraction that are to draw us toward one person or away from another. Nor are we to be fueled by the level of psychological strength or weakness we might have in a given social situation. We are not to fall back upon our natural abilities to create constructive feelings or to avoid conflict. Our personalities are not to be the public face upon which our relationships are built. And it is not the natural powers of our charisma and authority that are to determine the direction that our relationships with one another should go.

Rather, the fellowship we share is to be identified as the Spirit of God acting in our midst for our edification and the edification of our fellow believers. Is there joy in our midst? The source of this joy is the result of our identifying and sharing in the providential work that God has done in our lives. It should be recognized as such by the interpretive powers of the Spirit. Is there conflict in our midst, as there will naturally be? It is through the wise movement of the Spirit in our midst that it is to be resolved. Is there discouragement? The Holy Spirit is there for our comfort rather than any psychological home remedies we might try to use.

Further, the authority needed for our orderly life should not come from the functional sources of power and authority around us. Its source should be the charismatic authority of spiritually wise women and men who are led by the Spirit in their deliberations through the gifts they possess. This kind of authority rests on prayer, even as the Spirit guides us into all truth.

The Spirit should be the shaping force at every level of our relationships with one another. Let me give you a simple illustration of what I mean by this from my own life. About thirty-five years ago Cec and I entered into a uniquely Western-shaped relationship: we began dating. My parents and grandparents from a different age called it courtship. I am not sure what they call it now.

This is how dating works in the West: The first stage requires getting to "know" another person. Cec and I began to observe each other's personalities as we expressed them in the various circumstances we shared. We asked other people about each other. Eventually we began to get to "know" each other better and better and better. Today, they have this stage down to a science, literally. If it isn't the precision of speed dating, then it is the standardized tests behind computer dating.

This getting to "know" each other was hard but fun work. Eventually we got to "know" each other as persons well enough to the point where we were ready to move to stage two and make a choice. In actuality, Cec and I had "known" other people for many years as we dated. But this time was different. Somehow our knowing each other—measuring our mutual attraction to each other, observing our personalities, exploring shared values—finally brought us to a point of prioritizing. She chose me over all those other gorillas she had previously dated. I chose her over the lovely ladies I had been dating.

We were ready for stage three: we were ready to make a commitment to each other. This commitment, based upon selective knowing, followed by choosing, finally led to marriage. We decided to commit ourselves permanently to each other: "For better, for worse . . . for richer, for poorer . . . in sickness and in health . . . to love and to cherish . . . until death do us part."

A good case can be made that most other kinds of relationships follow exactly this same pathway—from knowing to choosing to committing. Identifying and selecting friends certainly follows along this track. And is not this what we find ourselves doing in our polling booths? Is it not all about knowing, choosing, and committing as we elect our officials? What about commercial relationships? This was the process I took the last time I bought a car, when I entered into a relationship with my car salesman. I researched my options, and I choose my gray Honda over all the other options, which finally led me to the beautiful commitment I now have with my car dealer, or should I say banker?

What sets the body of Christ apart is that it does not follow this same pathway in the same way. First, the "knowing" in our relationships with our brothers and sisters is not built upon criteria commonly used in these other forms of relationships: common attraction, measured attributes, and shared values. Putting aside all other personal characteristics our brothers and sisters might possess, we are to "know" them in light of the Spirit indwelling them. Our relationships with them should be measured by the degree to which they manifest characteristics of the fruits of the Spirit, as Paul defines them: "love, joy, peace, forbearance, kindness, goodness, faithfulness, gentleness and self-control" (Gal. 5:22–23). Further, we are to "know" them in light of the authority placed upon them by certain gifts given them by the Spirit (1 Cor. 12).

Because the object of our knowing is different, so too the nature of our choosing and commitment is different. As we discussed previously, our relationships with our brothers and sisters are really not about choice. We are obligated to them no matter what characteristics they possess. The light of the Spirit should blind us to all manner of personality traits, levels of status, or the degree to which we are benefited by them. Our choice is only to love our brothers and sisters in Christ in whatever state we find them. This, in fact, is to be our commitment to one another as a community bound by the Spirit. We are to love one another unconditionally and through the power of the Spirit.

On an institutional level, this kind of relationship of the Spirit seems distant from what we see in many of our churches, where relationships are too often expressed as one might find them in any other organization—such as the Lions or Elks Club or our place of employment. In these settings, relationships are defined by personality and common interests. They are organizations that are run formally and informally by those with the most power or at least the most persuasion. Further, these relationships tend to be ends in themselves; that is, the goals of most relationships outside of the church are for individuals to be happy or to make money.

Not so the church. Our churches should be fundamentally different kinds of institutions, because the relationships that shape these institutions are to be different. The way we wear authority over others should be different. The way we socialize should be different. The way we make decisions together should be different. All these things should be different within the church, because the church is to be where the Spirit of God completely controls all of our personal and social impulses.

This is an amazing reality with significant implications for us. Christ is to be at the center of our fellowship with one another. To want more than the Spirit as the basis for our communion together is to want less than Christian fellowship. Or, as Bonhoeffer says, "One who wants more than what Christ has established does not want Christian brotherhood. He is looking for some extraordinary social experience which he has not found elsewhere; he is bringing muddled and impure desires into Christian brotherhood."[21]

Because this relationship is defined uniquely by the work of the Spirit, we come finally to a hard truth of Christian fellowship: Christian fellowship is, by nature, *an exclusive relationship*. This seems to contradict what we discussed earlier in terms of fellowship being nonexclusive. However, our previous conversation centered on our community being nonexclusive in terms of the breadth of those within the body of Christ. Here, we must address its limitations in terms of those who do not share in the work of the Spirit in their lives. Christian fellowship is defined, in part, by who is not a member of the community.

Perhaps a simple analogy sets this distinction between Christian community being nonexclusive in terms of its *breadth* and, on the other hand, being exclusive in terms of its *reach*. Blink back the sunlight as you enter into the nave inside of St. Peter's Basilica in Rome. Adjust your eyes. What you will find in that grand expanse—which stretches for 730 feet north and south and 500 feet from east to west, with a dome stretching upward for 452 feet—is nothing short of spellbinding. There is nothing within its great walls that would prevent people from all parts of the world from entering and gazing at its great expanse. People coming from every nation and people group are free to enter. Big people, skinny people, white people, black people, wealthy people, impoverished people, smart people, not-so-smart people, people with annoying personalities, gregarious people—all types are welcome.

But to speak of the breadth of the types of people who can freely enter into its four walls does not contradict the fact that St. Peter's is, in the end, a building with certain limitations. At some point the press of the marble walls on the shoulders of the crowd will say something about what it is not. The building is not the outside. It is defined by its nature as a building, and in this it resembles the church as a community of Jesus Christ. In the case of the latter, as nonexclusive as it is in allowing all manner of people in, it is by nature limited to those who have the Spirit within them.

From beginning to end, the Scriptures describe God's people as set apart as a "faithful remnant" from those on the outside (Ezra 9–10). Early on, we see God calling a pagan moon worshipper from Ur to separate himself from that world: "Go from your country, your people and your father's household to the land I will show you" (Gen. 12:1). It was with Abraham that God covenanted to make a great nation that was to be set apart in order to be a blessing to all other people (12:2–3). And it is this original covenant that God made with this, his chosen people, which continued to set them apart from their neighbors throughout the rest of the Old Testament. Faithful judges, committed priests, righteous kings, and the cries of the prophets all were used as the means by which God separated his people from their unfaithful neighbors.

Perhaps surprising for some, this message of exclusivity is especially evident in the Gospels. Over and over again in his teachings and through his example, Jesus drew lines in the sand between those who were in the kingdom of heaven and those who were not. He spoke often of wheat and weeds (Matt. 13:24–30), sheep and goats (Matt. 25:31–46), and the narrow gate of life versus the broad road that leads to destruction (Matt. 7:13–14). Most dramatically, for example, there was for Jesus to be little hospitality offered for those who chose not to celebrate with him in his kingdom, as in the parable of the wedding banquet in Matthew 22, where the king gives instructions concerning the uninvited guest to "tie him hand and foot, and throw him outside into the darkness, where there will be weeping and gnashing of teeth. For many are invited, but few are chosen" (Matt. 22:13–14).

The apostle Paul continues to draw an equally sharp line in the sand between the people of God and those in the world. In Ephesians, he calls those in the church "saints," as those who are "holy" and set apart (Eph. 1:1). They are, he says, being raised up to be a "holy temple," built up as a dwelling for God by his Spirit. He states, "Don't you know that you yourselves are God's temple and that God's Spirit dwells in your midst? If anyone destroys God's temple, God will destroy that person; for God's temple is sacred, and you together are that temple" (1 Cor. 3:16–17).

As saints, Paul admonishes believers to act like the holy people they are. To walk in holiness is to walk by means of the Holy Spirit in two ways. First, they are to abstain from sin, which characterizes their former lives and those from the outside. He admonishes them "to put off your old self, which is being corrupted by its deceitful desires; to be made new in the attitude of your minds; and to put on the new self, created to be like God in true righteousness and holiness" (Eph. 4:22–24). Second, the holiness that is to set believers apart is to be marked by the life of Christ being reproduced in them through the power of the Holy Spirit. Paul says, "Follow God's example, therefore, as dearly loved children and walk in the way of love, just as Christ loved us and gave himself up for us as a fragrant offering and sacrifice to God. . . . For you were once darkness, but now you are light in the Lord. Live as children of light" (Eph. 5:1–2, 8).

The danger in seeing ourselves as set apart, of course, is that it might tempt us to think that this somehow makes us special. But Paul is quick to remind us that our status as an exclusive community is no basis for thinking ourselves as better than others. On the contrary, he asks the church at Corinth to look at their own position in society as a basis for understanding their status: "God chose the lowly things of this world and the despised things—and the things that are not—to nullify the things that are, so that no one may boast before him" (1 Cor. 1:28–29). The very reason why God chose the foolish and weak in this world for his own is precisely because it is this realization that keeps us from boasting.

Rather than the source for our boasting, the exclusive nature of our community is really to be the basis for our mission. John Stott beautifully describes this thought when he says of the church, "Our calling is to be 'holy' and 'worldly' at the same time." On the one hand, he says,

> If we are not "the church," the holy and distinct people of God, we have nothing to say because we are compromised. If, on the other hand, we are not "in the world," deeply involved in its life and suffering, we have no one to serve because we are insulated.[22]

Our mission as the church rests on our "double identity" as a church, both as ones set apart as holy and as those who are intricately involved in the world. We can serve the world only if we haven't assimilated its standards and values.

9 ⸱ Fellowship Is for Strangers

Do not forget to show hospitality to strangers.—(Heb. 13:2)

Most of them were probably strangers. Although the text indicates that all of them were God-fearing Jews, their religious orientation tells only part of the story. The three thousand who were visited by the Spirit that day of Pentecost were themselves visitors to Jerusalem. Coming from all parts of the known world to celebrate the fifty days from Passover to Pentecost, they probably had more to do culturally and relationally with their pagan next-door neighbors from their own countries than they had to do with one another in the temple courts that day. At the very least, their assumed languages set them apart by place of origin—that is, until they began speaking to one another in various tongues as the Spirit enabled them.

The reality that the Spirit brought strangers from all the nations together at Pentecost and that they could be heard and understood is amazing. But the reality that many of these strangers displayed the kind of community described at the end of Acts 2 is all the more amazing. It is one thing for individuals who have honed their relationships with one another through long years of mutual experience and trust to express the kind of fellowship we find displayed here; it is quite another thing to observe newly minted acquaintances, now fellow converts, giving so freely of themselves and their possessions to one another. Imagine, recent strangers daily breaking bread together, many of them selling their possessions and giving freely to those they hardly knew until recently by "having all things in common."

A further trait not to be overlooked in understanding the uniqueness of Christian community is that it is a *relationship dominated by strangers*. As counterintuitive as it may seem, brothers and sisters in Christ need not actually know one another to be in a relationship. That is, actually knowing another person is not a necessary criterion for entering into Christian fellowship. Come again? Put differently, Christians have the liberty of entering into fellowship with one another completely in the abstract.

Jesus certainly had a special relationship with strangers, and he makes it plain that we are to as well. Who does he say are to be blessed inheritors of the kingdom of God? He declares,

> "Come, you who are blessed by my Father; take your inheritance, the kingdom prepared for you since the creation of the world. For I was hungry and you gave me something to eat, I was thirsty and you gave me something to drink, *I was a stranger and you invited me in*, I needed clothes and you clothed me, I was sick and you looked after me, I was in prison and you came to visit me." (Matt. 25:34–36; italics added)

It is we who invite strangers into our midst who will inherit God's kingdom.

In parallel fashion, the writer of the book of Hebrews makes a similar invitation to us:

> Keep on loving one another as brothers and sisters. *Do not forget to show hospitality to strangers*, for by so doing some people have shown hospitality to angels without knowing it. Continue to remember those in prison as if you were together with them in prison, and those who are mistreated as if you yourselves were suffering. (Heb. 13:1–3; italics added)

There is something about entering into relationship with those we do not yet know that is especially built into the mandate of the gospel.

The implication of being free to relate to others in Christ without having a direct personal relationship with them is significant. The church and our culture, in fact, would be quite different today if this were not the case. Max Weber, in his second volume of *Economy and Society*, observes that one of the keys to the rise of urbanization and population flow in the West rests with the social barriers that were broken down by Christianity in the centuries of the Middle Ages.[23] Put simply, prior to the growing influence of Christianity, people lived geographically and culturally in proximity to their extended clan. Society was largely defined by blood relationships.

A new social order came about with the growth of the influence of the church. The early church described a whole new way of understanding what it means to be brothers and sisters, and this new definition extended beyond actual blood relationships. "Who are my mother and my brothers?" Jesus asked as his human family stood nearby. Looking at the crowd he said, "Here are my mother and my brothers! Whoever does God's will is my brother and sister and mother" (Mark 3:33–35). This new way of relating to one another, says Weber, eventually allowed individuals freedom to roam geographically and circumstantially far beyond the boundaries of traditional society, which had been pooled in clans and tribal settings.

Taking Weber's observation one step farther, the limits of Christian community in the early centuries not only extended beyond family, but they extended beyond friendship and acquaintanceship as well. The reason the early church community grew so dramatically is precisely because it was not predicated upon individuals having actual firsthand knowledge of others. Brothers and sisters in Christ could be complete strangers.

The apostle Paul's own missionary ministry is a testimony to this phenomenon. Where would the churches in Antioch and Corinth, Philippi, Asia Minor, and Rome be if it had not been for a stranger—let alone a Jewish stranger—introducing himself to complete Gentile and Jewish strangers? Every one of his letters bears the marks of Paul introducing himself and others to complete strangers.

Following Paul's example, buried deep in this understanding that we are a community of strangers is the very impulse central to the spreading of the gospel. The gathered community is always to be in service to the scattered community. Serving strangers rather than those we know offers us freedom to proclaim the good news. Toward that end, in all due respect for the best intentions behind our current nomenclature, perhaps the language that needs to be mastered in evangelistic settings should be less that of "friendship" and more of "stranger-hood." This is what we are called to do: Proclaim the good news to complete strangers, whoever and wherever they might be.

Finally, in terms of the quality of fellowship we share with one another, we would do well to refocus our eyes and look beyond those we know around us. The church—our church—extends well beyond our own oftentimes myopic understanding of the community of which we are a part. Of the over two billion Christians in the world today, 28.9 million live in Uganda alone; 4.4 million of our brothers and sisters live in Norway; 3 million live in New Zealand; between 70 and 80 million live in China, with on average nine thousand new Chinese brothers and sisters being baptized every day.[24] And 375,000 of them live in Peoria, Illinois. Although not all necessarily claim to be born again, many of these are our brothers and sisters in Christ. Although few of us will ever really know any of these people, we can be assured that every Sunday they stand before the same God and worship him, that they bear the same marks of God's grace in their lives, and that they seek to serve the same Savior. All these things should make a profound impression upon us. Just as we strive to gain a deeper and deeper knowledge of the greatness of God and his character, so we should grow in a greater and greater understanding of the enormity of his church.

10. Fellowship as Full Transparency and without Secrets

All the believers were together and had everything in common. —Luke (Acts 2:44)

What is it that so attracts us to the description of that first little church of Jerusalem recorded at the end of Acts 2? Have you ever found yourself caught up into something extraordinarily special, something larger than yourself, a situation that you could not altogether control but that actually controlled you? The sense from this passage is that these believers were swept up into just such an experience, and as a result they did not walk but ran to enter into the fellowship of their newfound brothers and sisters.

It says that they met, not periodically, not weekly, but daily in the temple courts as a large group and in twos and threes in their individual homes. They ate together, they broke bread together, they prayed together, and they worshipped together. They soaked in all of what the apostles had learned at the feet of Jesus, pre- and post-resurrection. At points, the passage says, they found themselves just sitting together wide-eyed in wonder as they experienced miracles performed by the apostles. Their fellowship was so sincere that they were willing to give freely to anyone who had need. They did this with open transparency with one another, enjoying the favor of everyone's company.

It is this transparency we find most inviting. Of course, the antithesis of this openness was soon to follow in the sad story of Ananias and Sapphira. Unlike others in the church, this couple withheld part of the proceeds from a piece of property they sold (Acts 5:1–11). But it wasn't greed that was their problem. The source of the judgment that was soon inflicted on them through the hand of the apostle Peter was their deceit. Because Ananias secretly held back some of the money, Peter said to them, "You have not lied just to human beings but to God" (v. 4). Later, after being asked by Peter whether the price given was the actual price, Sapphira lied and said it was. Into the garden of their hearts came the evil one. Like Adam and Eve, these two thought they could lie to God, and as a result they offered a partial truth. They were judged accordingly.

Ananias and Sapphira were not the only ones afflicted with self-deceit and the dishonesty that inevitably follows. To reconstitute the old maxim

"Beauty is in the eye of the beholder," "Deceit is in the eye of the beholder" as well. Look back throughout the gospel story and gaze into the eyes of the scribes and Pharisees as they daily positioned themselves with Jesus in front of the crowds, and you will see deceit, maybe even self-deceit (Matt. 16:1–4). Or look into the eyes of Peter himself after Jesus was taken; three times his eyes must have lowered in shame as he denied knowing Jesus. Or what about Judas and his betrayal of the Savior? We know that the deception revealed in the garden of Gethsemane had been developing for some time.

It is the transparency of this first church of Jerusalem—and the lack of it by these other characters—that leads us to the final characteristic of fellowship we find displayed in the New Testament. The language of the gathered community must be one of *openness and transparency*. Brothers and sisters are to communicate with utter honesty.

There is no place for secrets in the church—no place for privatized language, for that matter. If there is power in secrets between friends, then the opposite is true of brothers and sisters in Christ. The sideways glance, the private smirk and nod between individuals, the inside story, the talking behind one's back, the caucusing in dark corners of the church—all these things work against Christian fellowship. Their effect is to segment brothers and sisters into small pockets in the church, rather than to bring brothers and sisters together into the light of God's Spirit in their midst.

Scripture is filled with passages that admonish us to protect ourselves from such behavior. In his letter to the Ephesians, Paul reminds us to avoid the kind of conversation that so often goes on behind closed doors: "Do not let any unwholesome talk come out of your mouths, but only what is helpful for building others up according to their needs, that it may benefit those who listen" (Eph. 4:29). And James declares,

> Brothers and sisters, do not slander one another. Anyone who speaks against a brother or sister or judges them speaks against the law and judges it. When you judge the law, you are not keeping it, but sitting in judgment on it. There is only one Lawgiver and Judge, the one who is able to save and destroy. But you—who are you to judge your neighbor? (James 4:11–12)

Further, there is no place for secrets even in our public life together. The Masonic Lodge may have secrets, and fraternities and sororities may have secrets, but there is no place for the church of Jesus Christ to ritualize such behavior. You want to become a member of the church? No secret handshake is required. There is no backroom ritual you must go through. There is no special key offered to open a mysterious door. Against every impulse toward esoteric specialized language, we should build into our liturgies the simple message of the gospel, clearly and openly proclaimed.

Bonhoeffer, in considering life together with his community of ordinands at Zingst, Germany, was particularly aware of the critical need for transparency between brothers and the parallel dangers of withholding something from the community at large. To protect himself and his brothers from such, he built daily into their lives a rule for living: Never was one brother to speak about another brother in his absence. He declared,

> But to speak about a brother covertly is forbidden, even under the cloak of help and good will; for it is precisely in this guise that the spirit of hatred among brothers always creeps in when it is seeking to create mischief.[25]

So concerned was he for living with transparency that he even went so far as to reinstitute the formal practice of confession for the entire community. Everyone, including himself, was assigned to a confessor.[26]

Churches that lack this kind of openness tend to be unhealthy communities. Conflict that begins quietly in the back recesses of the church often eventually explodes in public with open discontent! It doesn't take long to realize that the source of the conflict began well before the explosion, when members of an apparently aggrieved party had talked out their problems in private. And how many churches have been victimized by a pastor who lived a life of quiet desperation for months and even years while nurturing his or her own private indiscretions? Churches divide over such matters, or they begin to wither on the vine and die a thousand deaths.

Further, what of ruling boards that failed to be open and honest about important matters with their people? Many held secrets, and churches with something to hide ultimately do not thrive. This is not to say that there isn't a place for appropriate forms of confidentiality, particularly in the area of church discipline. There is a place for discretion in the life of the community, but this discretion of information should be rare and served with purpose. Churches should not bear secrets—period.

Healthy churches, on the other hand, are filled with openness and transparency. Brothers and sisters are free to be honest with one another, confident that what is said in private could equally be said in public. If there is conflict between members, then these disagreements should be dealt with systematically, and in good order according to the admonitions established by Jesus in Matthew 18: in person, with two or three, and, if necessary, with the church. The natural impulse of our communication together should be: "Everyone should be quick to listen, slow to speak and slow to become angry" (James 1:19).

FRIENDSHIP	FELLOWSHIP
1. Exclusive *Not everyone can be a friend*	1. Nonexclusive *Universal love*
2. Preferential *Hierarchy of relationships*	2. Nonpreferential *"Neither Greek nor Jew . . ."*
3. Reciprocal/mutual *Friendship requires being a friend in return*	3. Nonreciprocal *"A nonreturnable cloak . . ."*
4. Equal status *Mutuality, eye to eye*	4. Without concern for status *"Love thy neighbor as thyself . . ."*
5. Freely chosen *Without obligation, non-role relationship, without institutional constraints*	5. Divine obligation/calling *God's commandment, constraints, toward a higher end*
6. Self-benefiting *Demanding of a specific response*	6. Self-giving *Good Samaritan, love without return on investment*
7. Dynamic *Ever changing, open to termination*	7. Static *Unchanging, eternal*
8. Not necessarily spiritually based	8. Christ-based *Mediated relationship, exclusive*
9. Direct personal "knowing" required	9. Indirect knowing *Relationship of strangers*
10. Communication that is secretive, informal, privatized language	10. Communication of transparency, without secrets

CHAPTER SIX

GREAT EXPECTATIONS

W hat are we to make, then, of this new relationship that binds us all together as the community of Christ? Here is a relationship that is universal in its scope, nonpreferential in its choices, one-sided in its commitments, completely without concern for status, expressing itself in radical giving of the self without concern for anything in return, operating out of divine obligation rather than free inclination, unchanging in its eternal nature, indirect and mediated in its connectivity, not requiring direct knowing, and demanding complete transparency. Where else do we find such a relationship?

Further, what are we to make of the startling realization that the river flowing through this relationship runs in the exact opposite direction from the relationship the church often wrongly represents as Christian community? Completely different headwaters! Friendship and even being "friendly" does not a Christian community make.

But friendship has so many of the qualities we strive for in the church. It represents informality, intimacy, and a wonderful sense of commonality. It is wonderfully expressive and heartfelt. How can this be? To hum a few bars of an old country song, "How can something that feels so right be so wrong?"

Perhaps a look again into the five little windows we mentioned in chapter 1 will provide some clarity.

Five Windows into the Soul of Community Revisited

Window One: Thursday Night Live Revisited

Mary Beth left our Thursday Night Live Bible study without warning. She snuck out the backdoor, as it were, and never came back. None of us were sure what became of her. Maybe she found another Bible study where she felt more welcome. Maybe she moved and found another church. It is possible, however, that she just gave up on the church altogether. What if her short time with us was her last hope of feeling accepted, and when friendships in our group didn't materialize, she slid off into a place where many socially awkward, needy people go? Maybe she returned to a place of loneliness from which she will never escape.

What thoughts did she have as she left? How did she make sense of the Bible as it was genuinely and sincerely taught? How did she relate it to her own lonely life? Surely, having a vital, satisfying faith in Jesus Christ somehow meant something. But what did it mean from a relational perspective? Why was she still so isolated, and why were these otherwise sincere, well-meaning people not willing to accept her for who she was? Even if she didn't fully know herself that well, perhaps she sensed down deep her limitations to seek change in herself. Certainly, she could do a bit more to make herself more presentable, but in the end she was who she was. Shouldn't that be enough?

The Mary Beths of our world are not that uncommon. We see them on the street corners and bus stops of our big cities. We are perhaps more personally aware of them in our smaller cities, at least by reputation. We tend to know them by name in more rural areas. They circle around the outer edges of our "societies" at all levels, whether on a geographically national level, or in any number of social institutions—including, unfortunately, our churches. They live out there, many times not because they don't desire to be in the center of things, but because they do not have the capacity to move toward the center of activity.

There is a word used almost always as a derogatory term: *clique*. We use it most often to describe a group of which we are not members. Churches are filled with cliques. A pastor with any sense of social adeptness will see his or her church filled with roaming hoards of cliques. They begin early. We can see them in our youngest in our Sunday school classrooms: "Susan, Annie, and Ruth play together and refuse to include Mary." We see them in our youth programs, accentuated especially perhaps by a combination of adolescent angst and the reality that many groups include young people from multiple school settings. We see them in the fellowship halls between worship services as adults circulate among themselves. We see them in our sanctuaries. And we apparently see them in young adult Bible studies.

What are cliques? Read first what C. S. Lewis describes as friendship: "Friendship must exclude. From the innocent and necessary act of excluding to the spirit of exclusiveness is an easy step; and thence to the degrading pleasure of exclusiveness."[1] Cliques are another word for friendships, but friendships wrongly contextualized: exclusive, preferential, mutual, freely chosen, filled with secrets—you can recite the rest.[2]

Cliques, we say, are intentionally built on a sense of superiority. But is this not the point? Superiority is a matter of perception. How would someone from the outside view you and your friends as you sit around a table enjoying one another's latest inside joke or intimate conversation? Your time together seems harmless, so very healthy. Intentional or not, friendships tend to take on the sense of superiority by the mere nature of being exclusive and preferential. Isn't this the subtle tyranny of relationships?[3] Depending on where you stand, inside the group or outside, one person's band of brothers and sisters is another person's clique.

Returning to our Thursday Night Live Bible study, I don't want to be too hard on its members, perhaps partially because I was a member in good standing. This was a group with all the best intentions. What could be more inspiring than to see a group of twenty- and thirty-year-olds who could have been off doing other things but instead arrived weekly in my living room to study Scripture and pray together? And as they did so week after week and month after month, they found themselves committing to deep, growing relationships. Many of them became dear friends with relationships that are sustained to this day. Some even found their marriage partners as a result of the group.

But friendship, by itself, was not enough to include Mary Beth in the group. By nature, this type of relationship just does not have it in itself. The center collapses under the weight of its own natural predilections toward exclusiveness and preferentiality. Mary Beth could probably never have found friendship in this group in the way she longed, even if she had stayed.

But does this mean that she could never, then, partake in true Christian community? No. The relationship that could have bound Mary Beth to others on those Thursday nights, if rightly expressed, would have brought her weekly into meaningful relationships with her brothers and sisters in Christ. Christian community did not have to be limited to the narrow requirements of friendships in the group. We could have been more careful not to allow our friendships to get in the way of our relationship with her. We could have been more openly inclusive of her in our company as a true sister in Christ.

Genuine Christian community requires more of us than friendship can give. Extended to the church in general, this means that the demands on us must go deeper than any friendly inclinations or expressions we have toward others, as honorable as they might be. Being a part of the community of Christ requires that we live under an altogether different set of relational guidelines.

Window Two: One Happy Family Revisited

The service ended, I packed up my robe, one of the ladies kindly handed me an envelope containing my speaker honorarium, and I walked back to my car with a story to tell my future grandchildren: Seven people in attendance—amazing! The reality of the situation was hardly softened when one of the ladies self-consciously explained that perhaps thirty of the congregation were not in attendance that day. In the twenty-mile drive north to my home, I probably drove by thirty-five other small New England churches where the experience of their preacher was in varying degrees not too different from my own.

Certainly every tangible measurement would suggest that this church was not in a healthy state. Take its endowment away and this once-proud Presbyterian church would have collapsed under its own weight long ago. Their once-impressive building was crumbling under their very feet. The church had no real program to speak of, although it still maintained all the old vestiges of institutional structure and all that it required. The old committee framework remained "theoretically" in place. Further, the church was caught in that vicious cycle that afflicts so many churches: New people didn't come to the church, because there were no programs to attract them; yet there were no programs, because there were no people to run them. And a mission statement? You have got to be kidding!

Although I did not stick around that morning long enough to confirm this reality in any real depth, the example of other churches of this kind is striking in its irony. Far from lacking friendliness, they are accommodating places in so many ways. These small churches are filled with friendships. Described differently, the language of "one happy family" fills the air. Indeed, many of these churches are run out of the back pockets of one or two extended families or a small gaggle of friends. Although the foreheads of those who lead these faithful remnants are periodically creased with concern for their church's future, there is nothing like a good potluck supper or church fair to put things back into perspective (or out of perspective, as the case may be).

What do we make of these churches? Speaking broadly, they are churches that tend to be defined in terms of a concept of friendship rather than true Christian fellowship as we have defined it. Look closely and you will find these churches filled with exclusive, preferential, and mutual relationships. Many in the church are linked by deep, abiding friendships that go back years, sometimes all the way back to shared childhoods. The people in these churches tend to be self-selected; that is, they are chosen. As a result, most often people in these churches tend to all "look alike" in one way or another.

Further, their leadership comes from a small group of people who choose to maintain the privileges of long years of exercising authority based on an almost mythical standard characterized by "this is the way we have always done things." The language used in these churches tends to be highly secretive, based on accumulated inside stories from the past. Nevertheless, these churches are wonderfully intimate places. These people will do anything for one another.

There is a reason why small churches stay small despite their professed desire to grow. Trust me on this; every day I work with pastors who serve these kinds of churches in New England. The reason they stay small is because they live out of a concept of friendship rather than genuine Christian fellowship. Why don't new people tend to become a part of these congregations? It is because the cultures of these churches are highly selective. Of course, very little of this is translated intentionally, but it does not take long for new people to get the subtle impression that it will be difficult to be included in the inner circle of these communities, especially if they seek to become part of their leadership. Beneath the language of friendliness is the reality that friendliness has its limits.

To illustrate this, I know of a small church in the Midwest that struggled for many years to reclaim a lost vitality. A sanctuary that once held 150 now contained forty on any given Sunday. What the leadership of that church did is a story written many times over: Claiming a desire to grow, they hired an energetic young pastor willing to put in the time and effort to make this happen. In God's providence, this little church did, in fact, see significant growth in the next seven years. The sanctuary was filled to capacity.

But why then was the pastor asked to leave after his tenth year by these same core members of the congregation? Going out into the highways and byways of this little farming community, the pastor had invited all sorts of people into the life of the church. Some of these people were not "well-churched" families. Some didn't fit the profile of the core group. The kind of community being formed was not what the original members had hoped for. This church illustrates an important reality that small churches rarely comprehend: growth is a messy business. It cannot happen without expanding one's notion of community. What happened in this little church is a story that has been replicated a hundredfold in other places.

There is a bit of irony in the relationships found in larger growing churches as well. For all the talk about seeking to be friendly, the reason big churches are growing is, in fact, because they are not strangled by the limitations of exclusivity and preferentiality represented in friendship. The invitation extended in these churches tends to be far more inclusive of others, no matter the social or ethnic class. As proof of this, we even find whole programs designed to intentionally "assimilate" others as a central part of their strategy. Many of these churches actually hire pastors of assimilation.

Further, the language often used by these churches tends to be nonselective and purposefully designed to communicate effectively to a wide variety of individuals. This is especially true for new church plants. For lack of warm bodies, they tend to "let anyone in the door." A culture of inclusivity arises in these new communities out of necessity. For these churches, the "community from within" is forever linked to the "community from without." These congregations are always welcoming new people in; they are porous.

So what does it mean to be "friendly" in both of these kinds of churches? For the people in the small church, it is an expression of who they really are rather than what they want to become. Small churches unconsciously tend to reach the limits of friendship and therefore stop thriving. Large, growing churches tend to live out of a different relational perspective, in part because they may not be old enough to have established a deep culture of friendship, or perhaps because they make their growth and vitality such a high priority that they intentionally or unintentionally seek not to be governed by limitations that exist in friendship. They may speak a great deal about being friendly and seek to institutionalize it programmatically, but (ironically) they do not live under its strictures.

Finally, it takes great intentionality to remain fellowship-driven as opposed to friendship-driven. Once a church begins to grow, it's easier to stop by the side of the road and have a picnic with friends rather than to continue offering the more meager meal to total strangers. Just as small churches can become big churches in a heartbeat, so too the opposite can occur. Big churches can become small in a heartbeat. The power of friendship is extremely strong, much more so than the impulse to reach out in fellowship to those we do not know.

Window Three: Magical Mystery Tour Revisited

So we returned the bus, tucked away our bell-bottomed pants, brushed the Cheez Whiz and Twinkies from lips, and turned our CD players back to artists better appreciated by our teenage children. The Magical Mystery Tour was a success in every way for the forty-five of us now fifty-year-olds. We all had a great time recalling our pasts.

And part of that past involved, again, recalling the excitement during those few short years when we were caught up into something larger than ourselves in helping to revitalize our 275-year-old church. None of us had planned on being on the front end of all this growth. Only in hindsight did we really see how we as a group of people entering into relationships with one another had shaped, and were being shaped by, a common set of desires that in time translated itself into institutional changes in the church.

Set aside the vision statements and business plans—churches tend to thrive and grow because of relationships, not because of these institutional contrivances. Certainly good preaching and sound teaching, meaningful worship, and growing resources that eventually translate into programs are all central ingredients to the ongoing growth and vitality of a church. But at the eye level of any thriving church, we see deep-seated relationships that are vital to that church's long-term sustainability.

None of us were fully aware of this as we got off the bus that night, but the vitality of the future of our church community rested upon our willingness to allow a sense of community to be redefined by others, even in our wake. It was an interesting situation as we traveled in that bus for those two hours, as we found ourselves already talking about "the good old days" of the church. Imagine, "the good old days" being only ten years behind us.

Already an impulse was forming in us to do things in the church because "we always do it this way." And why do we do it this way? Because we saw how well it worked during a time when there was so much vitality. Already we had in our minds the types of people who could carry on the vital mission of the church. How did we know who they were? They were our peers on the bus, and we knew that we could bestow authority and leadership on them because we had been right there with them when the church started growing.

This is a dangerous period for any church community. Churches rise and fall through time in relational pockets. They ebb and flow in large measure by how the community of relationships in churches is forever changing. More to the point, the path that churches take through time is determined by how the community of relationships is allowed to change.

Churches that quit growing tend to get caught in the spin cycle of their generational washing machines. One generation begins to dominate, and all the rest tend to get lost in the spin. But the measure of a thriving community is the degree to which community is shared through the generations. Vital churches always have a healthy balance of those who have been present in the church over the long haul and new people who are allowed to enter into the life of the church freely and with encouragement. Always behind the wake of the boat there needs to be a new wave forming. If not, churches tend to get stuck with results already mentioned above.

Nowhere is this more apparent than in the way communities allow leadership to be shared by old members and new members alike. The vision of a church needs to be continuously shared by those with a perspective from the past, as well as those with new voices continuously being vested with authority. This is certainly not an easy transfer of authority of vision. It can be done only through respectful relationships passing down a sense of common community from one generation to the next.

Window Four: Pastor as Friend Revisited

It was those in the front row I was most aware of at the funeral. They all had gray hair, or no hair at all, depending mostly on their gender. They knew each other in fours and fives, but they all came from different churches. The one thing they held in common was their relationship with my father as their onetime pastor. I could see it in their eyes; they came there with deep affection and gratitude to honor my father and his years of ministry. These were genuine brothers and sisters in Christ, salt of the earth, no-nonsense true believers. They represented everything you could hope for in terms of what churches should be relationally.

But were they friends to my father? Certainly many of them were. Certainly all would have been considered friends. Certainly it is dangerous to speak for someone now deceased for how he considered these parishioners. But based upon the voracity of his oft-spoken maxim—"my best friends are ex-parishioners"—I can only assume that the relationships my father most treasured in these folks had less to do with friendship than it had to do with his commitment to them as their brother in Christ.

Should pastors have friendships within their congregations? Perhaps my father overreached in his views, and my guess is that he was not always consistent in what he thought was something worth abiding by at this point. But behind his often quoted maxim was an intense determination to minister to the full body of Christ within his church.

This meant that he was responsible to everyone, regardless of who they were. It included the deeply troubled and needy woman who, if my father let her, could have taken up his entire ministry. (And don't all pastors and churches have these people?) It included the young teenager with whom he would never really have a relationship because of generational differences. It included even, I suppose, the attractive young woman who showed up regularly whom he had the sense to minister to from a distance. And it included the man just about his age who happened to have all the same interests as him, who laughed at all the same jokes, and who could easily have taken up the rest of the time not consumed by the needy woman, if he allowed it.

Should pastors have friendships in their congregations? Many indicators suggest that pastors live lonely lives.[4] On the one hand, there is no greater calling, and most pastors find themselves flourishing in this reality, give or take a day or two a week. But the combination of the demands of public leadership, motivating largely volunteer organizations, hours of study—and did I mention the needy lady?—make the pastorate challenging. In the end, Henri Nouwen confesses that "too many of us are lonely ministers practicing a lonely ministry."[5] Consequently, pastors need to be sustained by deep-seated relationships that can replenish their souls. Spouses and children can do this to a point; but as we discussed, thinkers from Aristotle to Lewis have described for us the wonderful delights of companionship that only friendship can bring.

Again, I ask, should pastors have close friendships in their congregations? This is too subjective a question to be answered categorically for all persons in ministry. It is the kind of question that provokes long discussions at monthly ministerial meetings. Behind the question, however, is a universal responsibility all must meet. Pastors are responsible relationally to their entire flock. This requires that friendships must take a backseat to their pastoral commitments.

Friendships can be dangerous business for pastors in their churches. What do people in the church say, for example, after the third Sunday in a row when Pastor Peterson and his wife are seen heading off after church for lunch with their friends, the Kaboskis? How does it look when the pastor plays golf weekly with the same foursome? What does it look like when a pastor continuously sides with a certain group in his congregation, who also happen to be persons he is close to?

Pastors would do well to be sensitive to the relational expectations of their congregations, even if these expectations are wrong. The relational expectations that most shape parishioners is, understandably, what they see described in Scripture, and what they find in Scripture is a description of what it means to be the community of Christ: nonexclusive, nonpreferential, nonreciprocal, unconcerned about status, radically unselfish—a nonnegotiable divine command, eternal in its scope, distinctly Christian, and fully transparent. Right or wrong, the need for friendship by pastors is not easily distinguished from their requirements to care impartially for the entire body.

It behooves pastors, then, to be careful how they express friendship publicly within eyeshot and earshot of their congregations. Friendship needs to be expressed prudently and respectfully. This may mean that supper with the special Kaboski couple be made more irregular and held at the restaurant two suburbs away. Or it may mean that pastors spread their golf game partners around to others in the church. It certainly means that pastors should be aware of how alliances are perceived during moments when decisions need to be made in the church. Might this be inconvenient at times? Absolutely. But for pastors living in the context of the church, friendship must always be expressed secondarily to Christian community. This concern, I think, was the shadow cast behind Dad's relationships for all those years.

Window Five: "Friendship Evangelism" Revisited

Andy still faithfully attended church every Sunday morning. Most weeks he even made it to a Saturday morning men's Bible study. The pastors and others continued to be nice enough, but the friendships he longed for those months back did not seem to have materialized. People in the congregation were friendly to him, although he did sometimes get the sense that he rubbed some the wrong way. To this point in time, he still has not found someone willing to spend quality time with him outside of the formal events held in the church. He has not found a true friend.

Although he could never articulate this, the "friendship evangelism" of his now-fellow brothers and sisters in Christ has not fulfilled everything it promised him. These deeply committed followers of Christ certainly valued the most important thing in seeking him out. From the perspective of eternity, his salvation is his most treasured gift. Even he can acknowledge this, but he admits sometimes that his new growing faith in Jesus Christ does not cover the loneliness he continues to feel. What he thought he had found in entering into relationship with the people of the church just never happened.

Andy's situation begs a larger set of questions related to the church's responsibility to relate honestly to the nonbelieving world. First, what kind of relationship does the world see when it looks in the windows of the sanctuaries of our churches? Do they see a set of relationships not too dissimilar from what they might find anywhere else, at the American Legion Hall for example, or even—minus the alcohol—at a really friendly neighborhood bar? Can the intimacy that is supposed to be reflected in the church be easily replicated in these other settings? If so, what makes the church so radically different?

Is not one of the marks by which we are to be known our love for one another (John 13:35)? What if the nonbelieving world was able to see a community of people who loved one another unconditionally and without preferences, from the oldest to the youngest, each member valued equally? What if they saw a community that had an unusual—some might even say supernatural—capacity to love the most unlovable? What if they saw a community of complete transparency where persons showed a willingness to give completely to one another without expecting anything in return?

Even if the nonbelieving world could not make complete sense of it, could the church offer a relationship without the limitations of exclusivity and preferential treatment found in friendship? Even if wonderfully intimate, would we have to "sell" them a relationship shrouded in secrets? Would we have to be "selling" friendship to nonbelievers, when we really want to be inviting them entry into a community that offers so much more?

In saying this, certainly I recognize that a phrase such as "friendship evangelism" is only a description. But words mean something; and just as it is important to clarify more precisely the relational types that fill our lives, so we would do well to clarify more precisely the language we use to describe these relationships. If the invitation to enter into the community of Christ is to be honest for those who seek it, then we need to be clear in how we describe it evangelistically lest we promise more than—or different from—what we deliver. So we find Andy entering into the life of the church—but, really, what kind of community is he entering?

Friendship and Fellowship as Strange Bedfellows

Great Expectations

There may be yet other windows we can peer into in order to understand how community is to be formed in the body of Christ. But these five provide sufficient perspective for us to understand some key issues facing congregations every day in developing authentic relationships.

Buried deep in all five of these relational situations is the identical seed of potential confusion. Left to germinate, I can assure you that this confusion will grow into frustration, and if not attended to, will eventually flower into full-blown conflict in our churches. The title of Charles Dickens's wonderful nineteenth-century novel *Great Expectations* describes this seed beautifully.

At the core of all relationships lies "great expectations." What are our work relationships, for example, if not a bundle of expectations? Your employer expects a full day of work from you and your colleagues, a day that allows for perhaps a few moments at the water cooler; but make a habit of lingering too long, and you will get an earful of expectations. In return, as an employee, the expectation is that there will be good communication between you and your boss, that you will be treated with a degree of respect, and that you will get paid fairly.

Commercial relationships bear the same expectations. Who doesn't expect great things from the person who sells us a new set of sheets or a washer and dryer in which to wash and dry them? If the sheets don't fit right or the washer breaks down, then our great expectations for our relationships with the salespeople who sold us these things quickly become self-evident. The same holds true with our relationships with our lawyer, hairdresser, or insurance agent.

And we could go on: If we marry a lovely, sensitive bride or groom, then we expect certain things as the marriage progresses through the years. If we are fortunate to have children, then we expect certain great things from them. Picture those children as they grow from being sweet little bundles of joy to the angst-filled teenagers who are only too ready to leave the nest. Perhaps some of the yelling that goes on in the house during the teenage years has something to do with ever-so-subtle shifts in expectations on both sides of the generation gap.

Every relationship is defined by expectations. So what great expectations lie beneath the surface of Christian community? Wipe away the morning dew from each of our five little windows, and we find Mary Beth daring to enter into a living room filled with total strangers because she has certain expectations of what it might mean for her in her loneliness. She represents on a small scale the larger drama that goes on every Sunday, as new people stand on the thresholds of our sanctuaries big and small. Stop for a moment with them and picture what is in their minds as they peer into a worship space or a fellowship hall for the first time—places filled with individuals bustling about, laughing, talking, and relating to one another. What expectations need to be met for these new people to enter and eventually stick around?

Some of these new outsiders might be like our recent convert, Andy, who finds himself in a situation where being a Christian is such a new, untried experience that he, and they, enter church life with unformed, even clumsy expectations of what it might mean to be brothers and sisters in Christ. These expectations don't stop once they initially enter the church. What about the expectations that long-time attendees and members have to eventually enter into the ebb and flow of the church, even to the point of becoming leaders? And, finally, what of the expectations surrounding the relationships attendees share with their pastors?

Isn't this the source of most of the confusion, frustration, and conflict in our churches? Listen closely to the tightly parsed discussions about what color to paint the sanctuary, or whether to replace the one-hundred-year-old organ with a new set of amps, or the more substantive theological conversations that reflect differences between members in the church. Observe the nonverbal subtexts of these discussions. As legitimate as the discussions might be on the surface, they are all surrounded by relational contexts. How persons in churches successfully resolve the conversations within their life together is the result, in part, of how they read the relational drama that goes on beneath the words spoken. Text and subtext, both must be listened to carefully to get the whole story of what is going on in the life of the church.

All the more, it is important to identify the right expectations with the right relationships—which brings us back to our central distinction between friendship and fellowship. More often than not these two relationships coexist in the same room together. And herein lies the deception. Contrary to the stark differences we have found in them when viewed more abstractly, in real life they seem to mimic each other. Smell them. Taste them. Touch them. Listen to them. Hear them. If these two relationships are not, in fact, the same, then they at least appear to be deeply compatible.

But they are not. In fact, they are exact opposite relationships with opposite goals, and this is the source of the problem. Mary Beth, the stalwart old women who have kept alive the timeworn semi-comatose church, the members of the Magical Mystery Tour, congregants seeking a closer relationship with their pastor, and Andy the new convert—all are potentially afflicted by great false expectations. They may very well expect something relationally from the church that was never promised to them in the first place. The relationships we find described as central to the New Testament certainly are not friendship. But is this what we expect? And from the churches' perspective, is this what we wrongly offer?

Fourfold Comparison

To answer these questions, it is important to put the two relationships side by side, as we have done. How do they measure up against each other? Line them up heel to heel and head to head. Mark them up against the kitchen door, as it were. Are they the same height? If they are as different as I have suggested, then is one relationship more important than the other? Is one less important? Should one be eliminated for the sake of the other? Can one be eliminated? Four points need to be made here, lest we have misconceptions about how these two relationships are to coexist within the church.

Comparison One

First, although in real life it might be tempting to suggest that these two relationships operate on parallel tracks, or that given time they might eventually run on the same track, they never become the same relationship. Put in geometric terms, the axis of friendship and fellowship never cross one another. They forever run on nonintersecting tracks. They are always different relationships.

This is an important concept to understand in seeking to develop authentic forms of community in our churches. What are we seeking to do in nurturing a sense of "fellowship," for example, in our small group ministries? What is our ultimate goal in putting individuals together in our children's ministry or youth group? What are we seeking to accomplish in our assimilation strategies as a deacon board for new members?

Is the relational intimacy we find in friendship to be the goal? If so, are we then not tempted to assume that, if these individuals are left to marinate long enough in the obligations surrounding Christian fellowship, they might eventually get to know one another well enough to become friends? The pastor might say, "If I can only get our people in the same room together long enough, thinking and doing the same things, I just know they could become good friends."

Might our relational goals for one another as Christian brothers and sisters reveal the fact that we really do act as if friendship is a higher form of relationship and that Christian fellowship is only a means to a higher end? This is often our dilemma: If we act as though we seek Christian fellowship among ourselves as a means to get at the real intimate good stuff—that is, close friendship—then how does the transition transpire from this lower form of relationship to the higher? To put it in quantitative terms, how many quarts of the former does it take to finally reach the brim of the latter? In practice, how do we as church leaders get everyday, run-of-the-mill Christians to become best friends?

The answer to this question is that we should not. Nor are we obligated to in Scripture. Contrary to our temptation to think otherwise, fellowship is not a lower form of friendship, nor is it a higher form. The relational intimacy found in friendship is not to be the ultimate goal of our efforts to develop Christian community in our churches.

This has significant implications for how we seek to develop meaningful relationships within our churches. And it has significant implications for those seeking those relationships. On the one hand, imagine this: Healthy forms of community in our churches need not lead to friendship, nor should this be the expectation. God commands us to be in fellowship with one another, but this does not necessarily constitute that we become best friends or, for that matter, friends at all. Fellowship, as a distinct, God-ordained relationship, is an end in itself and need not lead anywhere else. Put more positively, the gathered community is not limited to mere friendship. In fact, our community of brothers and sisters extends so much larger and includes even those we would not naturally befriend or even know.

On the other hand, neither is friendship to be viewed as a relationship lesser than fellowship in the sense that friendship, too, is an end in itself. To the extent that they are completely different relationships, friendship need not be viewed as the means toward other ends. That is, friendship need not become merely a spiritualized form of what is naturally a part of our world.

As an aside, this realization points us directly to the dilemma the medieval monastic brothers, such as Aelred and de Sales, confronted us with when they conceptualized their shared life together as "friendship" or, more precisely, "spiritual friendship." In describing friendship as synonymous with Christian fellowship, these brothers spiritualized friendship. For these "spiritual friends," relationships apart from those within the cloister were viewed as lesser forms of friendship.

One of the unintended consequences of this spiritualizing of friendship is that this relationship, which is otherwise more naturally universal in expression, became cloistered within the safe confines of the abbey. What they lost in spiritualizing friendship was one of the authentic connecting points with their world from a relational perspective. This should be a warning to us as well as we engage the larger culture around us. If anything, we need to be more intentional in nurturing the vital umbilical relationship that binds us to our brothers and sisters, both Christian and non-Christian.

Comparison Two

This leads us naturally to the second point of clarification. To speak of friendship and fellowship as never being the same does not mean that they are mutually exclusive, even when expressed within the confines of the gathered Christian community. Friendship remains an important relationship when expressed carefully and with sensitivity within the church.[6]

Not only does friendship have value within the church, but it is irreplaceable. Friendship provides us something relationally that no other relationship can provide us, even as marriage, for example, offers us a relationship unique from Christian community but also complementary to it. As the supreme example of this, we can well imagine that Jesus benefited greatly from friendship with his disciples—maybe even certain of his disciples over others—in ways that could not be expressed otherwise. Although not explicitly stated in the Gospels, we can picture that one of the things that sustained Jesus throughout the life of his ministry was the genuine friendships of his followers. Not only were the disciples his students, not only were they his apostles, not only were they those he came to redeem, but some, if not all, were—perhaps in varying degrees—certainly also his friends.

Friendship has an important place within the church. As we have already illustrated, however, to speak of its importance reminds us again of the dangers of expressing friendship indiscriminately within the gathered community. In this, it must be said that friendship is a "wonderful, terrible relationship." To the extent that friendship draws people together in uniquely transformative ways, it also has the power to pull them apart in deeply destructive ways.

For this reason, in an important sense, there is a priority of relationships that must occur in the way relationships are expressed openly within the gathered community. Returning to our discussion from chapter 1, just as every relationship has a primary context characterized by a common language and set of conventions, so fellowship is to have the pride of place within the confines of the gathered Christian community.

In this sense, friendship is no different from any other kind of relationship when expressed within the context of the gathered community. Employers are called to temporarily set aside the way they express authority over their employees at the door of the church. Fathers and sons sitting next to each other are called to reflect their true natures as coequal brothers in Christ when expressing their fellowship with one another in mutual worship of God, rather than to express themselves in terms of the hierarchy that normally characterizes their place in the family.

And so it is with friendship. Friends are called to leave aside the benefits of their relationships for the sake of the body of Christ when they are together with their brothers and sisters in Christ. All other relationships might legitimately be expressed in some measure in the life of the church, but fellowship is to have primacy over them all.

This setting aside of the rights and privileges of another relationship for the sake of our brothers and sisters in Christ may very well be one of the lost disciplines of the church. It requires a consciousness, intentionality, and humility often lacking in many of our churches. Evidence of this, perhaps, can be found in the nature of the tensions and conflict that beset us. Strip away the rhetoric surrounding what we fight over in our congregations, and we may find misplaced sources of authority characterizing relationships other than fellowship that informs our priorities and behavior.

What is it, again, that is to characterize our life together? It is a mutuality and sense of equality that obligates us to love one another with radical self-giving. As Christians, we are to be an inclusive community, reflecting complete transparency with one another, wholly unconscious of status, dominated in everything we say and do by the mediated power of the Holy Spirit. It is these characteristics that should override all other relational priorities whenever and wherever the gathered fellowship expresses itself, whether in the church sanctuary, the fellowship hall, a small group gathering in our homes, or wherever two or more are gathered in the name of Christ.

Comparison Three

The third point of clarification concerning how friendship and fellowship relate to each other is that it would seem at first blush that fellowship is a far less intimate relationship than friendship, at least conceptually. Friendship seems so much more bright and light and user-friendly than its grumpier counterpart as we have described it. Overall, the heartfelt, interpersonal varnish that covers friendship, as it were, seems far glossier than that of fellowship.

Friendship, after all, is characterized by a small group of handpicked relationships that allows for more intense and targeted shared experiences. Friends are freely chosen. They carry with them a discriminating eye and a clear sense of who is in and who is out of the group. Friends don't need to give their hearts to just anyone. They can bask in a private, intimate world of their own making. We find them most often tucked away into discrete corners, communicating secretly to one another. It would seem that all this should make for deeper, more intense experiences.

On the other hand, those in Christian fellowship are obligated to give themselves to virtually anyone who might walk in the door—that is, anyone who names the name of Jesus. It is a relationship of obligation. As such, the rules of fellowship don't even require that a fellow brother or sister in Christ be someone we actually know directly. How personal and intimate can one be with a total stranger?

So, does friendship carry with it a more natural power of intimacy than what can be expected in Christian fellowship? In one sense, yes—at least on the surface. Without directly comparing the two relationships, John Stott rightly reminds us of the true source of Christian fellowship. This source, he says, exists separate from the emotional trappings that we commonly associate with it:

> In common usage fellowship [friendship, as we have described it] describes something subjective, the experience of warmth and security in each other's presence, as in "We had good fellowship together." But, in biblical usage *koinonia* is not a subjective feeling at all, but an objective fact, expressing what we share together.[7]

At its core, the source of fellowship is not the natural affections of the heart as is the case in friendship.[8] True Christian fellowship springs objectively from an altogether different source. It springs from God himself.

With these words from Stott, we are reminded again that the fellowship we share as brothers and sisters in Christ is first and foremost a mediated relationship that depends upon a third party for its point of intimacy. In terms of its source of expression, it goes well beyond the affections of the human heart and rests upon a mutual encounter with the living God through the work of the Spirit.

This reminder of the objective nature of fellowship—in striking contrast to its subjectively charged counterpart in friendship—is an important corrective for us as we seek authentic relationships with one another as a gathered community. What are we truly seeking in our life together as Christians? A confession is in order here. Too often I am prone to succumb to what might be called the "intimacy fallacy." Perhaps you are, too. That is, we find it so easy to measure the quality of fellowship with our Christian brothers and sisters by the level of subjective intimacy evoked.

While true fellowship between our brothers and sisters can easily be seen in a highly charged worship service together, it is not so obvious in the hard, tedious giving of ourselves, day after day, in serving with a few others in the back room. Why is it we call it "fellowship hour" when we stand around on Sundays with our friends and eat donuts and drink coffee together, but not "fellowship" during the hour later in the week when, at the least opportune time, we get that call from the person in our congregation whose needs are as fathomless as a dry well in the desert. Can we see ourselves experiencing "fellowship" during those moments being squeezed from our lives as the person drones on and on?

A sense of fellowship can so easily be evoked—maybe even manipulated—when life is looking up, everything is going just right, and people are in good spirits and cooperating; or when we are with people with whom we are socially comfortable, and when we can readily see ourselves getting something tangible from our relationships, even if that something is a legitimate, mutual deeper sense of God. But more often than not, true Christian fellowship is hard work. It rarely comes easily. It requires a cost. What does fellowship look like when we don't readily feel it or, for that matter, even desire it? We are called to live in Christian community with *all* of our brothers and sisters in Christ *all* the time, whether we feel like it or not!

And herein lies the danger. If we find ourselves addicted to the subjective benefits of our fellowship with one another, and if this is how we measure whether it really is occurring in our lives, then might we run the risk of missing some of what God is asking of us in our relationships? Transfixed by all the emotional benefits of fellowship, we may never commit ourselves to the length, breadth, and depth of what living in community requires of us, in both good times and bad.

I was reminded of this a few years ago when I was dragged down to New Orleans on a mission trip in the aftermath of Hurricane Katrina. On the surface, the entire experience seemed to have little value for me from a relational perspective. The days were hot. The no-see-ums were out. The work fluctuated from being dirty to downright monotonous. Rarely did we get a thank you from those we helped. There was little time left in the day to do the things that normally account for good community building, such as worship or Bible study.

But something happened during those rare moments in the week when Cec and I, and the students from the seminary—all of us complete strangers at the beginning of the trip—were able to be together. Surprise of all surprises, we were captured by a profound sense of deep commitment to one another I can only describe as reaching the level of heartfelt worship. In having an opportunity to serve others less fortunate than ourselves, by the end of our service together our fellowship had become truly transcendent.

So just as true fellowship does not rest on the natural human affections of the heart but on the mediating relationship we share together through the Spirit of God, so fellowship may have less to do with how and when we seek it than when the Spirit chooses to offer it to us. A sense of true fellowship may ultimately sit outside our control. In Christian community, we are required to rest in the Spirit for our own relational nourishment. And herein lies the mystery surrounding fellowship: Can fellowship match the intimacy of friendship? Absolutely. But it is up to the Spirit, working in our midst, when and how he chooses to offer it to us as a gift of his presence.

Comparison Four

Fourth and finally, I only wish it were as easy to parse these two relationships—friendship and fellowship—in real life as it appears in my typology. It is not. My exercise here in extrapolating one of these relationships from the other in a highly conceptual way is a luxury only a sociologist dare make. For the brief period you have been reading this book, I have sought to allow us to stand above the high grass as we looked at the sharply honed distinctions between friendship and fellowship. But you understand, in the real day-to-day life of the church these two relationships get tangled together like the thick undergrowth of an overgrown forest.

Or to mix my metaphors in the worst way: Like a small child busy coloring in a coloring book, rarely do the distinctions I have been making between friendship and fellowship stay within the lines in real life. Did I mention that life is messy? And nowhere is life messier than in the way we conduct our relationships with one another. We rarely live our lives within the lines. So it is with these two relationships. In our consciousness, the two bleed together, sometimes in ways that almost make them indistinguishable from each other.

Returning now to our central point, with these four statements of clarification in mind, we might ask ourselves: What are our great expectations for the fellowship we are to share in Christ? Do we have great expectations? Thus far we have been flying the plane of our understanding of these relational concepts at a fairly high altitude. We turn now to what I hope will be a more concrete picture of how our life together looks at ground level—that of extending true hospitality to one another.

CHAPTER SEVEN

THE HOSPITALITY OF SOJOURNERS AND ALIENS

T he moment stands out as if it were yesterday. It probably stands out so vividly because I became self-consciously aware of the moment as it happened. It was actually a small moment as moments go—nothing to write home about—but there I was one of nine or ten sitting around a table—second chair on the left side of the room—eating otherwise forgettable food while conversing with a group of almost-complete strangers. I cannot even remember what we were discussing. All I knew at that moment was that what I shared in Christian community almost overwhelmed me.

The moment washed over me, but I had a profound sense that these almost-strangers and I were locked together as fellow believers in a way that was utterly transformative for me personally, and that I sensed was transformative to them as well. As these kinds of experiences go, I did not want it to end.

Perhaps you have experienced a sense of community in this way as well. There have certainly been other times for me other than this moment in the little living room of Chateau Beu Site that winter of 1976 in Huemoz, Switzerland. I periodically sense this link between my brothers and sisters in Christ, if less intensely, as I sit in my creaky old New England Congregational church on Sunday mornings.

Our natural impulse is to want to string these high moments of relational intensity together into a predictable and regular pattern. If only we could capture these moments of community in a bottle for our ongoing consumption! Evidence of this desire to make our sense of community conform to our beck and call can be found in bookstores filled with how-to books on mastering formulas for keeping the romance of community alive: *Five Easy Steps to Effective Community Building.*

Perhaps I have unintentionally misled you thus far to believe that this Christian community we share is a set of individualized relationships that can actually be controlled in this way. I may have left the impression that fellowship—and friendship, for that matter—consists of highly personalized entities that somehow well up subjectively from within us and are manipulated by us.

If this is the impression given thus far, let me now set the record straight by suggesting that relationships like these two are far more complex. Christian community and friendship are as much products of a culture we have little direct control over as psychological and social ones that we do, perhaps even more so. As such, these relationships are inextricably embedded in a thick soup of "language, habits, ideas, beliefs, customs, social organization[s], inherited artifacts, technical processes, and values," all of which Richard Niebuhr says makes up culture.[1] We wear these cultural phenomena as the "artificial secondary environment" that is draped over the natural world we live in. To say we create culture is only a half-truth in that just as we are about the business of creating culture, so we are bound to using these same cultural phenomena as tools for its further development. And just as we say we are entering into and experiencing relationships, these relationships are being formed for us by multiple social factors beyond our control.

Therefore, as a cultural phenomenon, at any given moment we are captured by a sense of community as much as capturing it. Consequently, we need to realize that our very thinking about community—the values we put around it, the expectations we have for it, even the feelings that surround it—are not completely our own. They are being shaped for us even as we are a part of their shaping.

So embedded are our perceptions, in fact, in the "taken for granted" nature of the relational culture surrounding us that we are rarely conscious of how these relationships affect us and those around us. Like an iceberg in the North Atlantic Ocean, we may be able to see and understand only a small part of how our relationships work and affect our lives, but it is the vast underworld beneath the waterline that is most telling. It is this underworld of culture that James Hunter says is most deceptively strong, because culture is "most powerful . . . when it is perceived as self-evident."[2]

Returning to our discussion from the last chapter on the "great expectations" that surround Christian fellowship, in the face of our honest efforts to develop for ourselves authentic, biblical models of fellowship for our churches, we need to be aware that the expectations behind these models will inevitably bear the marks of our cultural settings. Even as we seek to enter into Christian fellowship, we would do well to acknowledge that what we enter into is not solely of our own making but is being shaped for us.

Perhaps an illustration from an obvious source would be helpful at this point. What modern-day example of Christian fellowship is most often on our lips as we discuss the kind of Christian fellowship we desire for ourselves and our church community? Bonhoeffer's description of community in his *Life Together* most often comes to mind. Many of us silently rhapsodize on the great intensity and the profound commitments we find displayed in his book. If only our church community could share in the common cup of fellowship that these young men shared together in his experimental community at Zingst and Finkenwalde. Like Bonhoeffer, we are so bold as to begin our ruminations about how we want our community to be formed with the same psalm on our lips that was on his as he starts his *Life Together*, "Behold, how good and how pleasant it is for brethren to dwell together in unity!" (Ps. 133:1).[3]

Of course, the backdrop to these ruminations often corresponds to our frustrations as pastors and church leaders as to why we can't get our congregations to commit to being part of a small group, let alone a vibrant community. We often find so few willing to commit themselves to regular church attendance or Bible studies. And why is it that soccer and Little League now compete with our children's and youth ministries? As Dr. Cyril Wechte (played by Albert Brooks) says in the film *Concussion*, "The NFL owns a day of the week. The same day the Church used to own. Now it's theirs." We long for a community more akin to what we see in the above example.

In considering this example of community for ourselves, however, we perhaps neglect to take into consideration the historic-cultural context that shaped such a community. How is it that these men in Bonhoeffer's community could live with such intensity? How could they live such disciplined lives together that allowed them to be so committed to one another? At this point, we could expand our illustration and include the example of the Christian churches we might find in mainland China or in the Middle East where we see fellowship among brothers and sisters flourishing in such dramatic ways.

In seeking community for ourselves similar to these examples, however, we may have neglected the simple reality that any community we find ourselves in has a larger cultural framework that shapes it. In the case of the brothers at Zingst and Finkenwalde, their sense of "life together" was deeply shaped by the fact that they lived under the shadow of the Third Reich. We can see the same situation in China and the Middle East where the cultural forces around these communities of believers help shape the intensity of their common life together. Take the unique features of their historic-cultural settings away from any of these examples and chances are the nature of their communities would change as well.

Which brings us to our current cultural setting in the church in the West. What natural cultural cauldron do we find ourselves stewing in as we seek to relate meaningfully together as a community of Jesus Christ in America in the twenty-first century? Three cultural institutions come to mind as specific examples of aspects of life that subtly shape us in significant ways, though I am sure there are many, many more. We are the product of the insurance industry, the entertainment industry, and an economic system that has significant sway over our society.

First, the insurance industry: We in the West have for several decades found ourselves increasingly the beneficiaries of a culture that has done a phenomenal job of protecting us from the natural world around us. As a cultural tool we have constructed for ourselves, we have built an entire industry that hedges our bets against the unknown. Currently, for example, in this country there are more than 394,347 different insurance companies, including 2,826 accident and health insurance companies, 4,144 hospital and medical service plan companies, 8,585 life insurance companies, and 2,740 pension, health, and welfare companies, to name a few.[4] We have taken care to insure everything around us, from our health to the health of our property: cars, houses, copyrighted documents, current investments, future investments, even our gambling debts.

These policies act as fingers stuck in the dikes of everything from high-rising water, to mischievous cancer cells, to equally mischievous teenagers who might key our cars, to our impending deaths, to the weaknesses of our own vices. One can only wonder what we could do at the end of the year with the aggregate of all the money spent on insurance every year. All that money provides us with a sense of security, while it artificially protects us against the natural world that forever seems to intrude upon our best-laid plans.

Given this artificial world of security we have built for ourselves (a friend of mine likes to call it "a lifestyle lived between two mattresses"), how might this cultural climate ever so subtly shape our need for Christian community? I am not thinking here of a well-reasoned response to this question. Rather, I am thinking more viscerally, of the kind of immediate impulse we might feel for needing—or not needing, as the case might be—the fellowship of others. (For that matter, I wonder how this environment even shapes the way we express our need for trust in God, given our seemingly growing artificial control over our environment.)

Given our hedge against the natural occurrences of this world offered by the insurance bubble we have built for ourselves, do we really need each other in any immediate sense—that is, perhaps in the same way that two brothers from a church in the country of Chad need each other in their world where life is lived without any protective barrier? Let me say this again: Do we really "need" each other? Perhaps we do, but at the very least, this industry of our own making might have blunted the forces of community we say are so important to us.

What of the second industry that dominates our world? Regarding the entertainment industry, I was struck not long ago by a picture depicting the stands of Fenway Park in 1918. To scan the bleachers was to scan a sea of black suits, white shirts, ties, and hats. Not a Red Sox jersey in the place except on the players on the field!

Now, overlay this picture from 1918 with a picture of the bleacher seats today, and we find not only a far more colorful picture but one symbolically representing a culture now dominated by the entertainment industry in all its forms. A new type of wardrobe fills our closets: we call it "leisurewear," "sportswear," or "casual wear," and it ranges from sweat suits to other informal clothing that seems to fit every occasion imaginable. The shift in our clothing is nothing less than a reflection of a relatively new era where the time, money, and priorities of our culture are directed toward filling our free time with whole new sets of activities.

In 2007, Nike, the largest manufacturer of athletic shoes and apparel, made 16.3 billion dollars.[5] The combined revenue of U.S. professional sports teams is currently approximately $19 billion annually, including sales of $8,000 million for the National Football League, $3,800 million for the National Basketball Association, and $2,900 million for the National Hockey League.[6] Between 2005 and 2006, 17.1 million tickets were sold for Broadway plays at over two hundred theaters around North America. This does not include tickets sold on Broadway in New York.[7] In 2009, the video gaming industry and PC game software retail sales reached 20.2 billion.[8] I could go on, but you get the point. We have become a culture that has the luxury of being distracted by what entertains us and fills our lives with a variety of leisure and artificial forms of competition.

I wonder how this culture of entertainment has shaped our need for and our understanding of community. We decry what seems to be a lack of commitment to community, but given all the entertainment options at our disposal, our churches struggle to keep up. Put "easily-achievable-mild-distraction" next to "dealing-with-the pain-and-problems-of-another-person," and "mild-distraction" will win nine times out of ten. Given all the options, do we really feel the need for the kind of community we may once have required? We say we need community, but do we have the same sense of urgency we might have had in other times and places?

Finally, even in spite of recent ups and downs in our economy, in relative terms we live in an economic system that has worked well for most of us. I make this assessment from the perspective of how others live globally and historically. If we are honest, when we find ourselves at the checkout counter, our "wants" are oftentimes elevated in our minds to the "need" level. More broadly, we can measure the influence this system has on us when we realize that a primary indicator of the strength of our economy is based on our consumption: when consumption goes up, our economy goes up; when consumption goes down, we know we are in trouble.

Once again, given the cultural tools around us that shape every aspect of our lives in terms of how our needs are met, how might our cultural situation in terms of our economic situation shape our living in community?

Undoubtedly, our communities are filled with many needs, some of them concrete (financial) and others less concrete (more spiritual and emotional), but how we perceive these needs may be parsed quite differently now from how they once were.

There are certainly plenty of other culturally embedded influences that shape our lives besides these three. But imagine how each of the effects of these three cultural institutions have through the years seeped into our consciousness, most often through the backdoor so we hardly know how they impact our lives. The fact that some of us might not have insurance, or are not card-carrying season-ticket holders of any particular part of the entertainment industry, or are not particularly wealthy is beside the point. In relative terms, we live and breathe and are influenced by these cultural entities even as we may, some of us, reject them. Prick our fingers and we will find they are a part of our DNA. These three, among many other cultural influences, have certainly shaped the way in which we have developed community for ourselves as a church in the West.

Given our cultural situation, it might be tempting to seek answers for revitalizing our understanding of community in other places and times. Again, we may pine for a simpler time and place where community is thrust on us. But such looking over the fence at other cultural circumstances very much misses the point of what God is doing in our lives. It acts as a distraction. The point is that in God's providence he has placed those of us who live in our particular setting with all the advantages we have—including those mentioned above—along with the liabilities and temptations they bring, and he has called us to live lives of obedience in this context.

It is in this place and time—"safe," entertainment-crazed, affluent Western culture—that we are called to make for ourselves places of faithful community. What does God want to do here and now in our lives as the church of Jesus Christ? How are we called to live lives of faithful obedience? How are we to extend community to others here and now? These are the questions before us.

Building Cultures of Hospitality

As he has done in ages past and is doing now, God calls those in his church to live in fellowship within the specific places and cultures in which we find ourselves. For lack of a better term, let us call this extending of Christian fellowship "hospitality." We as the church are called to intentionally nurture *cultures of hospitality*, surely for those within our own doors, but also to offer hospitality to those standing outside our doors looking in.

Look into the family rooms of the normal suburban house on any given autumn Sunday afternoon. The entire afternoon is well orchestrated according to the agenda on the screen. Two or three couples and a single or two begin slowly with chips and salsa, followed by wings, topped off finally with three kinds of pizza and two kinds of beer. One would think at times that the big game is only a pretense for other things, big and small. Between plays of the game of the week, the conversations range from lighthearted ribbing to ruminations on politics, to workplace gossip, to complaints about chores around the house, to recommendations over the best way to take care of a problem septic system.

Or consider perhaps the hospitality displayed in this very same room on Thursday evenings when a couple invites a group over for a book discussion. It is a more genteel event, filled with discussions about a book by David McCullough, or a classic by Dostoevsky, or the most recent must-read from the *New York Times Book Review*. The fare for this evening is more calorie-sensitive, including tea, wine, and dessert. Between mouthfuls and literary observations, the conversation ranges for these couples between child rearing, a laundry list of house updates, and worries about the economy.

These two typical scenes should strike us in our churches as familiar. They describe what we might find on any given Sunday in most of our congregations, minus the beer and wine—depending upon one's denominational tradition. But the rest is generally there: we like to make our churches friendly places where we extend ourselves with small measures of light banter mixed periodically with more serious conversation. The goal of hospitality is to provide an informal environment where everyone feels comfortable and, if not accepted, at least tolerated in the least offensive way possible.

Many of our churches, in fact, have gone to great lengths to purposefully set the mood for this. We "measure the drapes," as it were, of the family room of our two examples, and we design our sanctuaries and worship services accordingly. We place hospitality on the middle shelf next to the coffee and pastries in order to be accessible for anyone who might walk by. At times, various forms of entertainment are used in our worship services to draw us in, both to keep those within the church interested and to attract those outside the church, possibly for the first time. All this, of course, is done with every good intention.

Certainly there is nothing wrong with these expressions of hospitality, but do these scenes really capture all of what God has for us as communities of believers? Really? Sure, the coffee is hot and almost everyone is mixing nicely. If gregariousness is a measure of success, then we can generally rely upon a few lighthearted individuals to keep things upbeat. And, most importantly, we feel entertained. We in the West love to be entertained.

But I wonder whether these expressions of polite sociability measure up to the admonitions we find in Scripture to extend hospitality to one another. What is the writer of the book of Hebrews really asking of us when he declares, "Keep on loving one another as brothers and sisters. Do not forget to show hospitality to strangers, for by so doing some people have shown hospitality to angels without knowing it" (Heb. 13:1–2). Or what is Peter calling us to in 1 Peter 4:8–9: "Above all, love each other deeply, because love covers over a multitude of sins. Offer hospitality to one another without grumbling."

Recently, I saw a sign inviting new customers to consider doing business at a local bank. The invitation on the sign simply read, "Good People Work Here." Interestingly nothing was said about the lowest interest rates in town, the convenience of multiple ATM machines on every block, the availability of car loans; there was not even a reference to a free iPad if you set up an account. The thin subtext behind the sign was that prospective customers should consider doing business at this particular bank because those who work in that bank are apparently wonderful, inviting people.

But is this invitation of hospitality enough? Imagine, as time went on, if all that the new bank customers received when they entered into a commercial relationship with this establishment was a happy, inviting face. How far would the kind, friendly handshake really take these customers if their first bank statement revealed that the bank offered 1 percent less yield on their savings account or that they offered car loans 3 percent higher than the less friendly bank down the road? In time, my guess is that these customers might privately want to wipe all that apparent friendliness off the faces of their new "best friend" bank tellers.

Now imagine if every church placed this sign on their front door: "Good people live and work and worship here." What might this thin message of hospitality really mean? In our sincere efforts to create places of hospitality for ourselves and others, perhaps we have unwittingly settled for something less than what God has called us to. Maybe we have settled for being exceedingly friendly, approachable, inviting, informal, user-friendly, and winsome when God has called us to be all these things but more, much more. And maybe even at times he has called us to express hospitality in ways that run crosscurrent to these very traits.

More is being asked of us. Hand in glove with the biblical understanding of hospitality is the idea of "caring for the sojourner and alien." We see this linkage throughout the Old Testament, most poignantly in the story of the life of Abraham as he moved from place to place as a sojourner in the land (Gen. 23:4; Heb. 11:9). This idea extends more universally as we see the general condition of God's people of Israel living as sojourners and aliens in Egypt (Gen. 15:13), to the hospitality extended by God time and again in the Exodus (notably, for example, with the offering of manna in Exodus 16), to when Israel finally inherited the land God had promised: "You reside in my land as foreigners and strangers" (Lev. 25:23).

God's people are viewed everywhere as aliens and sojourners in the land and, thus, as receivers of hospitality. But just as hospitality is rooted in a concept of the Almighty who "loves the foreigner" (e.g., Deut. 10:18), so he declares to the Israelites, "Do not mistreat or oppress a foreigner, for you were foreigners in Egypt" (Exod. 22:21). And elsewhere, it is said, "He defends the cause of the fatherless and the widow, and loves the foreigner residing among you, giving them food and clothing. And you are to love those who are foreigners, for you yourself were foreigners in Egypt" (Deut. 10:18–19).

This idea of receiving and offering hospitality to the sojourner and alien extends into the teachings of the New Testament as well, most notably in the life of Jesus. Interestingly, time and again, we find Jesus acting as host even as he was also a guest and stranger/alien (Luke 5:27–32; 7:36–50; 19:1–10). We find him as both in his relationship to the Samaritan, and with the little children he puts between his knees, the tax collector, and the prostitute. In so doing, he acts as the supreme example for us. Perhaps the most important passage that identifies who is to be the object of our hospitality is found in Matthew 25:31–46, where we, his disciples, are admonished to welcome those in greatest distress—those who are thirsty, hungry, the stranger, the naked, the sick, and those in prison.

Finally, this idea of hospitality expands into the life of the early church. It is not without significance that the New Testament word for hospitality (*philoxenia*) combines the general Greek word of love or affection (*phileo*) with stranger (*xenos*), and carries with it the need to care for those who are aliens to us, be it physically, socioeconomically, or religiously.[9] Time and again in Acts and the Epistles, we find the apostles as the recipients of hospitality from those they are called to serve (Acts 16:15, 32–34; 18:1–11), even as they admonish the church to express hospitality to others within the church, notably to those in physical need and the poor (Acts 24:17; Gal. 2:10). Sharing a common life together was, in fact, the means by which they created unity in a young church otherwise divided by religious and economic distinctions (Acts 10–11; 1 Cor. 11:17–34; James 2:1–13).

So it is throughout Scripture that this concept of extending hospitality to the sojourner and alien is inextricably linked to our awareness that we, ourselves, are alien sojourners. The two go hand in hand. We see Jesus himself as a sojourner and alien in this world in his incarnation (Luke 24:36–51); and just as Jesus experienced the vulnerabilities and rejection of being a stranger (Luke 2:7; 4:16–30; John 1:10–11), so we are to accept and offer hospitality as it has been given us: "Accept one another, then, just as Christ accepted you, in order to bring praise to God" (Rom. 15:7).

If we are serious about developing intentional places of hospitality in our churches for those aliens and sojourners among us, whoever they might be, we need to ask ourselves a couple of serious questions: What would it be like to transform the aliens and sojourners in our midst into guests? Using all of our senses, what might places of true Christian hospitality look like? What might they feel like? What would they sound like? What would they smell like? What might they even taste like? At least five things come to mind.

Making Sense out of Hospitality: Using Our Five Senses

The Look of Distinctive Hospitality

For some strange reason, it was the pointy shoes I noticed first when I got off the plane at the airport in Kiev. All the Ukrainian men seemed to be wearing pointy dress shoes, apparently a fashion phenomenon imported from Mother Russia I found out later. I am not sure what my second, third, and fourth conscious impressions were during that trip a few years ago. Starting with the pointy shoes, the rest of my early sensations of Ukraine came to me in an inarticulate rush, like being hit in the face with a splash of cold water.

Whether in distant, exotic Kiev, or visiting a new local restaurant or a person's house for the first time, new places provide opportunities to experience altogether fresh and unique sensations. Rarely do these experiences pass directly through the brain for conscious processing. More times than not, when I experience new places and events, they seem to wash over me as vague impressions. Without consciously thinking, I suppose my mind searches for points of similarity, for familiar places and times I can connect them to. It is the differences in these new experiences, however, that strike me first as most notable.

So it is with entering into places of true Christian hospitality. Displays of authentic Christian community should first and foremost have a distinctive look to them. They should hit us in the face as the product of relationships altogether unique to us as brothers and sisters in Christ. What we share together as Christian communities is absolutely distinctive to ourselves and foreign to others.

This statement is more radical than it might seem at first. What I am claiming here is that nowhere else should hospitality be expressed in the same way as in the midst of the gathered fellowship of believers. Nowhere! Not a wonderful fun-filled neighborhood bar "where everyone knows your name," not in a small town meeting where we might be surrounded by lifelong friends and neighbors, not at the local Kiwanis Club, not in an un-Christian home setting where extended families—as kind and wonderful as they might be—gather yearly around a roaring Christmas fire, and not in an evening book club or game day in front of a big-screen television. Christian hospitality should have its own unique texture.

When we walk into our churches, something altogether different should be displayed. The nature of these distinctions, of course, might not be that apparent at first, particularly for nonbelievers looking in. They may not even immediately observe any differences between what they find around their Christmas trees and bar tables and the hospitality among brothers and sisters in Christ. But given time, the fruits of true Christian fellowship should become apparent. Christian hospitality should be qualitatively and quantitatively different.

What is it that makes Christian hospitality so unique? We have spent most of this book painting the distinctions in broad strokes between friendship and fellowship. Central to our unique Christian fellowship is that it is the only relationship defined in terms of the work of the Spirit. It is the Spirit of God walking in the midst of his people that shapes the church. Where else can we find this claim being made? The Spirit alone makes displays of Christian hospitality altogether separate from all other social and cultural relationships.

The apostle Paul in his letter to the Galatians beautifully lays out the distinct nature of our relationships with one another by speaking of the freedom we are called to share as individuals to "serve one another humbly in love" (Gal. 5:13). What a wonderful description of Christian hospitality: "Serving one another in love!"

The source of this freedom, Paul claims, is through the life of the Spirit and by the power of the Spirit. Undoubtedly thinking of the strife and divisiveness in the church of Galatia, which is the backdrop to his letter, he goes on to say,

> For the entire law is fulfilled in keeping this one command: "Love your neighbor as yourself." If you bite and devour each other, watch out or you will be destroyed by each other.
> So I say, walk by the Spirit, and you will not gratify the desires of the flesh. For the flesh desires what is contrary to the Spirit, and the Spirit what is contrary to the flesh. (Gal. 5:14–17)

The freedom these Galatians have on the positive side (to love one another) and on the negative side (to not devour themselves), says Paul, comes only through the work of the Spirit dwelling within them.

Paul then proceeds to offer two lists of traits that contrast those who live in the flesh (*sarx*) and those who live in the Spirit (*pneuma*). Each list includes conduct that shapes our capacity to live together in relationship with one another. On the one hand, apart from the intervening grace of God in our lives through the Spirit, our default mode in life—and in our relationships—is toward the following: "sexual immorality, impurity and debauchery; idolatry and witchcraft; hatred, discord, jealousy, fits of rage, selfish ambition, dissensions, factions and envy; drunkenness, orgies, and the like" (5:19–21). By contrast, the Spirit offers us fruit to express our lives—and relationships—with "love, joy, peace, fortitude, kindness, goodness, faithfulness, gentleness and self-control" (5:22–23).

Of course, the full measure of the conduct indicated in each of these lists in Galatians 5 is not necessarily on full display at any one time, either by those who live by the flesh or by those who live under the power of the Holy Spirit. God's common grace and the universal consequences of the Fall are revealed in all of our lives and relationships. Consequently, there are many social settings outside the fellowship of believing Christians that are characterized by some measure of joy, patience, and heartfelt kindness. Likewise, not all relationships in the church are pure. Sadly, some manifest displays characteristic of the flesh, including hatred, fits of rage, and discord.

And, regrettably, we all know too well if we have participated in a typical church business meeting that the fellowship we display does not always shimmer with the joy, gentleness, and self-control described in the list of the fruits of the Spirit. On the contrary, all too often our relationships reflect dissensions, factions, and open displays of envy.

But Paul's claim here is that, in the end, it is only the Spirit who gives us freedom both to avoid conduct revealed in the former list and to express conduct manifested in the second list. Could he expect anything else of us? In speaking elsewhere of our lives and relationships, Paul reminds us that we are ultimately and inevitably enslaved to sin.[10] It is only through the Spirit that we can behave in any other way.

Ironically, it is this larger idea of enslavement that uniquely characterizes the hospitality we are to display toward one another as Christians. Not only are we naturally enslaved to sin—again considering Paul's claim "to serve one another humbly in love"—but we are also to serve one another. The word *serve* (*douleute*) has the sense that we are to "become slaves of one another." What a glorious thought: To the extent that our slavery to sin is inevitable and awful, our slavery to one another in our fellowship together is voluntary and wonderful.[11]

Free to be enslaved! Does this even make sense? Yes, but only through the work of the Spirit in our lives. Here is a radical freedom in relationships that does not spring from personal and subjective inclinations or prejudices toward or against others; it is freedom that comes from a Source outside of us. We are free to be completely obligated to one another in ways that are altogether different from any other form of human relationship, because of the Spirit within us.

It is this Spirit of freedom to be a slave to one another that makes our relationships so qualitatively and quantitatively unique. We are free to serve aliens and sojourners with whom we would not otherwise relate. Can you imagine die-hard Republicans and Democrats, even Socialists and Tea-Partiers in the same room together, but instead of debating national or world issues, they happily support one another in a church committee meeting? And the Andys of this world—young Christians—and the Mary Beths—the needy newcomers of the church—are right there in the center of our activities. So, too, individuals who would be considered enemies in any other setting—those who purposefully and persistently malign us—are accepted with great delight into the life of fellowship.

Those looking in from the outside should see completely unnatural forms of hospitality in our life together. They should be struck by how relationally tone deaf we are to social factors that in any other setting would matter—whether socioeconomic, temperamental, political, or ethnic. They should be puzzled by our radical forms of giving as we offer freely to those in need. Imagine giving freely to other persons without any thought of something in return! They should see justice displayed in ways that extend far beyond the mere thresholds offered by present-day jurisprudence. They may not understand, but those from outside our community should at least wonder, maybe even marvel, at the radical, unnatural life we share.

As I make this claim of the distinctive nature of our unnatural community life, however, I realize this emphasis is counterintuitive to certain trends found in our churches today. If we are, indeed, truly a different community of relationships, then this is not what we have tended to reveal. Quite the opposite—we have intentionally sought to be more like the cultural communities around us, not less.

For example, we have sought to make our sanctuaries more familiar to the social settings we might find elsewhere: less cluttered with sacred words and symbols that set us apart, and more relaxed and accommodating to language and decorum that helps us fit in better. Our sermons and worship modes have taken on the more evocative and less provocative character of our culture.

Even the signs outside our sanctuaries often reveal our hesitation to set ourselves apart. Gone now are those intrusive references to denominational affiliations that both clarify our communities as well as set them apart. Gone in some cases are even references to "church," replaced by more amenable, albeit more ambiguous, references to "assembly," "fellowship," "Christian center," and "faith center." There are certainly many good, well-intended reasons behind these efforts to mask the distinctive nature of our life together, but these intentions are built on certain assumptions that may need to be further tested. In an effort to draw the larger community to our doorsteps, we have tried to make ourselves more like them.

Maybe those from the outside are looking for something different—not more of what they already have in other parts of their lives. Maybe sojourners from the outside are looking for an altogether different set of relationships, a new way of seeing life being lived. Maybe the very things that make our life together as Christians so unique are the things for which they are longing, even if they don't fully know it. Consequently, maybe they need to be invited into a world radically different from their own world, a world that may be unfamiliar at first but inviting nevertheless. Maybe it is the "hospitality of difference" that needs to be offered them.

The Touch of Authentic Hospitality

Let us return to the hospitality on Thursday evenings with the book club mentioned earlier. And let us look under the furniture, as it were, and observe what might lie beneath all of the seeming pleasantries of the occasion of that typical evening. What might we see next to those dust bunnies hidden under the furniture?

The poet e. e. cummings (who chose to write his name in lowercase letters) offers us an ironic, biting picture of what lies beneath a similar, seemingly innocuous social occasion. With tongue squarely in cheek, he writes:

> the Cambridge ladies who live in furnished souls
> are unbeautiful and have comfortable minds
> (also, with the church's protestant blessings
> daughters, unscented shapeless spirited)
> they believe in Christ and Longfellow, both dead,
> are invariably interested in so many things—
> at the present writing one still finds
> delighted fingers knitting for the is it Poles?
> perhaps. While permanent faces coyly bandy
> scandal of Mrs. N and Professor D
> . . . . the Cambridge ladies do not care, above
> Cambridge if sometimes in its box of
> Sky lavender and cornerless, the
> moon rattles like a fragment of angry candy.[12]

What a powerful description of a social situation exposed for what it really is, all sophistication and civility on the surface and pettiness and pretense underneath: "shapeless," "comfortable," "coy," "unfurnished," and "unscented" individuals.

Perhaps this description too strongly characterizes the disparities we find in most of our social settings, but you get the point. Like the clothes we choose to put on every morning, so we make our choices based on the occasion. The brand-new sweater with the vertical stripes covers a multitude of sins, be it the new year's crop of fat caused by last year's Christmas feasting, or the unsightly skin blemish you want to hide. The "self" "put on" at the book club or the Sunday afternoon big game is not necessarily the most "authentic self." We wear our public selves like fashion statements that cover up a multitude of ulterior motivations, insecurities, and pretentious gamesmanship.

Of course, there is nothing wrong with wanting to present our best side to others in public. But the scene cummings illustrates reflects a danger we all face when the social contrivances we use when we are with others reach a tipping point, and we no longer recognize what we know to be the true selves we see in the mirror.

Gazing into the mirror, I wonder if the source of this lack of transparency doesn't lead us back to the garden of Eden. Be it at the book club, an afternoon watching the big game, the fellowship hall of our churches, or in our worship services, don't we find ourselves forever standing in some manner next to our original grandparents, naked as jaybirds? We were made to be naked, mind you, just like Adam and Eve; it is actually part of our natural DNA as creatures borne from the very hand of God. But that was before a snake and a piece of fruit entered the scene. After the events of the third chapter of Genesis, we lost our natural right to be unself-consciously naked.[13] (Not even a pledge card to a credible nudist club can offset the shame we now live under.)

But thanks be to God, the rest of the long story of Scripture is all about dealing with our unnatural shame—from the story of Noah, through the narrative of God's covenant promises with Abraham, Moses, David, and with God's chosen people living in exile, wandering in the wilderness, entering the Promised Land, and living under a nation of peace; and then on to the story of God's continuing faithfulness, echoing from the words of the prophets as God's people once again found themselves in exile. This great redemptive story culminates finally at the foot of the cross where all of our shame is ultimately taken on by the Savior.

As the church of Jesus Christ, we are the "community of the cross," undone and then redone by the death and resurrection of Jesus. This should make us a different type of community in every way. Since Jesus has taken care of our shame for good, we can stand freely before one another with a transparency and authenticity not found anywhere else.

The basis of this authenticity can be found in the apostle Paul's first chapter of the first letter to his brothers and sisters in Corinth. As those who "preach Christ crucified," Paul invites these Corinthians to consider the following:

> Brothers and sisters, think of what you were when you were called. Not many of you were wise by human standards; not many were influential; not many were of noble birth. But God chose the foolish things of the world to shame the wise; God chose the weak things of the world to shame the strong. God chose the lowly things of this world and the despised things—and the things that are not—to nullify the things that are, so that no one may boast before him. It is because of him that you are in Christ Jesus, who has become for us wisdom from God—that is, our righteousness, holiness and redemption. Therefore, as it is written: "Let the one who boasts boast in the Lord." (1 Cor. 1:26–31)

Foolish, weak, lowly, despised, "things that are not": this is who we are in Christ. What else do we have to hide of ourselves from one another? We are free to be utterly authentic and transparent because it is these characteristics in ourselves, which we would otherwise choose to hide from others, that are the very things that are to point us to Jesus. It is these things, in fact, that should be the source of our boasting.

Consequently, we should be a community in which our hospitality is marked by this freedom to be wholly honest and transparent, weak and foolish as we might sometimes feel. Surely, there is a place for wanting to reveal our best selves socially, but there are times for various reasons when we cannot. And there are some among us who do not have the natural capacity to do so very well. The hospitality we extend toward one another should be expansive enough—accepting enough—to include us at our worst. Self-conscious, depressed, unemployed, filled with sin, experiencing failure, facing rejection in a hoped-for special relationship—imagine the freedom this brings us as we gather regularly as a community, with the knowledge that we are measured by something or Someone other than ourselves at our worst. What a relief!

This freedom allows us to be truthful in unique ways. Should there be a place for flattery in our life together? Not really, in the sense we see it often displayed elsewhere. Our compliments toward one another should have a ring of authenticity to them. Certainly there should be plenty of room for humor, but even here our lightheartedness toward one another should be measured by how it reveals something of the best side of others rather than the worst. It should be used as a tool to build up and not tear down.

The hospitality we share with one another should even have room for admonishment. Imagine honest correction as an aspect of hospitality. But if we have confidence in one another that the motivation behind all such correction comes from a position of weakness rather than self-aggrandizement, and that it is for the betterment of the other, then admonishment should play a part of our public life together. Above all else, we should see sincerity in one another's eyes. Everything in our social context as brothers and sisters in Christ should have the genuine feel of sincerity and authenticity.

Seeing ourselves for who we are requires that we focus on the right things in understanding ourselves as an authentic community. For a moment, let's consider our current dependency on a partially authenticated, overly generalized social theory used to describe the church. I frequently hear about the phenomenon of Generation theory, in particular as applied to the church. From what I overhear, no longer is it (apparently) enough to just call ourselves Christians, or even human beings for that matter. The current climate now has us increasingly categorized into ever-smaller generational epochs, from Gen X to Millennial and NextGen.

It is not that Generation theory hasn't been a helpful paradigm, even truthful to a point. The simple reality that cultural values shift through time from one generation to the next is so self-evident, it is hard to conceive that it has only been in recent years that the idea has taken root in our social consciousness.

But have we not pulled the thin strands that hold this concept together almost beyond the breaking point as it describes the way our community is constructed? How many church communities have been completely reengineered in recent years on the basis of this concept alone? Worship services and small groups, evangelism, outreach, and teaching ministries—every aspect of church life is filtered through the generational lens. Pastors now look upon their congregations as if they are filled with generational subspecies roaming across the Serengeti. Each subspecies—Gen X, Y, or Z—thinks differently, speaks a different language, and responds to God differently in the most fundamental of ways.[14]

I think one of the most dangerous implications of our over-dependence upon generational theory is that it causes us to focus on the differences in individuals within our churches, at the expense of what unites us together. For example, my twenty-something-year-old son wears his pants a little lower than I do. He uses vocabulary at times that sends me scurrying for further explanation. He enjoys different forms of music. He actually can figure out the technologies that are currently in use. But when we talk about what touches us most intimately, when we speak about God, our family, and our mutual traditions, we are the same species.

Further, we share the same gospel. The things we both look for in Christian community—authenticity, honesty, winsomeness—are the same, exactly the same. Our similarities far outweigh the differences, and the current focus on what makes us so different prevents us—and prevents us as a community of believers—from focusing on what binds us together in Christ. The huge amounts of time spent on fine-tuning our churches into segmented parts has become a grand diversion from what really, really matters. And what really matters—for those inside our community, as well those outside—is that we are a community utterly transparent and fully authentic with one another.

The Sound of Hard Hospitality

We first take away their phones. We take away their phones, and then we take away their access to social media, followed by their access to e-mail and the Internet. We call it a Technology Sabbath. All of their forms of media are gone in a moment, in the twinkling of an eye. You can almost see the scratch marks on these items as we pull them away for thirty long days.

After this, we put them through one month of hard situations in which they, as a group, are required to crawl together over various obstacles. Some of these obstacles are solid and real, even terrifyingly real. They find themselves above the treetops on a high ropes course and dangling on the side of a mountain on a rope climb. Some of the obstacles are less concrete but every bit as real, as they are confronted with theologically rich questions they cannot answer easily. Finally, they are required as a group to confront the discomfort and dissonances of a cross-cultural setting in South America.

For many summers now, I have had the opportunity to observe cohorts of approximately thirty high school students each year in a challenging youth program called Compass. They move from living in a wilderness setting to the classroom, and finally to a missions context. It has been a laboratory of community of sorts for us as we have had the privilege of standing back, year after year, and observing intentional community in the making, where complete strangers are transformed into a lifelong community of brothers and sisters, all in the confines of one month. How long does it take for the awkward glances of a nervous stranger to become heartfelt eye-to-eye acknowledgements of a fellow believer in Jesus Christ? It doesn't take long, when these fellow believers are required to face hard times together.

It also doesn't take long for these young people to express authentic forms of hospitality toward one another. We see it everywhere, from simple words of encouragement to a sister trying to make it up the last twenty feet of the side of a mountain, to their small group conversations as they tell each other their stories, to sitting up all night next to a new friend sickened by unfamiliar food in a foreign land, to the worship they share that is deeply moving and instructive to their souls as brothers and sisters in Christ.

The lesson learned in simple ways is that extending hospitality to one another is not always easy. It is not easy for these young people on a one-month excursion into community building, and it certainly is not easy for us in our churches. Too often we relegate our expressions of hospitality to its entertainment value. Isn't this, in fact, what we point to in our culture when we talk of the "hospitality industry"? We point to entertainment in all its forms. Hospitality and entertainment have become synonyms in our cultural consciousness.

Unfortunately, they have become synonyms in our church lexicon as well.[15] Too often we build our lives together around entertainment. At worst, our times together serve as distractions; we use them like watching a good movie or a baseball game on television where the entertainment value of the experience becomes an end in itself. Too often, hospitality is relegated to self-selected venues where we invite those we feel most comfortable with to share a common experience of mutual gratification. Oftentimes not much is required of us outside of the effort it takes to make a salad or, in the case of a typical men's ministry, pancakes. We like to keep things light and conversational.

There is nothing wrong with any of these forms of entertainment in themselves. However, the danger that entertainment brings to the topic of hospitality is when the entertainment value of our lives together takes over. The various enticements of the forms of entertainment at our disposal can easily serve as a distraction from the hard work required of expressing true hospitality to one another.

Listen closely to the stories in your churches, and you will discover hard choices being made: An unemployed brother trying to keep his credit rating from exploding; the teenager making decisions surrounding new temptations that could impact the rest of her life; the couple whose marriage secretly isn't going all that well; the single sister who is so lonely she can hardly keep herself together; and the elderly woman who needs to decide when to shut off the life support system of her lifelong spouse. If our hospitality only involves entertaining ourselves, then none of these stories will be heard, let alone responded to.

Entering into the life-giving discipline of extending hospitality to these, our fellow aliens and sojourners, is hard and intentional work. It asks something of us, but it doesn't need to be overly dramatic. In fact, hospitality displayed at its best does not draw attention to itself. It sits in the background, inconspicuous but always purposeful. Here are three examples I have observed in my own church context.

The first is of a couple who opens up their home to a huge number of guests every Christmas season. Preparation for the evening is impressive enough with all of the baking, cooking, cleaning, and decorating, but it is not these things that set their hospitality apart. It is their guest list. Their guest list has no logic to it. They fill their house with all manner of individuals from within our church and many from the community. The well-heeled executive who commutes into Boston in his town car is found standing next to the unemployed woman in our church who never seems to get her act together. The socially awkward stands next to the gregarious. The believer may find himself standing next to the nonbeliever. You would think our hosts would be more conscious of the things that otherwise divide us, even as a congregation. But they aren't. For a brief moment, they place us in the same set of rooms, crammed to the rafters, and invite us into the messiness of other people's lives and they into ours.

Similarly, every month you can find two couples in my congregation who invite a different couple or single person to their homes for dinner. Rather than fill their small group with familiar friends and faces from the church, they intentionally open themselves and their homes to people new to them. In so doing, they choose to dedicate the most important time in their social calendar at the church to awkward social moments of getting acquainted with individuals they would not otherwise get to know. As a result, many in our congregation who would not be invited into the lifeblood of our church now at least have an invitation.

Finally, there is a successful businessman in our church who for years has populated our congregation with the Andys of this world. I have no idea where he meets these less fortunate individuals, some of them fresh out of confinement. Given his income level, it doesn't seem likely that this highly prominent person would be anywhere near the social strata of the individuals he brings as guests to our church. But as simple acts of hospitality, he extends himself to these less fortunate, inviting them into his home and his life. As a result, our church has benefited greatly from many of them becoming new fellow brothers in Christ.

A packed Christmas party, a monthly dinner in the lovely dining room of a home, and a simple invitation to a guest—in all three examples, these individuals appear to be about the business of entertaining. At one level I suppose they are but, more circumspectly, they are about the business of exhibiting hospitality to the aliens and sojourners around them. I hasten to say that they do so in the midst of the messiness of their own lives as well. True hospitality doesn't always wait for the ideal moment for its expression. In fact, sometimes the most meaningful time to express hospitality is when it is least convenient, when there is a lump in your throat over facing some type of disappointment or failure, or when you are concerned for your own finances, or in a more immediate sense, when the house is not perfectly clean.

All of this brings us back again to the scene described earlier in the end of the second chapter of the book of Acts (2:42–47). This young upstart church of Jerusalem was finding its way instinctively into what we now understand as the community of believers we call the church. There was no manual, no three-ring notebook; only the work of the Holy Spirit in their midst. Through the Spirit, they taught one another and stood together in awe of the wonders and signs of the Spirit around them. They broke bread, worshipped, and prayed together. And they went about the hard business of extending hospitality to those in need. They appear to have been so busy with the work of the Spirit in their midst that they hardly had time to think about themselves. So it should be for us.

The Smell of Messy Hospitality

The best-dressed girl would get the special wreath with the daisies at the end of the nightly dance. They would then end the day with performing a "symbol of Universal Unity," in which they joined hands in a circle and vowed "truth to the cause of God and Humanity."[16] Just about every night they would do this; the same words spoken with the same earnest idealism of those around the circle.

Thus ended another day at the nineteenth-century Brook Farm experimental community. Started by George Ripley and his wife Sophia in the 1840s in West Roxbury, Massachusetts, Brook Farm was one of many utopian experiments begun at the time, designed to prove in practice that individuals could live in perfect harmony with one another. Hard labor was to be balanced with leisure and play; the working-class man would sit at the same table with the intellectual and artist; women and children would have the same rights as men and adults. The fuel that burned such assumptions into this fledgling little community was Emersonian Transcendentalism mixed liberally with socialist Fourierism. Such notables as Nathaniel Hawthorne, Henry David Thoreau, and Margaret Fuller dipped their toes briefly, if reluctantly, into the Brook Farm experiment.

Libraries are filled with compelling and not so compelling descriptions of utopian experiences like Brook Farm, stretching as far back as Thomas More's *Utopia* and beyond. What might a perfect community look like in real life? Soon after Brook Farm started and failed, Bronson Alcott sought to find out by earnestly living a subsistence agrarian lifestyle at Fruitlands. In like manner, in 1848 the Oneida Colony was started in upstate New York. The Shakers sought a form of simple perfectionism even earlier, and there was something going on in the 1960s that involved "free love."

What is it in the drinking water of these times and places that provokes this utopian impulse to create perfect, highly idealized communities, even up to the present in many modern-day cult experiments? Whatever it is, this impulse does not in the end characterize Christian community. Scripture certainly offers us high standards for our life together. No social theory can compete with Jesus' standard of love that sets the bar of loving others at the love we have for ourselves. None competes with the radical premise that our love should extend even to our enemies; we are to actually pray for those who would do us harm. The apostle Paul's great description on the "unity of the Spirit through the bond of peace" (Eph. 4:3) competes with any philosophical treatise on how humankind is to live a common life.

But even with these high ideas scripted as benchmarks for our life together, the biblical account never leaves us standing at the same front door of wistful utopian idealism as those at Brook Farm, Fruitlands, or the hippy generation. The New Testament ideas of how we should live our lives together are embedded deeply in a narrative reflecting less-than-perfect community. The Gospels and Epistles have as much to say about repentance and forgiveness, about conflict and resolving conflict, as they do about unity and the sweet fruits of *koinonia*. Indeed, take away the problems surrounding the early church—the coming together of the then unthinkable commonwealth of Jew and Gentile communities, the quibbles over how to worship, the more serious theological fights over the nature of Jesus and the Godhead, as it was being fought out in the early period of the church—and we would not, in fact, have the Epistles today. The New Testament leaves us with a complete picture of our life together, sin and all.

Christian community is not utopian in nature. In fact, the hospitality we are called to display among our brothers and sisters in Christ is characterized more like the bedroom of a typical American teenager. Walk by and take a glance, if you dare: T-shirts and blue jeans in relatively the same location from where they were last used, typically on the floor. What isn't actually in the opened dresser drawers is certainly draped elsewhere: sweatshirts, blouses, underwear, socks, flip-flops. Old CDs, unused textbooks, miscellaneous old movie and concert stubs, and dirty dishes complete the picture. If the universe is a place of harmony, don't look here for evidence of it.

So it is with our churches. Living in Christian community is messy business. Pastors know this best of all. If they allow their minds to wander as they stand up in front of their congregations on Sundays, they will see the woman in the choir whose life matches her voice. Her current situation is filled with disharmony, reflected in everything from the demise of her marriage, to the alienation she feels from her daughter, to her inability to make friends. *Who in the church is she going to have Christmas with this year?* And there is the unemployed young man who lives in what the poet has so aptly called "quiet desperation," even as he hears again the hope found in the gospel lesson for the day. *Do these words mean anything to him in a way that would settle the lump in his throat?* And there they are again this Sunday, two families sitting on opposite sides of the sanctuary because of some perceived slight from two months back. *How in the world can these people be so petty?* The people in our churches are hanging out of drawers everywhere, laying helter-skelter on the floor, sometimes hardly able to pick themselves up from where they last fell.

It is to these people that Christian hospitality is to be administered. More amazingly, it is *from* these people that hospitality is to be offered. How does this happen? How can community happen in the midst of the brokenness of our lives?

It begins first with a clear acknowledgement of our condition, which starts with admitting our brokenness as individuals. Pull back the brittle veneer surrounding our lives and we quickly find we are not all that put together. Even when we are on our best behavior, our motives for doing good end up being self-serving. Our best desires quickly get sidetracked toward wrong ends. Our public lives often cover up parallel universes of private ruminations and activities. We live with failure, misgivings, and feelings of inadequacy.

If this is who we are as individuals, we can only imagine what we are as a community. Multiply our own brokenness a thousandfold, then layer that messiness with multiple levels of relationships, and we find congregations filled with relationships characterized by false motives, unclear intentions, confused communication, and quiet sadness. It should not come as a surprise to any of us that we enter into relationships with our brothers and sisters in Christ already compromised.

Then why sometimes are we so unforgiving of one another? Why do we expect more of the aliens and sojourners we sit next to than we do ourselves? Not only do we not accept and love our brothers and sisters in the midst of their temptations and sin, but more destructively sometimes, we don't seem able to see beyond their own honest limitations, whether related to personality, fractured background, or temperament.

But is it not this very awareness of our own vulnerabilities and limitations that makes our lives together so wonderfully attractive and satisfying? Healthy congregations understand themselves for who they are. Rather than being driven by a false sense of altruism, they see themselves as communities of fallen individuals not that different from those outside their walls, except for the grace of God they share together. As a result, they are willing to be open continuously to the forces of inconvenience, acts of repentance and forgiveness, and ultimately the desperate need for the hope of a Savior.

One of my all-time favorite images from the vast storehouses of wisdom provided by Garrison Keillor in his radio show, *Prairie Home Companion*, as I can recall it, can be reduced to a single two-minute moment when a young Garrison, resisting all impulse to do otherwise, threw an overly ripe tomato toward his older sister, who just happened to be bending over looking south. The overly juicy tomato came in low and hard from the north and hit her squarely on the part of the anatomy where one normally sits. Can you hear the wonderful, big, juicy splat of that tomato?[17]

Putting aside the deviance of an adolescent boy, this is what we need to hear more in our churches: more splattering. We need to see and accept ourselves more in the context of the messiness of our lives. I realize this runs contrary to some of the efficiencies and professionalism many of us like to bring to doing church life, but we are not tidy people. Nor do we serve tidy people. In building our lives together—programmatically, institutionally, socially—should we not be more attentive to the actual condition of our lives outside of our gathered community? In our planning, should we not be attentive to the dangers of forcing square individuals into round holes?

Sometimes expressing hospitality to one another abhors the neatness we want to give it. We hesitate extending ourselves, hoping for the "ideal time" to invite someone into our lives, not realizing that sometimes the less-than-ideal time is actually the absolute right time. Sometimes we are so concerned about chipping our fine china that we don't extend hospitality even on paper plates. And on a more programmatic level, sometimes we have become so scripted that we have wrung all the spontaneity out of our life together.

Finally, the brokenness and messiness of the relationships within our communities should also be manifest institutionally and in the way we display leadership in our churches. There is currently a presumption that is so naturally a part of our thinking in our churches that to think otherwise almost seems irresponsible. Here it is: A big God requires that we think big. Perhaps the reason our churches aren't thriving is because we haven't thought big enough? Right?

So we set big goals for ourselves as communities: BHAG—Big Hairy Audacious Goals—is the current battle cry from a couple of years ago. Big Hairy Audacious Goals for prayer: It's not enough for a few people to pray. Imagine what God could do if thousands of people prayed for the same thing at the same time, preferably at the same place. Big Hairy Audacious Goals for evangelism: Pick a number, any number; how many can we save for Christ? Big Audacious Hairy Goals for missions: How can we strategize campaigns that would encompass whole countries, even entire continents? Big Hairy Audacious Goals for churches: Big churches require big programs and big budgets designed to bulge our imaginations. *We receive not because we ask not.*

To drive these goals, we, of course, need a vision. A neighborhood corner store kind of vision will not do. We need a megastore, Walmart/ Home Depot kind of vision. We need an expansive vision, a great vision that matches the bigness of God. Dare I say, to truly honor God, we need a vision that explores the very frontiers of God's providence in our lives. *"If there is no vision, the people perish."*

And, of course, a big vision requires a certain type of leader. Big, thick, deep voices are required not only to think and articulate big, deep, expansive thoughts, but also to provide the will to see these mega-visions through to their end. Leaders need to be out front—way out in front—of their organizations, calling their people to the kind of obedience required to fulfill these big visions. We need more big daydreamers, daydreamers for God's glory.

In the midst of all of this mega-vision casting we hear a thin small voice: "God hates visionary dreaming." Come again? A wisp of a voice it is—indeed, almost inaudible. Have we heard this right? The logic of the words runs so counter to the current orthodoxy of obedience. There it is again: "God hates visionary dreaming."

Allow me to put the words into context. In *Life Together*, Dietrich Bonhoeffer writes

> God hates visionary dreaming; it makes the dreamer proud and pretentious. The man who fashions a visionary ideal of community demands that it be realized by God, by others, and by himself. He enters the community of Christians with his demands, sets up his own law, and judges the brethren and God Himself accordingly. He stands adamant, a living reproach to all others in the circle of brethren. He acts as if he is the creator of the Christian community, as if his dream binds men together. When things do not go his way, he calls the effort a failure. When his ideal picture is destroyed, he sees the community going to smash. So he becomes first an accuser of his brethren, then an accuser of God, and finally the despairing accuser of himself.[18]

Bonhoeffer's creaky, sixty-plus-year-old words about Christian community fall like a thud on the current evangelical landscape. They just do not add up in our current economics of obedience. The words sound downright counterintuitive to what we know of the way God works in our lives and expects of us. But are they wrong?

Perhaps Bonhoeffer's words expose a growing theological presumption on our part, a presumption driven by a deficient understanding of who God is in the economy of his design for his world. As well intended as our big designs are on behalf of God and his kingdom, are they not sometimes tainted ever so lightly with our own hubris? Does God need us to fulfill his kingdom here on earth? Certainly. By an act of his grace, he has providentially written us into his grand redemptive story. But does he really need us in the ways we often think he does? I sometimes think that if God were somehow written out of the big plans we have for him in fulfilling his kingdom, it would take an uncomfortable amount of time for us to realize his absence. At the end of the day, our grand designs for God are wonderfully expendable.

Maybe the net effect of our well-intended pandering for doing great things for God is that our big goals, big visions, and big plans sometimes overshadow the hard work of obedience. Cast our eyes back to the narrative of Scripture and church history. What is the pattern we see? Do we really see the great imprint of God's work in redemptive history as the product of well-conceived, humanly orchestrated BHAG plans? Not really. More times than not, God's story is one of steadfast, obedient people being caught up and transformed by a divine plan that extends far beyond their own best intensions. It may be that God's work is periodically manifested in dramatic fashion. More often than not, however, the work of God is an exercise in plain, hard obedience.

Bonhoeffer's words are mostly directed toward church leaders. Leadership is a delicate thing, isn't it? Looking across the life of the church today, don't we see enough examples of leadership blinded by ambition falsely camouflaged as faithfulness? This is not to say that Christian leaders with big, deep visions aren't sincere, but isn't this the point? Sincerity is a dangerous gatekeeper to what is truthful and right. Our hearts are vulnerable to our own self-deceptive ways.

What is the antidote to this self-deception for those of us in leadership roles in the church? Contrary to what we would guess looking at the rows of books on leadership located at our local bookstores, the New Testament speaks very little about being a good leader. There isn't much biblical evidence for the need for big, visionary dreamers. The clarion call of the Gospels is all about being good followers. This is what Jesus asks of us: to be humble dreamers with enough sense to follow him.

All this to say, our life together as brothers and sisters in Christ, both interpersonally and institutionally, is far less predictable and far more complex than we often understand it to be. It resists the controls we frequently want to put on it. People live messy lives, and churches should bear some of that messiness with them. I leave it to you to decide what this might look like in your church.

The Taste of Compelling Hospitality

I love cooking shows on television. There, I said it. I don't know why, except there is something about a master chef putting just the right amount of butter into a sauté pan, and then adding the precise amount of chopped onion and—can you believe it?—cinnamon and basil leaves together to make a simple glaze in such and such a recipe. Oh, and don't forget the pinch of sea salt. All this effort ends in layers of nuanced taste designed to stimulate a three-centimeter flap of real estate we call the tongue.

To be honest, most of the layers of taste are wasted on us hungry souls. Many of us don't have the capacity or the patience to drill down through the layers of taste to appreciate the dishes we eat for their true value. It is a little bit like a friend of mine who brings a clean and experienced pallet to his wine tasting. I don't know how he does it, but he can smell, sip, and observe a vintage and tell the degree of pressure the grape was crushed under during such and such week of August of a certain year, grown on the south side—the sunny side—of a certain area of the south of France in a particular type of soil. For me, the wine is purple and wet. For him, it is musty and bruised.

Finally, there is something deeply compelling about the taste of Christian hospitality. I have already alluded a few times to my involvement at the L'Abri community many years ago in Huemoz, Switzerland. I do so here again, although L'Abri for me was by no means an ideal community. In fact, like many through the years, I found the community quite cold to the touch. In contrast to the familiarity to which we are accustomed, many have found it austere and quite unfriendly, at least initially.

Nevertheless, the hospitality displayed there had a significant impact upon me personally. In hindsight, in drilling down through the nuanced layers of the experience over the years, what I found so compelling was the community's seemingly naive openness to almost anyone who stood at the doorstep of one of its chalets. Everyone was welcome: strident fundamentalist, the "Cosmic Muffin" who offered nothing more than a far-off smile, the wandering troubadour who came with neither a purpose nor the money to pay for his seemingly meaningless reason for being there, the hot-headed arguer who had a chip on his shoulder as large as the granite boulders around him, the evangelical sightseer, and the confused seeker searching for something she could sense but hardly comprehend.

Here was a community that extended an invitation to everyone, an invitation that was genuinely open to whatever drew these sojourners there. It was an invitation that met each traveler somehow at the point of his or her longing, as clear or unclear as that inner impulse was to its bearer. There is something deeply inviting about a community shaped by yearning, but what is it?

Perhaps I am overreaching by connecting the impulses of those who showed up at the front door of L'Abri to what C. S. Lewis made of the German concept of *Sehsucht*, "yearning" or "craving"—what he eventually called inconsolable longing in the human heart for what is not easily known, "immortal longing."[19] There is in all of us, says Lewis, a source of longing that can hardly be put into words:

> In speaking of this desire for our own far-off country, which we find in ourselves even now, I feel a certain shyness. I am almost committing an indecency. I am trying to rip open the inconsolable secret in each one of you—the secret which hurts so much that you take your revenge on it by calling it names like Nostalgia and Romanticism and Adolescence; the secret also which pierces

with such sweetness that when, in very intimate conversation, the mention of it becomes imminent, we grow awkward and affect to laugh at ourselves; the secret we cannot hide and cannot tell, though we desire to do both.[20]

It is this yearning for something in all of us—a yearning so deeply embedded we find it hard to express in words—that brought many of these individuals to the side of a mountain in Switzerland.

If we are honest, this same longing rests in all of us, even if hidden deep under layers of other forms of yearning—some of them misplaced and misdirected; others more positive but buried in the monotony of everyday life. Born of both suffering and its opposite, this supreme sense of longing is bittersweet to the tongue. It at once satisfies us and leaves us craving for more.

Shouldn't the hospitality we display toward one another in Christian community be that of longing? Or more to the point, shouldn't our hospitality display opportunities for us to explore the longings of our own hearts while exploring the longings of others as well? After all, we are a community made for eternity, and there is part of eternity built into us even now. On this, I appreciate what St. Therese de Lisieux says in her autobiography:

> Let me suppose that I had been born in a land of thick fogs, and had never seen the beauties of nature, or a single ray of sunshine, although I had heard of these wonders from my early youth, and knew that the country wherein I dwelt was not my real home—there was another land, unto which I should always look forward. . . . From the time of my childhood I felt that one day I should be set free from this land of darkness. I believed it, not only because I had been told so by others, but my heart's most secret and deepest longings assured me that there was in store for me another and more beautiful country—an abiding dwelling place. I was like Christopher Columbus, where genius anticipated the discovery of the New World. And suddenly the mists about me have penetrated my very soul and have enveloped me so completely that I cannot even picture to myself this promised land . . . all has faded away.[21]

We truly are all aliens and sojourners, caught betwixt and between lives lived together now and lives promised for us together in the future.

There is, indeed, something deeply compelling about interacting with others at the depth of the longings of their hearts. To explore with others the headwaters of their personal yearnings, to drill down deep through layers of what we, together, long for and explore the depths of what God has for us, to discover together what God's word has to say about what we are to yearn for, to lovingly admonish when competing and false yearnings take over, to wait patiently and expectantly for what we will become in the future, while living together responsibly in the present—these are not mere romantic notions but biblically grounded impulses that lie at the heart of Christian community. The hospitality we extend to one another ultimately is our invitation to enter into the shared longings of our hearts as a community, longings that bear the marks of this world and the next.

What is the evidence that this is happening in our churches? It is a small thing, but watch what happens after the formal program of your church ends, when there is no longer a good reason to be together in the building. Communities where brothers and sisters are truly in fellowship with one another are "lingering churches." They are churches where one persistently finds people lingering everywhere, scattered about, not yet ready to "go home." In some ways, they already see themselves at home. They are scattered about in the aisles of the sanctuary or on folding chairs in the fellowship hall. Their agenda is not that of the church program, but it is the agenda of the longings they share with one another.

Second, churches that display hospitality well are communities that value it highly as a gift they can give to one another. I was especially reminded of this many years ago when, as a young couple, Cec and I first started attending a church that offered itself to us like no other church has from that day to the present. From the moment we walked in on the first Sunday, there were people who purposefully extended themselves to us in a way that made it easy for us to make that church our home.

It probably took us three months to realize that what made this church so hospitable was actually the product of two people—let's call them Mr. Peterson and Mrs. Samuelson. Every Sunday we were greeted, but not with five or ten or twenty people as it felt. It was these same two individuals who extended themselves with warmth and genuine grace every Sunday. Their hospitality had the face of the entire congregation on it.

Their hospitality served as an example to us. Not everyone has the natural, inbred gift of gregariousness in their bones that lends itself to overt expressions of hospitality. However, every church that truly extends itself in hospitality acknowledges those who do have these gifts in their midst. They honor these individuals and their gifts, and they set them free to express them in ways that make their churches enormously compelling places.

Finally, what makes these kinds of communities so compelling to those nonbelievers looking in from the outside? When asked to describe my experience as a member of the community at L'Abri, I invariably say it was the kind of place where it took three months for me to realize how theologically narrow they were. Supremely open to any person and conversation on the front end, the community never gave up anything it stood for on the back. Open expressions of hospitality and commitment to biblical and theological principles are not mutually exclusive.

But sometimes biblical and theological truth is best simmered slowly on the back burner as a set of authentic questions that lead those at the front doors of our churches in time to the profound truths of the gospel. As I found at L'Abri, the yearnings in the hearts of those who showed up at its doorstep either drew them to the biblical truths of the gospel or, in the end, drew them away.[22] But it was the Spirit who did this work, not something forced or manipulated. There is something wonderfully inviting about this confidence in the work of the Spirit in the lives of those who desperately need to hear the gospel message. Churches with a compelling message have big front doors that allow longing hearts to enter gradually into the narrow road of the kingdom of God within.

Experiencing Hospitality

Let us approach the idea of hospitality using the five human senses. The hospitality we extend to one another as brothers and sisters in Christ should have a *unique look* to it. The Christian community we share together is unlike any other. Further, it should have the *touch of authenticity*. The freedom the gospel offers us allows us to be fully transparent and honest with one another. It should *ring with the sounds* of not just the good things in our lives but the *hard and difficult things as well*. It should *smell of the messiness* around us. We live in a broken-down world, and we all bear some of that brokenness. Finally, there is something in our life together that should be deeply compelling. It should *taste of something sweet* of this world and the next.

I am sure there is more that can be said about Christian hospitality. Regrettably, there are only five senses we know of, and I have run the length and depth of my metaphor. But the larger point is that the experience of extending and receiving hospitality goes well beyond our reasoning of it. Our expressions of hospitality are meant to capture our hearts and imaginations, not just our thought processes. And any discussion of it is meant not so much to elicit a plan to follow as to evoke an impulse within us that requires our response. We are meant to engage in hospitality, not just talk about it. Indeed, there has been far too much talk surrounding the topic of the meaning of Christian community and not enough action.

How are we to experience hospitality in our churches? I close with three simple admonitions:

First, particularly for you practitioners in ministry, anchor yourselves in a clearly thought out set of working definitions of what you mean by friendship and what you consider to be "Christian community" in your context. To do otherwise sets you adrift on the high seas of emotionalism. This is the hazard of any discussion about relationships, especially subjectively charged informal relationships. By nature, their habitat is oceans of mush, and unless you set sound bearings for yourself that point you toward solid ground, you will find yourself drifting aimlessly.

Of the topic of friendship, I am especially grateful for the opportunity to focus for a time on an area of life that often is such a part of the common woodwork of our lives that we can lose sight of it. The classical writers on the subject have it right when they talk about friendship as central to the very meaning of life itself. As I seek for clarity on the subject here, it is the faces of my own friends that have made the topic come so alive for me. I may not have written of them by name, but if they look deep between the lines of this book, they will find themselves right here on the page, in black and white.

Of the topic of Christian community specifically, I am reminded of a *Far Side* cartoon in which the master is saying to his dog (what cartoonist Gary Larson titles, "What we say to dogs"), "Okay, Ginger! I've had it! You stay out of the garbage! Understand, Ginger? Stay out of the garbage or else!" The bubble over the head of the dog (titled "What they hear"), however, tells the real story of the conversation. What the dog is hearing of the seemingly clear message of his master is "blah blah GINGER blah blah blah blah GINGER blah blah blah . . ." When I hear much of the talk about Christian community that surrounds me, I can only add an additional "blah . . . blah . . . blah . . . blah . . . blah." I don't know what it all means. Such talk demands a clear set of definitions.

Second, our understanding of God's great gift of shared community needs to be anchored more specifically in Scripture. We are above all else people of the word. All we need to understand our common life together is clearly laid out for us in the Bible, both descriptively and prescriptively. It describes for us in rich detail the story of God's people marching through the events of the Old Testament into the New. It describes with clarity the teachings of Jesus' great kingdom of heaven here on earth in the gospel story. And it describes for us the story of his great church, from its dramatic beginnings at Pentecost to its culmination in the age to come. Further, it is prescriptive in that it offers in fine detail all that is required of us to live faithfully before God and with one another.

Finally, who we are as a community of God's people matters more now than ever in today's world. I didn't need to wait to the very end to remind us of the obvious: the Christian faith we find currently expressed in the Western church has become dangerously privatized. If they were alive today, the New Testament writers would be appalled by the way we in the church in the West have driven the rich truths of the gospel message they so carefully laid down for us into the narrow culs-de-sac of our own personalized faith. Now more than ever we need to grow in our understanding of the saving work of God's grace in the context of our lives together as a community of believers and not just in terms of our personal relationships with Jesus.

Our life together as the church should matter to us because it matters to God. We are his bride (Eph. 5:25), his very body (Eph. 5:30), his own people (1 Pet. 2:9–10), his new creation (2 Cor. 5:17), his building (1 Cor. 3:9), his temple (2 Cor. 6:16), designed to be the salt of the earth (Matt. 5:13), and a letter written on hearts "known and read by everyone" (2 Cor. 3:2–3). These are only a few of his descriptions of us, plural. We should act accordingly—accordingly in terms of our faithfulness to him in return for the grace he so richly bestowed on us, and in terms of our faithfulness to the community of grace to which he has called us.

Further, the church should matter to us because it matters to a dying world. The world may not clearly see it this way. More times than not we may be the object of its curiosity, even at times the object of its ridicule. But we are God's people, the living embodiment of his saving grace in this dying world. If we are known for anything, I trust it is that we are known by our genuine love for one another. It is this, our compelling commitment to one another as his body, that more than anything will make the difference to a world so desperately in need.

BIBLIOGRAPHY

Aelred of Rievaulx. *Spiritual Friendship*. Translated by Mary Eugenia Laker. Washington, D.C.: Consortium Press, 1974.

Alexander, T. Desmond, et al., eds. *New Dictionary of Biblical Theology*. Downers Grove, IL: InterVarsity Press, 2000.

Aristotle. *The Nicomachean Ethics*. Translated by H. Rackham. Cambridge, MA: Harvard University Press, 1926.

Augustine. *The Confessions of St. Augustine*. Translated by John Ryan. Garden City, NY: Image Books, 1960.

Bacon, Francis. *Essays, Civil, and Moral and the New Atlantis*. Vol. 3 of Harvard Classics. New York: P. F. Collier and Son, 1909.

Banks, Robert. *Paul's Idea of Community: The Early House Churches in Their Historical Setting*. Grand Rapids, MI: Eerdmans, 1980.

Barna, George. "Survey Explores Who Qualifies as an Evangelical." In *The Barna Update*. January 18, 2007. http://www.generousgiving.org.

Barr, William R., and Rena M. Yocom, eds. *The Church in the Movement of the Spirit*. Grand Rapids, MI: Eerdmans, 1994.

Barton, S. C. "Hospitality." In *Dictionary of the Later New Testament and Its Developments*. Edited by Ralph P. Martin and Peter H. Davids. Downers Grove, IL: InterVarsity, 1997.

Bell, Julian. "The Samaritan Concept of Befriending." *British Journal of Social Work* 5, no. 4 (Winter 1975): 414–21.

Berger, Peter. *Sacred Canopy: Elements of a Sociological Theory of Religion*. Garden City, NY: Anchor Books, 1969.

Berkeley, George. "Friendship and Benevolence." In *Periodical Essays of the Eighteenth Century*. Edited by George Carver. Garden City, NY: Doubleday, Doran & Company, 1970.

Blue, Ron, with Jodie Berndt. *Generous Living: Finding Contentment through Giving*. Grand Rapids, MI: Zondervan, 1997.

Bonhoeffer, Dietrich. *Life Together: A Discussion of Christian Fellowship*. Translated by John Doberstein. New York: Harper and Row, 1954.

Brown, Colin, ed. *The New International Dictionary of New Testament Theology*. Vols. 1–2. Grand Rapids, MI: Zondervan, 1967.

Cicero. *Letters of Marcus Tullius Cicero with His Treatises on Friendship and Old Age.* Translated by E. S. Shuckburgh. Vol. 9 of Harvard Classics. New York: P. F. Collier and Son, 1909.

Connell, Jack. "Ministry Mulligans." *Leadership* (Winter 2011): 89.

Cummings, E. E. "[the Cambridge ladies who live in furnished souls]." *The Norton Anthology of Modern Poetry.* 2nd ed. New York: W. W. Norton and Company, 1973.

De Sales, Frances. *Introduction to the Devout Life.* Translated by Michael Day. London: J. M. Dent and Sons, 1961.

Dunn, James D. G. *Jesus and the Spirit: A Study of the Religious Charismatic Experience of Jesus and the First Christians as Reflected in the New Testament.* Philadelphia: Westminster Press, 1975.

Emerson, Ralph Waldo. *Essays First Series. The Complete Works of Ralph Waldo Emerson.* Vol. 2. Boston: Houghton Mifflin Company, 1865.

Eskridge, Larry. *Defining Evangelicalism.* Wheaton, IL: Institute for the Study of American Evangelicals. n.d.

Fee, Gordon. *1 and 2 Timothy, Titus.* New International Biblical Commentary. Peabody, MA: Hendrickson, 1984, 1988.

———. *Paul, the Spirit, and the People of God.* Peabody, MA: Hendrickson, 1996.

Felton, Todd R. *A Journey into the Transcendentalists' New England.* Berkeley, CA: Roaring Forties Press, 2006.

Gaebelein, Frank E., ed. *Romans, I Corinthians, II Corinthians, Galatians.* The Expositor's Bible Commentary. Vol. 10. Grand Rapids, MI: Zondervan, 1976.

Gager, John G. *Kingdom and Community: The Social World of Early Christianity.* Englewood Cliffs, NJ: Prentice-Hall, 1975.

Gish, Arthur G. *Living in Christian Community.* Eugene, OR: Wipf & Stock, 1998.

Godwin, William. *Thoughts on Man: His Nature, Productions, and Discoveries.* London: Effingham Wilson, Royal Exchange, 1831.

Gottman, John M., and Jeffrey G. Parker, eds. *Conversations of Friends: Speculations on Affective Development.* Cambridge: Cambridge University Press, 1986.

Harrison, Everett F. *Interpreting Acts.* Grand Rapids, MI: Zondervan, 1975.

Hawthorne, Gerald F., and Ralph P. Martin, eds. *Dictionary of Paul and His Letters.* Downers Grove, IL: InterVarsity Press, 1993.

Helvetius, C. A. "Of Friendship." In *De L'spirit or Essays on the Mind.* Albion Press, 1810.

Hipps, Shane. *Flickering Pixels: How Technology Shapes Your Faith.* Grand Rapids, MI: Zondervan, 2009.

Hunter, James Davidson. *To Change the World: The Irony, Tragedy, and Possibility of Christianity in the Late Modern World*. Oxford: Oxford University Press, 2010.

Joseph, Abbot. "The First Conference of Abbot Joseph." Vol. X. A Select Library of Nicene and Post-Nicene Fathers of The Christian Church. 2nd ser. New York: The Christian Literature Company, 1894.

Kant, Immanuel. "Friendship." In *Immanuel Kant: Lectures on Ethics*. Translated by Louis Infield. New York: Harper and Row, 1930.

Keener, Craig S. *The IVP Bible Background Commentary: New Testament*. Downers Grove, IL: InterVarsity Press, 1993.

Kittel, Gerhard. *Bible Key Words: Love, The Church, Sin, Righteousness*. Translated by J. R. Coates. New York: Harper and Brothers, 1951.

Kurth, Suzanne B. "Friendships and Friendly Relations." In *Social Relationships*. Edited by George J. McCall. Chicago: Aldine, 1970.

Lewis, C. S. *The Four Loves*. San Diego: A Harvest Book, 1960.

———. *The Pilgrim's Regress: An Allegorical Apology for Christianity Reason and Romanticism*. London: Geoffrey Bles, 1956.

———. *The Weight of Glory*. Grand Rapids, MI: Eerdmans, 1949.

Leyton, Elliott, ed. *The Compact: Selected Dimensions of Friendship*. University of Newfoundland: Institute of Social and Economic Research, Newfoundland Social and Economic Papers, no. 3 (1975).

Linton, E. Lynn. "The Ethics of Friendship." In *The Universal Review*. Edited by Harry Quilter. London: Swan Sonnenschein and Co., 1889.

Lofland, John, and Rodney Stark. "Becoming a World-Saver: A Theory of Conversion to a Deviant Perspective." *American Sociological Review* 30 (1965): 863–74.

MacDonald, Gordon. *Who Stole My Church?* Nashville: Thomas Nelson, 2007.

Maxwell, Herbert. "The Conduct of Friendship." In *The Eclectic Magazine of Foreign Literature*. New York: E. R. Pelton, 1893.

Meilaneder, Gilbert. *Friendship: A Study in Theological Ethics*. Notre Dame, IN: University of Notre Dame Press, 1981.

Metaxas, Eric. *Bonhoeffer: Pastor, Martyr, Prophet, Spy*. Nashville: Thomas Nelson, 2010.

Minear, Paul S. *Images of the Church in the New Testament*. Philadelphia: The Westminster Press, 1960.

Montaigne, Michel de. "Of Friendship." In *Montaigne: Selected Essays*. Edited by Blanchard Bates. New York: The Modern Library, 1949.

Niebuhr, H. Richard. *Christ and Culture*. New York: Harper Colophon Books, 1951.

Ridderbos, Herman. *The Coming of the Kingdom*. Philadelphia: The Presbyterian and Reformed Publishing Company, 1962.

Social Investment Forum. *2003 Report on Socially Responsible Investing Trends in the United States*. Washington, D.C., 2003.

Stott, John. *God's New Society: The Message of Ephesians*. Downers Grove, IL: InterVarsity Press, 1979.

———. *The Living Church: Convictions of a Lifelong Pastor*. Downers Grove, IL: InterVarsity Press, 2007.

———. *The Spirit, the Church, and the Word: The Message of Acts*. Downers Grove, IL: InterVarsity Press, 1990.

Streamer, Volney. *What Makes a Friend?* New York: Prentano's, 1892.

Taylor, Jeremy. "The Measures and Offices of Friendship." In *The Whole Works of the Right Rev. Jeremy Taylor, D.D*. Vol. 3. London: Reeves and Turner, 1880.

Therese of Lisieux. *Autobiography of St. Therese of Lisieux*. New York: P. J. Kenedy and Sons, 1958.

Thoreau, Henry David. "A Week on the Concord and Merrimack Rivers." In *Walden and Other Writings*. Edited by Brooks Atkinson. New York: The Modern Library, 1937.

Tilberg, Cedric W. *Revolution Underway: An Aging Church in an Aging Society*. Minneapolis: Fortress Press, 1984.

Weber, Max. *Economy and Society*. Edited by Guenther Roth and Claus Wittich. Vol. 2. Berkeley: University of California, 1968.

———. *Methodology of the Social Sciences*. New York: Free Press, 1949.

Wells, David F. *Above All Earthly Pow'rs: Christ in a Postmodern World*. Grand Rapids, MI: Eerdmans, 2005.

———. *The Courage to Be Protestant: Truth Lovers, Marketers, and Emergents in the Postmodern World*. Grand Rapids, MI: Eerdmans, 2008.

———. *Losing Our Virtue: Why the Church Must Recover Its Moral Vision*. Grand Rapids, MI: Eerdmans, 1999.

———. *No Place for Truth: Or Whatever Happened to Evangelical Theology*. Grand Rapids, MI: Eerdmans, 1993.

Wenk, Matthias. *Community—Forming Power: Socio-Ethical Role of the Spirit in Luke-Acts*. Sheffield, UK: Sheffield Academic Press, 2000.

World Christian Database. Center for the Study of Global Christianity. Gordon-Conwell Theological Seminary. Accessed May 3, 2011.

Wright, N. T. "The Holy Spirit in the Church." Paper presented at Inciting Insight: The Holy Spirit Fulcrum Conference, Islington, April 29, 2005.

NOTES

Preface

1. In particular, I commend to you the works of my colleague, David Wells, whose critique of the contemporary evangelical church has been of enormous help to most and a minor annoyance to a few. His trilogy of books, plus one, describes a church that has given itself over to sound business practices and marketing, often at the expense of Scripture and theology. His four books include: *No Place for Truth: Or Whatever Happened to Evangelical Theology, Losing Our Virtue: Why the Church Must Recover Its Moral Vision, Above All Earthly Pow'rs: Christ in a Postmodern World,* and *The Courage to Be Protestant: Truth Lovers, Marketers, and Emergents in the Postmodern World.*

2. Throughout the length and breadth of this book, I will be using this otherwise oft imprecisely used term "community" to describe a specific type of relationship that exists uniquely within the Christian church. I use the term many times in contrast to other forms of human relationships, notably, "friendship." Other synonyms will be used to identify the same relational phenomenon throughout the book, including "fellowship," "body of Christ," "fellowship of believers," "community of Christ," "church of Jesus Christ," and in the last chapter, "Christian hospitality." Each of these terms is intended to describe the same relationship type.

3. Max Weber says, "My use of ideal types are indispensable for heuristic as well as expository purposes." As such, ideal types are not descriptive of reality, but are conceptual ideas that give unambiguous expression to such a description. To identify a type having certain characteristics gives an orientation with a continuum of social action. These types are reflective as much of the interests and prior commitments of the observer as they are of the actual data. *Methodology of the Social Sciences* (New York: Free Press, 1949), 90.

4. Michel de Montaigne, "Of Friendship," in *Montaigne: Selected Essays*, ed. Blanchard Bates (New York: The Modern Library, 1949), 69.

Chapter 1

1. The best example of this type of conversion theory is Lofland and Stark's world-saver model. Their world-saver model first emphasized the importance of social relations to recruitment of individuals to cults. Becoming a convert, according to Lofland and Stark, is "coming to accept the opinions of one's friends" as the first of many conditions that influence converts to change their religious commitments. The fundamental assumption of this sociological theory centers on the basic appeal residing within all individuals to meet the need for emotional

attachments. Although rooted in the internal structure of individuals, this strong emotional arousal for relationship is not sufficient for change to occur. The impulse to actually make religious changes is manifest only when triggered from outside influences, when strong enduring interpersonal relationships surround the convert. John Lofland and Rodney Stark, "Becoming a World-Saver: A Theory of Conversion to a Deviant Perspective," *American Sociological Review* 30 (1965): 863–74.

Chapter 2

1. See http://www.experiencefriendship.com/about/2015.

2. C. S. Lewis, *The Four Loves* (San Diego: A Harvest Book, 1960), 58.

3. Aristotle, *The Nicomachean Ethics*, trans. H. Rackham (Cambridge, MA: Harvard University Press, 1926), 451.

4. Cicero, *Letters of Marcus Tullius Cicero with His Treatises on Friendship and Old Age*, trans. E. S. Shuckburgh, vol. 9, Harvard Classics (New York: P. F. Collier and Son, 1909), 44.

5. Ibid., 25.

6. Augustine, *The Confessions of St. Augustine*, trans. John Ryan (Garden City, NY: Image Books, 1960), 100.

7. Montaigne, "Of Friendship," 69.

8. Francis Bacon, *Essays, Civil, and Moral and the New Atlantis*, vol. 3, Harvard Classics (New York: P. F. Collier and Son, 1909), 69.

9. Aelred of Rievaulx, *Spiritual Friendship*, trans. Mary Eugenia Laker (Washington, DC: Consortium Press, 1974), 65.

10. Ibid., 53.

11. Frances de Sales, *Introduction to the Devout Life*, trans. Michael Day (London: J. M. Dent and Sons, 1961), 143.

12. Jeremy Taylor, "The Measures and Offices of Friendship," in *The Whole Works of the Right Rev. Jeremy Taylor, D.D.*, vol. 3 (London: Reeves and Turner, 1880), 32.

13. George Berkeley, "Friendship and Benevolence," in *Periodical Essays of the Eighteenth Century*, ed. George Carver (Garden City, NY: Doubleday, Doran & Company, 1970), 113.

14. Immanuel Kant, "Friendship," in *Immanuel Kant: Lectures on Ethics*, trans. Louis Infield (New York: Harper and Row, 1930), 202.

15. C. A. Helvetius, "Of Friendship," in *De L'spirit or Essays on the Mind* (Albion Press, 1810), 269.

16. Ralph Waldo Emerson, *Essays, First Series: The Complete Works of Ralph Waldo Emerson*, vol. 2 (Boston: Houghton Mifflin, 1865), 194.

17. Lewis, *Four Loves*, 58.

18. Volney Streamer, *What Makes a Friend?* (New York: Prentano's, 1892), 50.

19. Cicero, *Letters*, 14.25; Aristotle, *Ethics*, 565.

20. Aristotle, *Ethics*, 565.

21. Berkeley, "Benevolence," 114.

22. Sir Herbert Maxwell, "The Conduct of Friendship," in *The Eclectic Magazine of Foreign Literature* (New York: E. R. Pelton, 1893), 539.

23. Lewis, *Four Loves*, 89.

24. Ibid., 66.

25. Henry David Thoreau, "A Week on the Concord and Merrimack Rivers," in *Walden and Other Writings of Henry David Thoreau*, ed. Brooks Atkinson (New York: The Modern Library, 1937), 378.

26. E. Lynn Linton, "The Ethics of Friendship," in *The Universal Review*, ed. Harry Quilter (London: Swan Sonnenschein and Co., 1889), 340–41.

27. Kant, "Friendship," 206.

28. Speaking more broadly, C. S. Lewis's essay on "Membership" in *The Weight of Glory* says, "But the function of equality is purely protective. It is medicine, not food. By treating human persons (in judicious defiance of the observed facts) as if they were all the same kind of thing, we avoid innumerable evils. But it is not on this that we are made to live. It is idle to say that men are of equal value" (37–38).

29. Kant, "Friendship," 208–9.

30. Emerson, "Essays," 213.

31. Taylor, "Measures and Offices," 34.

32. Ibid., 35.

33. Augustine, *Confessions*, 100.

34. Montaigne, "Of Friendship," 69.

35. Aelred, 77.

36. Streamer, 47.

37. Aristotle, *Ethics*, 457.

38. Lewis, *Four Loves*, 66–67.

39. Thoreau, *Walden*, 379.

40. Emerson, *Essays*, 215–16.

41. Quoted by Aelred, 117.

42. Aristotle, *Ethics*, 517.

43. Taylor, "Measures and Offices," 39.

44. Linton, "Ethics of Friendship," 333.

45. Cicero, *Letters*, 32.

46. Aelred, 115.

Chapter 3

1. Helvetius, "Of Friendship," 269.

2. Aristotle, *Ethics*, 469.

3. Ibid., 465.

4. Ibid.

5. Kant, "Friendship," 201.

6. Cicero, *Letters*, 19.

7. Streamer, 71.

8. Montaigne, "Of Friendship," 61.

9. Lewis, *Four Loves*, 71.

10. Taylor, "Measures and Offices," 44.

11. Streamer.

12. Thoreau, *Walden*, 385.

13. Ibid., 380.

14. Aristotle, *Ethics*, 463, 465.

15. Emerson, *Essays*, 209–10.

16. Aelred, 93.

17. Streamer, 9.

18. Kant, "Friendship," 208.

19. Cicero, *Letters*, 35.

20. Taylor, "Measures and Offices," 43.

21. Ibid., 43.

22. Aelred, 26.

23. Cicero, *Letters*, 13.

24. Aristotle, *Ethics*, 461.

25. Ibid., 465.

26. Taylor, "Measures and Offices," 33.

27. Ibid., 33.

28. Cicero, *Letters*, 13.

29. Aelred, 54.

30. Ibid., 59.

31. Ibid.

32. Ibid., 92.

33. Ibid., 64.

34. De Sales, *Introduction to the Devout Life*, 143.

35. Ibid., 136.

36. Taylor, "Measures and Offices," 33.

37. Aristotle, *Ethics*, 457.

38. Lewis, *Four Loves*, 72.

39. Conversations surrounding the virtues and vices of the brave new world of social networking now being thrust upon us could very easily divert our attention here. I will leave you only with cautionary words, shaped by Marshall McLuhan, that Shane Hipps offers us of the limitations inherent in the media: "When we realize, for example, that digital space has the extraordinary ability to create vast superficial social networks, but is ill-suited for generating intimate and meaningful human connection, we may treat it more like dessert than the main course." Shane Hipps, *Flickering Pixels: How Technology Shapes Your Faith* (Grand Rapids, MI: Zondervan, 2009), 183.

40. Streamer, 43.

41. Thoreau, *Walden*, 383.

42. Streamer, 25.

43. Taylor, "Measures and Offices," 43.

44. Aelred, 97.

Chapter 4

1. Even as Jesus ascended into the heavens, as recorded in Acts 1:6–7, we find the disciples puzzling over what it all meant, "Lord, are you at this time going to restore the kingdom to Israel?" Left flatfooted as he ascended, they had to make strange, incomplete sense of Jesus' words, "It is not for you to know the times or dates the Father has set by his own authority."

2. Herman Ridderbos, *The Coming of the Kingdom* (Philadelphia: The Presbyterian and Reformed Publishing Company, 1962), 353–55.

3. John Stott, *The Spirit, the Church, and the Word: The Message of Acts* (Downers Grove, IL: InterVarsity Press, 1990), 53.

4. J. Schattenmann, "Fellowship," in *The New International Dictionary of New Testament Theology*, ed. Colin Brown, vol. 1 (Grand Rapids, MI: Zondervan, 1967), 635–44.

5. Gordon Fee makes the case that the indwelling of the Spirit for the new community of faith looks both backward and forward: "The Spirit represents both continuity and discontinuity between the old and new covenants. The continuity is to be found in the promised renewal of God's presence with his people; the discontinuity lies in the radically new way God has revisited them—indwelling them individually as well as corporately by his Spirit." *Paul, the Spirit, and the People of God* (Peabody, MA: Hendrickson, 1996), 10.

6. In Galatians 2:11–21, we find the story of Peter, who separated himself from eating with Gentiles in Antioch for fear of those Jews who were part of the circumcision group. His example was so influential on the others, it says that even Barnabas was led astray and joined in the hypocrisy. Paul would have none of this and admonished his colleagues that this was not right. He said to Peter, "You are a Jew, yet you live like a Gentile and not like a Jew. How is it, then, that you force Gentiles to follow Jewish customs?"

7. John Stott, *God's New Society: The Message of Ephesians* (Downers Grove, IL: InterVarsity Press, 1979), 91–92.

8. World Christian Database, Center for the Study of Global Christianity, Gordon-Conwell Theological Seminary, accessed May 3, 2011.

9. Ibid.

10. Craig S. Keener, *The IVP Bible Background Commentary: New Testament* (Downers Grove, IL: InterVarsity Press, 1993), 694.

11. There are several who have rethought some of these values that have become so central to our view of church life. Two who have especially rethought the role of the elderly within our churches are Gordon MacDonald, *Who Stole My Church?* (Nashville: Thomas Nelson, 2007), and Cedric W. Tilberg, *Revolution Underway: An Aging Church in an Aging Society* (Minneapolis: Fortress Press, 1984).

12. Hostility between Jews and Samaritans was so great that Jesus' opponents could not think of anything worse to say of him than, "Aren't we right in saying that you are a Samaritan and demon-possessed?" (John 8:48).

13. John G. Gager, *Kingdom and Community: The Social World of Early Christianity* (Englewood Cliffs, NJ: Prentice-Hall, 1975), 70.

Chapter 5

1. John Stott suggests we need to put meaning and priority back into the word *fellowship*: "It is an overworked and undervalued term. In common usage it means little more than a genial friendliness, a superficial gregariousness, what Australian Methodists call PSA (Pleasant Sunday Afternoon) or a good gossipy get-together over a nice cup of tea." Stott, *The Living Church: Convictions of a Lifelong Pastor* (Downers Grove, IL: InterVarsity, 2007), 86.

2. Taylor, "Measures and Offices," 32.

3. There are some noted exceptions in the New Testament where these two words are used interchangeably, which prevents us from leaning too heavily on the New Testament distinctions between the two words alone, most notably in Peter's words in John 21:15–17, as he stood before the resurrected Jesus, where both words

are used but unevenly: "'Simon son of John, do you love me more than these?' 'Yes Lord,' he said, 'you know that I love you'" (v. 15). Another example where the two words are used and a common setting and distinction in usage is not always maintained is Matthew 6:5, where we find descriptions of hypocrites loving (*phileo*) to pray on street corners. In a similar context, *agapao* is used in Luke 11:43. A further important exception is in Paul's use of *phileo* in 1 Corinthians 16:22, where one would expect *agapao* as a means of describing love of the Lord as a condition for salvation. Colin Brown, ed., *The New International Dictionary of New Testament Theology*, vol. 2 (Grand Rapids, MI: Zondervan, 1967), 548.

4. Ibid., 547–50.

5. To elaborate on this much-used passage, which seems to imply that Jesus is calling all of us to be fast friends in the sense that they have described in the previous chapters, Jesus describes in John 15 the relationship of discipleship between himself and his disciples. The larger context here is the parable of the vine and the branches, which describes the essential relationship that exists between the outer foliage and the thick source at the center in Jesus Christ. He goes on to say, "My command is this: Love each other as I have loved you." In this context, Jesus says,

> "You are my friends if you do what I command. I no longer call you servants, because a servant does not know his master's business. Instead, I have called you friends, for everything that I learned from my Father I have made known to you. You did not choose me, but I chose you and appointed you so that you might go and bear fruit—fruit that will last." (John 15:14–16)

Jesus' use of "friendship" here is meant to elicit the essential relationship between Jesus and his followers as disciples, perhaps even as apostles, as "sent out ones." They are no longer to be viewed as servants in the sense that servants do not carry with them the business of the master in the same way friends, who are chosen, carry with them what is learned from the Father. The source of the love these friends share is not their own; it is love that comes from Jesus: "as I have loved you." With this love, Jesus calls these friends/disciples to "go and bear fruit—fruit that will last."

6. Gerald F. Hawthorne and Ralph P. Martin, eds., *Dictionary of Paul and His Letters* (Downers Grove, IL: InterVarsity Press, 1993), 575.

7. Ron Blue, with Jodie Berndt, *Generous Living: Finding Contentment through Giving* (Grand Rapids, MI: Zondervan, 1997), 201.

8. This information is taken from three different sources: *Social Investment Forum, 2003 Report on Socially Responsible Investing Trends in the United States* (Washington: 2003), 4; Larry Eskridge, *Defining Evangelicalism* (Wheaton, IL: Institute for the Study of American Evangelicals, n.d.); George Barna, "Survey Explores Who Qualifies as an Evangelical," *The Barna Update*, January 18, 2007, http://www.generousgiving.org.

9. "The United Methodist Foundation of Los Angeles, Money and Religion," *Lifestyle Stewardship: Learning the Freedom of Generous Giving*, Alliance Life (January 2001): 13.

10. American Pet Products Manufacturers Association, Inc., Industry Statistics and Trends, 2007; 120 Market Data Enterprises, US Weight Loss Market to Reach $58 Billion by 2007 (2007).

11. 120 Market Data Enterprises.

12. Gerhard Kittel, *Bible Key Words: Love, The Church, Sin, Righteousness*, trans. J. R. Coates (New York: Harper and Brothers, 1951), 45.

13. To a question posed by the Sadducees, Jesus replies, "When the dead rise, they will neither marry nor be given in marriage; they will be like the angels in heaven" (Mark 12:25; Matt. 22:30).

14. Stott, *God's New Society*, 35.

15. Ibid., 44.

16. Lewis, *Weight of Glory*, 14–15.

17. Ibid., 15.

18. The great hymn writer Ignaz Franz says it beautifully in his "Holy God, We Praise Thy Name": "Lo! The apostolic train, / Join Thy sacred name to hallow; / Prophets swell the glad refrain, / And the white-robed martyrs follow; / And from morn to set of sun, / Through the church the song goes on."

19. Dietrich Bonhoeffer, *Life Together: A Discussion of Christian Fellowship*, trans. John Doberstein (San Francisco: Harper and Row, 1954), 21.

20. Gordon Fee, *1 and 2 Timothy, Titus: A Good News Commentary* (San Francisco: Harper and Row, 1976), 29.

21. Bonhoeffer, *Life Together*, 26.

22. Stott, *Living Church*, 53–54.

23. Max Weber says of the growth of the city in the West, "When Christianity became the religion of these peoples who had been so profoundly shaken in all their traditions, it finally destroyed whatever religious significance these clan ties retained; perhaps, indeed, it was precisely the weakness or absence of such magical and taboo barriers which made the conversion possible. The often very significant role played by the parish community in the administrative organization of medieval cities is only one of many symptoms pointing to this quality of the Christian religion which, in dissolving clan ties, importantly shaped the medieval city. Islam, by contrast, never really overcame the divisiveness of Arab tribal and clan ties" (1244). Later he says, "But the *sib* had been deprived of all ritual significance by Christianity, for by its very nature the Christian congregation was a religious association of individual believers, not a ritual association of clans" (1247). *Economy and Society*, vol. 2, ed. Guenther Roth and Claus Wittich (Berkeley: University of California, 1968), 1243–48.

24. World Christian Database.

25. Bonhoeffer, *Life Together*, 92.

26. Eric Metaxas, *Bonhoeffer: Pastor, Martyr, Prophet, Spy* (Nashville: Thomas Nelson, 2010), 273.

Chapter 6

1. Lewis, *Four Loves*, 86.

2. In stating the dangers of friendship, Lewis articulates everything we understand as behavior characterizing cliques: "But the dangers are perfectly real. Friendship (as the ancients saw) can be a school of virtue; but also (as they did not see) a school of vice. It is ambivalent. It makes good men better and bad men worse" (*Four Loves*, 80).

3. In *Weight of Glory*, Lewis spends significant time exploring the hazards of forever seeking to be on the inside, of what he describes as the desire for the "inner ring." Of this enterprise that tends to be in all of us, he says, "To a young person, just entering on adult life, the world seems full of 'insiders' . . . full of delightful

intimacies and confidentialities, and he desires to enter them. But if he follows that desire he will reach no 'inside' that is worth reaching." Further, he warns, "The quest of the Inner Ring will break your hearts unless you break it" (65–66).

4. A 2005 George Barna study on pastors suggests that 61 percent of pastors did not have a close friend. About one-sixth feel underappreciated within their congregations. This data is based upon a nationally representative sample of 627 senior pastors of Protestant churches conducted during the fall and winter of 2005. "Pastors Feel Confident in Ministry, But Many Struggle in their Interaction with Others," July 10, 2006, http://www.barnagroup.org.

5. Henri Nouwen, quoted in Jack Connell, "Ministry Mulligans," *Leadership* (Winter 2011): 89.

6. In spite of the already stated potential hazards that friendships bring to the goals of fellowship, they need not be necessarily detrimental to the higher ends of building community. In fact, when expressed carefully and even strategically, they have the potential to become a significant asset. A practical example of this is in using friendships as a building block for small groups; that is, using a core of natural friendships as the basis upon which a diverse group of others—"those you would not naturally invite"—are invited to participate in a group together.

7. Stott, *Living Church*, 91.

8. Returning to our earlier discussion on the comparisons between the two words for love mentioned at the beginning of chapter 5, this understanding of the distinction here relating to the affections of the heart is reinforced by the biblical usage of *phileo* versus *agapao*. *Agapao* carries hardly any of the warmth that *phileo* carries in its normal classical usage.

Chapter 7

1. H. Richard Niebuhr, *Christ and Culture* (New York: Harper Colophon Books, 1951), 32.

2. James Davidson Hunter, *To Change the World: The Irony, Tragedy, and Possibility of Christianity in the Late Modern World* (Oxford: Oxford University Press, 2010), 211.

3. Bonhoeffer, *Life Together*, 17.

4. *Manta: We Do Small Business*, http://www.manta.com.

5. http://www.internetretailer.com.

6. http://www.hoovers.com.

7. http://www.broadwayleague.com.

8. http://www.npd.com/press/releases.

9. C. D. Pohl, "Hospitality," in *New Dictionary of Biblical Theology*, ed. T. Desmond Alexander, et al. (Downers Grove, IL: InterVarsity, 2000), 563.

10. What a powerful description Paul gives us of the condition of our hearts every morning we wake up to the sad state of our lives separate from our freedom in Christ. We are slaves to our sin:

We know that the law is spiritual; but I am unspiritual, sold as a slave to sin. I do not understand what I do. For what I want to do I do not do, but what I hate I do. And if I do what I do not want to do, I agree that the law is good. As it is, it is no longer I myself who do it, but it is sin living in me. For I know that good itself does not dwell in me, that is, in my sinful nature. For I have the desire to do what is good, but I cannot carry it out. For I do not do the good I want to do, but the evil I do not want to do—this I keep on doing. Now if I do what I do not want to do, it is no longer I who do it, but it is sin living in me that does it. (Rom. 7:14–20)

11. James Boice, "Galatians," in *Romans, I Corinthians, II Corinthians, Galatians*, ed. Frank E. Gaebelein, The Expositor's Bible Commentary, vol. 10 (Grand Rapids, MI: Zondervan, 1976), 493.

12. e. e. cummings, "[the Cambridge ladies who live in furnished souls]," in *The Norton Anthology of Modern Poetry*, 2nd ed. (New York: W. W. Norton and Company, 1973), 551.

13. Alas, from the very moment our first father and mother succumbed to the temptation by the serpent, it is said, "Then the eyes of both of them were opened, and they realized they were naked; so they sewed fig leaves together and made coverings for themselves" (Gen. 3:7). Prior to this time, these "helpmates" whom God created for each other were unself-consciously "one flesh." Fig leaves were to be their natural protection from the unnatural sense of nakedness and shame they now sensed as they were cast out of their garden home.

14. Not long ago, I met with the leadership of a national parachurch organization, and I made the fateful mistake of questioning the veracity of generational theory. The silence around that table of leaders was deafening. For a moment, I thought perhaps I had questioned the resurrection. To question it as a concept is not so much to diminish its usefulness as to caution us of its limitations. How much now rides on this conceptualization in your church?

15. S. C. Barton contrasts this conception of hospitality as entertainment with what we find in Scripture:

For [most Westerners today,] hospitality is personal and individualistic and has to do with entertaining relatives and friends with the prospect of the hospitality being reciprocated. In the first-century Mediterranean world, however, hospitality was a public duty toward strangers where the honor of the community was at stake and reciprocity was more likely to be communal rather than individual.... [F]urthermore, whereas contemporary Western hospitality has become secularized (so that a common synonym is "entertainment," hospitality in antiquity was a sacred duty ("Hospitality," in *Dictionary of the Later New Testament and Its Developments* [Downers Grove, IL: InterVarsity, 1997], 501–2).

16. Todd R Felton, *A Journey into the Transcendentalists' New England* (Berkeley, CA: Roaring Forties Press, 2006), 125–26.

17. Garrison Keillor, *A Prairie Home Companion* radio broadcast, May 15, 2008.

18. Bonhoeffer, *Life Together*, 28–30.

19. C. S. Lewis, preface to *The Pilgrim's Regress: An Allegorical Apology for Christianity Reason and Romanticism* (London: Geoffrey Bles, 1956), 10.

20. Lewis, *Weight of Glory*, 4.

21. St. Therese of Lisieux, *Autobiography of St. Therese of Lisieux* (New York: P. J. Kenedy and Sons, 1958), 254–55.

22. Are these not the two fundamental responses from Paul as to how individuals will inevitably respond to the same gospel message? "For we are to God the pleasing aroma of Christ among those who are being saved and those who are perishing. To the one we are an aroma that brings death; to the other, an aroma that brings life" (2 Cor. 2:15–16).